BULLY BOY

BULLY BOY

THE TRUTH ABOUT
THEODORE ROOSEVELT'S LEGACY

JIM POWELL

CROWN
FORUM

NEW YORK

To Madeline, Frank, Marisa,
Justin, Kristin, and Rosalynd

Copyright © 2006 by Jim Powell

Published in the United States by Crown Forum, an imprint of the
Crown Publishing Group, a division of Random House, Inc., New York.
www.crownpublishing.com
www.crownforum.com

Crown Forum and the Crown Forum colophon are
trademarks of Random House, Inc.

Library of Congress Cataloging-in-Publication Data
Powell, Jim, 1944–
Bully Boy: the truth about Theodore Roosevelt's legacy / by Jim Powell.—1st ed.
Includes bibliographical references and index.
1. Roosevelt, Theodore, 1858–1919—Influence.
2. Roosevelt, Theodore, 1858–1919—Political and social views.
3. Roosevelt, Theodore, 1858–1919—Philosophy.
4. United States—Politics and government—1901–1909. I. Title.
E757.P86 2006
973.91'1092—dc22   2005032330

ISBN-13: 978-0-307-23722-4
ISBN-10: 0-307-23722-2

Printed in the United States of America
Design by Robert C. Olsson
10 9 8 7 6 5 4 3 2 1
First Edition

CONTENTS

CONTENTS

THE REAL THEODORE ROOSEVELT

I don't think that any harm comes from the concentration of power in one man's hands.

—Theodore Roosevelt

THEODORE ROOSEVELT was a bold, unforgettable character—cowboy, big-game hunter, Rough Rider, champion of the "strenuous life." Now immortalized among the presidential sculptures on Mount Rushmore, he was a vibrant figure who fascinated the American public during his life. The trademark wire-frame spectacles, mustache, and toothy grin appeared in photographs everywhere.

Biographers and political historians, too, have been captivated by Roosevelt's dynamic personality. Soon after Roosevelt's death, William Roscoe Thayer called the former president "the supreme American," saying he "spoke for America and for the civilization which he believed America fulfilled."[1] Six decades later, biographer Edmund Morris wrote, "No Chief Executive, certainly, has ever had so much fun. . . . His famous 'presence' charges the air about him. It is, in the opinion of one veteran politician, 'unquestionably the greatest gift of personal magnetism ever possessed by an American.'"[2] Historian David McCullough commented, "Mainly Theodore Roosevelt was interesting, interesting as no President had ever been. He was someone who could make things happen."[3]

Even when biographers have looked beyond Roosevelt's personal magnetism, they have tended to accept his stated aims at face value. In the book *Theodore Roosevelt: A Strenuous Life*, for example,

Kathleen Dalton wrote, "He wanted to use the federal government as a moral force to serve the public good, to defend what he called social justice."[4] Like most biographers and political historians, Dalton described what Roosevelt did rather than reporting the consequences of his actions.

But one cannot properly assess an individual, especially a U.S. president, without understanding the consequences of his decisions. In my book *FDR's Folly*, I explained the unintended consequences of Franklin Delano Roosevelt's New Deal that political historians had long ignored—namely, how it prolonged the Great Depression. In *Wilson's War*, I explained how Woodrow Wilson was determined to do good by entering other people's wars and building other people's nations, but how the unintended consequences of his decisions included the rise of Hitler, Lenin, and Stalin, and ultimately the outbreak of World War II.

Though it has been ignored, the evidence against Theodore Roosevelt is just as persuasive as the cases against Franklin Roosevelt and Woodrow Wilson. Contrary to what the many worshipful books written about him would have us believe, Roosevelt has proved to be a scourge rather than a salvation.

Bully Boy presents the real Theodore Roosevelt.

THE ROOSEVELT LEGACY

So what did Theodore Roosevelt actually *do*?

- Roosevelt declared that the United States must carry out "the proper policing of the world."[5] To him can be traced the doctrine that America should enter other people's wars. Since his time, the United States has become involved in dozens of wars, and hundreds of thousands of American soldiers have died in wars that had little, if anything, to do with U.S. national security.

• Taxes are the biggest financial burden for most Americans—bigger than housing, food, health care, or anything else.[6] Theodore Roosevelt inspired the successful campaign to enact one of the biggest and most intrusive of our taxes, the federal income tax. Originally intended to "soak the rich," this tax ended up soaking all Americans.

• Roosevelt has enjoyed a reputation as a "trustbuster," a foe of monopoly, but in fact he *promoted* monopolies. He authorized price-fixing, and his antitrust policy turned out to be an anti-competitive weapon for high-cost producers to secure benefits they couldn't gain in the marketplace. The policy has disrupted markets and destroyed jobs.

• Roosevelt demanded regulations that crippled America's biggest industry—the railroads—by undermining its ability to raise capital. The trend toward more and more costly government regulations, creating obstacles to growth and jobs, began with him.

• He signed a "pure food" law that led to increasing numbers of federal regulations pertaining to food and drugs. Regulations did little for pure food and a lot for special interests (like dairy farmers) who wanted to strike blows at their competitors (like margarine producers). To protect people from bad drugs, the federal government has sharply increased the costs of developing new drugs, and it has blocked access to good drugs, contributing to the deaths of thousands.

• In the name of "conservation," Theodore Roosevelt squandered huge amounts of money and degraded much of our natural environment. He launched a federal dam-building program that flooded canyons, disrupted natural water flows, silted up waterways, raised water temperatures, lost huge amounts of water through evaporation, and increased the salinity of irrigated soil so much that very little could grow on it. Roosevelt's national forest policies contributed to overgrazing of grasslands and to forest fires of unprecedented ferocity.

Those and other disasters have been consequences of Roosevelt's "progressive" ideology. Believing that politicians could solve the problems of the world if only they were given enough power, Roosevelt reinterpreted the Constitution to permit a vast expansion of executive power. In his autobiography he said that he "declined to adopt the view that what was imperatively necessary for the Nation could not be done by the President unless he could find some specific authorization to do it." Reflecting on the U.S. president's power, he wrote that "it was not only his right but his duty to do anything that the needs of the Nation demanded unless such action was forbidden by the Constitution or by the laws."[7]

According to biographer Henry Pringle, "It seldom occurred to Roosevelt that the duty of the executive was to carry out the mandates of the legislative. . . . Congress, he felt, must obey the president."[8] He wished to be both president and Congress at the same time. Roosevelt boasted, "I did greatly broaden the use of executive power."[9]

Indeed, Roosevelt ushered in the practice of ruling by means of executive orders, bypassing the congressional legislative process. There had been presidential directives since the beginning, but they had seldom been used. During the presidency of Abraham Lincoln, they became known as executive orders. From Lincoln to Roosevelt's predecessor, William McKinley, there was a total of 158 executive orders. Roosevelt, during his seven years in office, issued 1,007. It was under Roosevelt that the State Department first identified and numbered presidential executive orders.[10] Only two other presidents issued more executive orders than he: his fellow progressive Woodrow Wilson (1,791) and his distant cousin Franklin Delano Roosevelt (3,723).[11]

Historians have gushed over Roosevelt's sharp mind and his grasp of history and politics. He was, after all, a Harvard man, an omnivorous reader, the author of a couple dozen books. Biographer Dalton marvels that "his mind seemed to work double-time, absorbing books, knowledge, facts with lightning-quick understanding."[12] H. W. Brands reports that "he had read more than any [previous president] save possibly Jefferson and was broadly traveled both in the United States and overseas. He was as familiar with the West as with the East. A native northerner, he was by birth half a southerner. He understood local and state politics, from Manhattan's Mulberry Street to the governor's house in Albany. He knew the bosses and—more important—they knew him. He knew national politics, both from holding office in Washington under Republicans and Democrats and from frequent campaign tours across the land. He knew international affairs about as well as anyone other than a practicing diplomat."[13]

For all his knowledge, however, Roosevelt failed to recognize the dangers of political power and war. He ignored the warnings of observers going as far back as Cicero, who wrote some two thousand years earlier. Instead, Roosevelt recklessly intervened in the lives of Americans and in the affairs of other nations, and we have seen the policy backfire. The more power government has had over people, the more intense the struggles to control it. Small issues became the occasion for big political battles. As a seemingly simple idea for reforming society played out through the political process, it was distorted by "logrolling" in Congress, by pressures from affected interest groups, and by bureaucrats who pursued their interests— lobbying for bigger staffs, bigger budgets, and more power. This is why laws frequently took on a life of their own and had consequences very different from what was intended.

DANGEROUS FOREIGN ADVENTURES

The most serious risks arose when the United States entered other people's wars. Theodore Roosevelt claimed that war would make better men and a better world. He longed for the excitement of war, as he showed clearly in the Spanish-American War, when he resigned from his position as assistant secretary of the navy to enter the fighting and secure a measure of glory. Roosevelt declared that "we should regard with contempt and loathing the Americans . . . crying on behalf of peace, peace, when there ought not to be peace," and he warned against "the Menace of Peace"—this from a man awarded the Nobel Peace Prize (for brokering a settlement between Russia and Japan).[14] As we will see, he promoted war and conquest before, during, and after his presidency. His many targets over the years included Cuba, Hawaii, Venezuela, China, the Philippines, Panama, Chile, the Dominican Republic, Nicaragua, and Canada.

As president, Theodore Roosevelt reversed the traditional U.S. foreign policy of refraining from intervention in the affairs of other nations. Intervention had been the exception, but Roosevelt began to make it the rule. His motto was "Speak softly and carry a big stick." Roosevelt realized it might be awkward for the United States to seize territory just because he wanted it, so he offered a high-minded rationale. He asserted that the United States must intervene in Central America and South America when a nation failed to "behave." He declared, "Brutal wrong-doing, or an impotence which results in a general loosening of the ties of civilized society, may finally require intervention by some civilized nation, and in the Western Hemisphere the United States cannot ignore this duty."[15] This bold new policy, which became known as the Roosevelt Corollary to the Monroe Doctrine, marked a radical departure from American tradition.

Roosevelt put muscle behind these declarations. First, he promoted a big navy, not to defend the country from a specific threat but to be a tool for an expansionist foreign policy. "The primary concern of Roosevelt and his fellow-expansionists," observed historian Howard K. Beale, "was power and prestige and the naval strength that would bring power and prestige."[16] In addition, he concentrated political power in the hands of presidents, making it much easier for him and his successors to pursue interventionist foreign policies. By expanding the use of executive agreements with foreign governments, he did an end run around the U.S. Senate's power to approve treaties. In 1909, while he was still president, Roosevelt wrote, "The biggest matters, such as the Portsmouth peace, the acquisition of Panama, and sending the fleet around the world, I managed without consultation with anyone; for when a matter is of capital importance, it is well to have it handled by one man only."[17]

Historian Arthur M. Schlesinger Jr. explained, "In this spirit Roosevelt sent American forces into the Caribbean countries and, in some cases, even installed provisional governments—all without prior congressional authorization. Though protection of American citizens and property remained the pretext, the result in the Roosevelt and Taft administrations was a series of challenges to sovereign states."[18]

Roosevelt's most controversial intervention involved the seizure of the Isthmus of Panama. He had resolved to build a canal connecting the Atlantic and Pacific oceans so that the U.S. navy could be more easily mobilized in either ocean. Panama, then controlled by Colombia, was chosen as the best site, and when Colombia demanded more money than Roosevelt wanted to pay, he supported a revolution in Panama and made a $10 million deal with the new regime. He later boasted, "I took the Isthmus." But as historian David McCullough said, "Roosevelt's haste, his refusal—his inability—to see the Colombian position on the treaty as anything other than a 'holdup,' were tragically mistaken and inexcusable."[19] Is it prudent to have a U.S. president who seizes foreign territory when convenient?

Roosevelt's other interventions—in Venezuela, the Dominican Republic, and Nicaragua—were small by later standards. But Roosevelt's aggressive advocacy of intervention undoubtedly made his successors feel more comfortable about entering foreign wars. And his concentration of political power in the presidency certainly made it easier for them to do so.

In the past century, the American people suffered catastrophic consequences because Theodore Roosevelt established a new model of aggressive American interventionism abroad. His immediate successor, William Howard Taft, dispatched troops to Latin America. Soon thereafter Woodrow Wilson authorized an invasion of Mexico to catch a bandit and install a proper government (he ended up doing neither) and then ordered the occupation of Haiti and the Dominican Republic. Worst of all, Wilson entered World War I—a decision that, far from making "the world safe for democracy," as he promised, paved the way for the rise of Hitler in Germany and Lenin in Russia. Following Roosevelt's and Wilson's interventionist policies, in 1950 President Harry Truman pursued an undeclared war in Korea, even though there had been no attack on the United States. Truman's secretary of state, Dean Acheson, had previously acknowledged that Korea was of no strategic value for us, yet more than thirty-eight thousand American soldiers were killed there. A decade later, another progressive president, Lyndon Johnson, escalated U.S. intervention in Vietnam, and more than fifty-eight thousand Americans were killed in that undeclared war.

THROTTLING COMPETITION

One of the enduring images of Theodore Roosevelt is as the great "trustbuster," the president who bravely faced down evil corporations to protect the American people. As president, Roosevelt championed antitrust laws on the premise that a free market, if left alone, tended to develop monopolies and only government intervention could maintain true competition. He denounced big businessmen as "malefactors of great wealth," a phrase later used by Franklin D. Roosevelt during his antibusiness crusades.[20] Theodore Roosevelt warned, "The fortunes amassed through corporate organization are now so large, and such vast power in those that wield them . . . to insure a healthy social and industrial life, every big corporation should be held responsible by, and be accountable to, some sovereign strong enough to control its conduct."[21]

But for more than two decades before Roosevelt became president, output had been expanding and prices had been falling—the *opposite* of what one would expect if there were a lot of monopolies. Despite Roosevelt's allegations about railroad monopolies, in the previous half century railroad mileage in the United States had increased more than 250-fold, and railroad rates were falling. Cheaper railroad rates undermined local monopolies by giving people the choice of buying economically priced goods from far away. Supporters of antitrust laws pointed to the "great merger wave" of the late 1890s as evidence of monopolization, but in fact, the total the number of commercial and industrial firms in the United States increased from 1.11 million in 1890 to 1.17 million in 1900 and 1.51 million in 1910, according to the U.S. Bureau of the Census. The business failure rate among commercial and industrial firms, and the average liability per failure, actually declined between 1890 and 1910.[22]

Contrary to Roosevelt's claims, mounting evidence shows that monopolies are rare in free markets, as changing consumer tastes, changing business conditions, new technologies, and new competitors both foreign and domestic relentlessly challenge established companies. John D. Rockefeller earned his fortune refining kerosene from western Pennsylvania, but rivals discovered oil fields in Kansas, Louisiana, Oklahoma, Texas, and California as well as overseas. Among the new rivals who emerged before Roosevelt's antitrust laws went into effect were Burmah Oil (1886), Union Oil (1890), Pure Oil (1895), Associated Oil & Gas (1901), Gulf (1901),

Texaco (1902), and Royal Dutch Shell (1903). Rockefeller's Standard Oil thrived because it was a low-cost competitor, investing in cost-cutting technology. Yet so intense was the competition that its market share declined.

Why, amid such circumstances, would anybody have been concerned about monopoly? Roosevelt was alarmed about the increasing size of major industrial corporations, even though they were dwarfed by rapidly expanding, competitive markets. In many cases corporations themselves, not consumers, were calling for intervention. "Competition was unacceptable to many key business and financial interests," historian Gabriel Kolko observed, "and the merger movement was to a large extent a reflection of voluntary, unsuccessful business efforts to bring irresistible competitive trends under control. . . . As new competition sprang up, and as economic power was diffused throughout an expanding nation, it became apparent to many important businessmen that only the national government could rationalize the economy. . . . Contrary to the consensus of historians, it was not the existence of monopoly that caused the federal government to intervene in the economy, but the lack of it."[23]

And what were the consequences of Theodore Roosevelt's antitrust crusade? Far from protecting the consumer, antitrust laws have had the perverse effect of protecting politically connected companies from competition. With very few exceptions, monopolies have persisted only when government has enforced obstacles to competition, such as licensing restrictions or trade barriers. The companies that became the main targets of Roosevelt's antitrust lawyers were those that created millions of jobs and brought a broader range of lower-priced, higher-quality products and services to millions of American consumers. Trust-busting became a major disruption in the American economy.

It has been that way ever since Roosevelt's time, especially with the explosion of private antitrust lawsuits. For many years, more than a thousand private antitrust suits have been filed annually—

perhaps fifteen to twenty-five times the number of antitrust lawsuits filed by the government.[24] Private suits have been filed overwhelmingly by small, high-cost companies against larger, lower-cost rivals. The appeal of a private antitrust lawsuit is the potential to win triple damages. The effect of antitrust laws, promoted vigorously by Theodore Roosevelt, has been to restrict competition.

CRIPPLING INDUSTRY

The antitrust crusade accounts for only part of the damage Roosevelt did to the American economy. Insisting that private business posed a threat to the economy, he and other progressives in the government intervened in America's largest industry, the railroads.

It didn't matter that earlier government intervention in business had been a disaster. During the 1820s, many states subsidized construction of canals, hoping to promote commerce, but almost all of these projects lost money, and states defaulted on their debts. Then in the 1830s came a frenzy of state-subsidized railroad building. Taxpayers' money financed bad decisions about railroad routes, bad construction, and, of course, corruption. The biggest American financial scandal of the nineteenth century, Crédit Mobilier, developed when crooked politicians and contractors exploited the government's effort to build a transcontinental railroad. At the time, there wasn't enough commercial demand for transcontinental shipping for the railroads to earn operating profits.

By the 1870s, it had become abundantly clear that government should stay out of the railroad business. But many farmers and small businessmen resented the railroads' practice of discounting their rates for shippers sending goods long distances. Undoubtedly more than a few disliked railroads because they were a big business and because some railroad men had cozy relationships with politicians. Antirailroad agitation increased, and by the late 1880s, progressives were calling for a federal agency to regulate the railroads, allegedly in the public interest. The top priority was to stop railroads from discounting their shipping rates. As it happened, railroad rates had been going down, in part because of a monetary contraction that began during the 1870s and in part because government subsidies had encouraged the overbuilding of railroads. There were more railroads and more track than the market could support at that time. Railroads were desperate for business, and discounting was one way to get it.

Nowadays, nearly everybody appreciates the obvious consumer benefits of discounting, but a century ago progressive reformers like Theodore Roosevelt believed that bargains were bad for people. Progressives portrayed discounting from the standpoint of producers who resented competition. Discounting was denounced as unfair and "predatory"—an evil. The most reviled discounts were those given to big-volume customers. So when the Interstate Commerce Commission (ICC) was created in 1887, it began to suppress railroad-rate discounting, making rates more expensive for everybody.

Theodore Roosevelt didn't begin the federal government's interference in the railroad industry, but when he became president, he made it much worse. Roosevelt signed two restrictive laws, the Elkins Act (1903) and the Hepburn Act (1906). This government interference in the railroads' standard long-haul/short-haul rate pricing discouraged cooperation among railroads—which might be construed as monopolistic—and prevented the development of a nationally integrated railroad system. By limiting the railroads' ability to adapt their rates to changing supply-and-demand conditions, the ICC made it harder for them to consolidate different lines into rational systems that would simplify long-distance shipping for customers.

The unnecessary government intervention crippled America's largest industry. Railroad rates of return declined, and railroads became less attractive as investments. According to railroad historian Albro Martin, from 1897 to 1907 an estimated $5.6 billion of capital that might have gone into railroads went elsewhere. "The great tragedy" of the government's intervention, Martin wrote, was that it cost "the spirit of enterprise which had produced such remarkable results and which had seemed then to stand on the threshold of even greater accomplishments."[25] American railroads deteriorated, in dramatic contrast with automobiles, whose manufacturers were not subject to the same kind of suffocating regulations. By the 1970s, there were major railroad bankruptcies, government takeovers, and mounting losses.

THE CONSERVATION MYTH

Roosevelt is now celebrated in many quarters as a conservationist, a forerunner of today's environmentalists. The National Park Service, for instance, hails him as the "father of conservation."[26] As in his other crusades, Roosevelt made it seem as if his calls for government control over the land represented a necessary—and noble—fight. The impetus for the conservation effort, he said, was that the nation was running out of its precious natural resources. Only the federal government could step in to preserve the environment.

But Roosevelt's "conservation" schemes actually squandered resources and degraded the environment.

By establishing federal control over so much U.S. land, he defied the prevailing American view that land use decisions were best made by private individuals who had a stake in improving the value of their property. This view developed after common property regimes nearly destroyed the earliest colonies in Virginia and Massachusetts and strengthened in the eighteenth and nineteenth centuries as America transferred a quarter-billion acres of land to private settlers. Opposing further privatization, Roosevelt issued executive orders to keep millions of acres off the market, under government control. He established the U.S. Forest Service to manage forestland. Because Roosevelt substantially limited privatization, the federal government today controls about a third of the land in the United States, including national forests, national parks, and other properties.[27]

Putting so much land under the control of the government really didn't conserve anything. Cattlemen overgrazed their herds on national forest lands, precisely because it was government property. In effect, nobody owned it. If one person's herds didn't eat all the grass, somebody else's herds would get it, so the incentive was to consume as much grass as possible. Nobody had an incentive to maintain the value of government-owned land, because benefits might go to someone else. Ever since Roosevelt established national forests and national parks, overgrazing has been a serious problem.

To justify government control of forests, Roosevelt and his supporters issued warnings about "timber famine." That problem never materialized, but many other problems did develop because of the conservation policies Roosevelt enforced throughout the country. Fire was considered bad for forests, so the Forest Service fought forest fires everywhere, and Smokey the Bear became famous. Forest fires were suppressed for decades and trees grew more densely. Moreover, Forest Service officials ordered reductions in logging, which accelerated the buildup of combustibles in national forests. As a result of these factors, instead of many small fires, there were huge conflagrations, which were hard to fight and terribly destructive. Intense forest fires have devastated Yellowstone National Park, for example. Millions of acres of forests have been destroyed as a consequence of "conservationist" Theodore Roosevelt's decision to expand federal control over American land. As James Ridenour notes in *The National Parks Compromised*, "The government has just not taken care of these beautiful treasures."[28]

Other environmental problems emerged as a result of the vast, government-subsidized irrigation projects that Roosevelt promoted to attract settlers to arid western states. Many of those settlers had little or no experience with irrigation farming. As journalist Marc Reisner explains in his book *Cadillac Desert: The American West and Its Disappearing Water,* these farmers "overwatered and mismanaged their crops; they let their irrigation systems silt up."[29]

Supposedly a foe of monopolies, Roosevelt approved unfair government practices that squeezed out private dam builders and helped the Bureau of Reclamation gain a dam-building monopoly. This government monopoly led to waste on a colossal scale. More water has been lost due to evaporation from reservoirs in hot deserts than has been needed for human consumption in major western cities like Los Angeles. Reisner has pointed out that California's livestock and cotton industries, which developed as a result of government-subsidized irrigation, "consumed much more water than everyone in urban California." He called the feeding of irrigated grass to cows "as wasteful a use of water as you can conceive."[30]

Roosevelt's conservation schemes certainly didn't make financial sense. Many of the government projects developed as ways to help western-state politicians gain political influence by increasing their states' populations. In the name of "reclamation," Roosevelt decided that eastern-state taxpayers should subsidize the vast irrigation projects necessary to attract people to farm arid western lands. After the Reclamation Act passed in 1902, reclamation projects had to be spread around to appease various senators and congressmen. Many of the locations made no sense and brought financial ruin to the inexperienced farmers who settled them. The American economy took a hit. Economist Robert H. Nelson, who worked in the Department of the Interior for many years, reported that "over the course of the twentieth century, the federal government would recover only 20 cents of every dollar of capital construction costs for the agricultural components of Bureau [of Reclamation] projects."[31] They transferred scarce resources from more productive uses to less productive uses, thereby making the United States less prosperous than it otherwise would have been.

Government water projects proved to be horrendously expensive. Rivers had to be dammed, vast systems were built to distribute the water, and sometimes siphon systems were built to make water flow uphill, over mountains, to reach a destination that might be hundreds of miles away. On top of all this might be added the cost of desalinization plants to reduce the salinity of used water.

If politicians had not bought into Theodore Roosevelt's quest for "conservation," the United States would not have been harmed with either the environmental degradation or the financial costs we endured in the past century.

CRAZY CRUSADES AGAINST GOOD FOOD

Theodore Roosevelt embraced the view that entrepreneurs were selling Americans bad meat, adulterated food, and spurious drugs. But the American food supply was safer than ever, thanks to new food preservation technologies, including canning, refrigeration, and freezing. More efficient railroad systems delivered food to markets faster, further reducing spoilage. Some great fortunes were made by nineteenth-century entrepreneurs who established reliable brand names such as Campbell's soup, Borden's condensed milk, Heinz's tomato ketchup, Post's Grape-Nuts, and Van Camp's pork and beans.

On June 30, 1906, Roosevelt signed the Meat Inspection Act largely in response to hysteria caused by Upton Sinclair's novel *The Jungle*, which depicted filthy conditions in small, local slaughterhouses. But those slaughterhouses were going out of business as big Chicago-based meatpackers (Swift, Armour, Morris, and Hammond) expanded by shipping lower-priced dressed meat in refrigerated railroad cars to distant markets. The big Chicago meatpackers actually welcomed more government inspection of meat, since it could help accelerate the decline of their undercapitalized competitors that were giving the American meat business a bad name, especially in export markets.[32] Indeed, the Chicago meatpackers had supported the original (1891) federal Meat Inspection Act for the same reason. When Roosevelt signed the 1906 law, there already were federal inspectors in slaughterhouses because of the 1891 law. Any problems that existed occurred in the presence of federal meat inspectors.

On June 30, 1906, Roosevelt also signed the Pure Food and Drugs Act, which mainly called for more truthful labeling. Who could possibly object to more information on food labels?

The agency responsible for enforcing the law, the Agriculture Department's Bureau of Chemistry, was run by Harvey Washington Wiley, who used his power to launch some crusades that had little to do with "pure food" and everything to do with politics. He attacked corn syrup, rectified whiskey, and even Coca-Cola (which he compared to strychnine and alleged was addictive) as "adulterated" substances. Wiley's wild claims about a crisis of adulterated foods were contradicted by his own Bureau of Chemistry, which took extensive food samples from around the United States and found that only 6 percent could be considered adulterated.

Roosevelt biographer Edmund Morris disparaged one opponent of the Pure Food and Drugs Act as a person who "believed government had no right to prevent consumers from poisoning themselves."[33] A more informed view came from economists Clayton A. Coppin and Jack High: "A striking fact about the Pure Food and Drugs Act of 1906, a fact with which every interpretation must come to terms, is that urban workers and families did not agitate for its passage or enforcement. No general outbreak of disease or death from food in the cities was recorded. No epidemic of malnutrition swept through the urban populace. No public outcry over food was ever heard from the working classes. The movement for a national food law came from food commissioners, agricultural chemists, manufacturers of expensive foods, representatives from rural agricultural states, and a small number of middle-class women. The rhetoric of regulation was 'pure food for the mass consumer,' but its impetus came from the professional classes."[34]

Roosevelt's federal "pure food" law blossomed into the Food and Drug Administration (FDA), which issued regulations making it increasingly difficult for pharmaceutical companies to get new drugs approved. In the name of safety, the testing requirements became tougher, and more than a decade could pass from the time a promising compound was identified until it gained FDA approval. While years of testing saved many people from taking drugs with terrible side effects, it also denied critically ill patients access to lifesaving drugs such as beta-blockers (for heart problems), and thousands died.

BLOOD MONEY

Theodore Roosevelt played a key role ushering in the graduated income tax.

After the Civil War income tax expired in 1872, western and southern state politicians began clamoring to bring it back so that the cost of the federal government could be pushed onto "the rich"—especially taxpayers in the East. Western and southern interest groups resented high tariffs, the principal source of federal revenue. Tariffs enriched politically connected interest groups and forced consumers everywhere to pay more for the goods they bought. The Panic of 1893 ushered in a depression, tariff revenue declined, and the federal government imposed a new income tax in an effort to avert a budget crisis. This flat tax—on 2 percent of net income above $4,000—affected less than 1 percent of earners.[35] The regional impact was likely to be much like that of the Civil War income tax: An estimated 80 percent of income tax revenue came from four states that had only 20 percent of representation in Congress.[36] In 1895, the Supreme Court struck down the income tax because it violated the constitutional requirement that a direct tax be in proportion to population. This ruling was intended to discourage some people from trying to exploit others with discriminatory taxes.

Progressives didn't see any way to "soak the rich" without encountering the same constitutional objection, and they turned their attention to other issues. For nine years, not much was heard about an income tax. Then, in April 1906, Theodore Roosevelt resurrected the idea. In his December 1906 State of the Union message he declared, "There is every reason why, when next our system of taxation is revised, the National Government should impose a graduated inheritance tax, and, if possible, a graduated income tax."

This proclamation energized progressive boosters of an income tax, and in July 1909 Congress approved an amendment to the Constitution permitting an income tax. The amendment was ratified on February 3, 1913. The first income tax law passed by Congress exempted about 98 percent of earners, but the income tax quickly became a people's tax, not aimed only at the rich. Democratic congressman Cordell Hull, who did more than anyone else to draft the law, claimed that the income tax would lead the government to be more careful about spending other people's money. But because the income tax made it easier for the government to get money, a spending spree resulted. Income tax rates became confiscatory during major wars, and though rates were reduced afterward, they never returned to prewar levels.

Today more than 130 million personal income tax returns are filed annually.[37] The income tax remains discriminatory—or, to use Roosevelt's euphemism, "graduated." The top 50 percent of earners pay an estimated 96 percent of income tax revenues; in other words, they are paying more for government services than others.[38] But everybody incurs the cost, time, and mental anguish of dealing with complex tax regulations, intrusive IRS agents, and sometimes audits, liens, and seizures. The income tax turned out to be a cruel joke on everybody who was expecting to get a completely free ride.

A BLIND SPOT FOR POWER

Generations of political historians have celebrated Theodore Roosevelt's good intentions, yet accumulating evidence makes clear that his policies backfired badly and harmed people who were supposed to have been helped.

In light of the hundreds of millions of people killed by governments during the past century,[39] it's chilling to realize that Roosevelt had a blind spot for the perils of political power and even became an apologist for dictatorship. The year he became president, for instance, he wrote a biography of Oliver Cromwell, the seventeenth-century British military commander who established a dictatorship and crushed the Irish. "Though it must be freely admitted that in its later years the government of Cromwell was in form and substance a tyranny," Roosevelt wrote, "it must be no less freely acknowledged that he used with wisdom and grandeur the power he had usurped. . . . On the whole, England and Scotland fared well under Oliver Cromwell."[40]

What made Theodore Roosevelt believe the problems of the world could be solved if only politicians had enough power? Why, since he didn't like private monopolies, did he promote government monopolies? Why did he demand more government interference in business, after government interference had led to corruption and waste? Why, after all the war horrors people had suffered through the centuries, did Roosevelt believe war was glorious? In this book, I attempt to answer these and many other questions about Roosevelt's doctrines that continue to cause serious problems for us today.

It's past time to evaluate Theodore Roosevelt not according to his intentions or personality but according to the consequences of his actions.

CHAPTER ONE

WHY DID ROOSEVELT BELIEVE MORE GOVERNMENT POWER WOULD SOLVE PEOPLE'S PROBLEMS?

THEODORE ROOSEVELT believed that if only politicians had enough power, they could solve the world's problems. Heralding the era of big government, he urged "far more active governmental interference with social and economic conditions in this country."[1] Although Abraham Lincoln dramatically expanded the power of the federal government during wartime, the peacetime expansion of federal power began with Theodore Roosevelt. Disregarding the dismal history of arbitrary and oppressive government, he declared, "I think [the presidency] should be a very powerful office, and I think the President should be a very strong man who uses without hesitation every power the position yields."[2] At another point he said, "I believe in a strong executive. I believe in power."[3]

Where did these beliefs originate? The defining event of Theodore Roosevelt's life was the American Civil War. It showed how a powerful federal government could forge people into a single nation. As the Harvard-educated poet and critic James Russell Lowell wrote, "every man feels himself a part, sensitive and sympathetic, of a vast organism."[4]

During the war, federal spending expanded by a factor of 20.[5] Even after postwar military cutbacks, the U.S. army remained about 50 percent larger than it had been before the war.[6] Postwar federal spending was four or five times higher than before the war, and spending never returned to prewar levels.[7] War debts forced the federal government and state governments to scramble for tax revenues.[8] Rather than pay off its debts, the federal government spent substantial sums to finance pensions for Civil War veterans and schemes such as a transcontinental railroad.

During the postwar years, many Americans looked to government for solutions to their problems. In 1865, Illinois governor Richard Yates remarked that "The war . . . has tended, more than any other event in the history of our country, to militate against the Jeffersonian idea, that 'the best government is that which governs least.' The war has not only, of necessity, given more power to, but has led to a more intimate provision of the government over every material interest of society."[9]

Before the Civil War, the most revered of the American Founders was Thomas Jefferson. His antislavery writings had inspired the abolitionists, and his other writings—especially the Declaration of Independence—articulated a compelling vision of a libertarian, democratic society with a government of strictly limited powers. But after the war, Jefferson's reputation plummeted. Nobody wanted to hear about Jefferson, who had defended the right to secede from the Union, after some 625,000 people had been killed in the war to preserve the Union. As Theodore Roosevelt's contemporary, the historian Henry Adams, remarked: It was "always safe to abuse Jefferson."[10]

After the Civil War, the most revered Founder was Alexander Hamilton, George Washington's secretary of the Treasury, who championed a strong central government. Hamilton helped establish a central bank and managed federal finances to make possible an expansion of government power. His efforts to impose a federal excise tax on whiskey—part of his plan to have the federal government assume responsibility for paying off state debts after the Revolutionary War—triggered the 1794 Whiskey Rebellion among Pennsylvania farmers. The writer and editor George W. Curtis wrote a friend: "Have you thought what a vindication this [Civil

War] is of Alexander Hamilton? He was one of our truly great men, as Jefferson was the least of the truly great."[11] Henry Cabot Lodge, for many years one of Theodore Roosevelt's best friends, produced a biography of Hamilton and an edition of his writings. Roosevelt declared, "I am a Hamiltonian in my governmental views, especially with reference to the need of the exercise of broad powers by the National Government."[12]

CHILD OF THE CIVIL WAR

Theodore Roosevelt's own family had split views about the Civil War. Born on October 27, 1858, in his family's New York City house at 28 East Twentieth Street,[13] Roosevelt was a toddler when President Lincoln authorized the attack against the South. Roosevelt's maternal grandmother Martha Stewart Elliott was from Georgia, her daughter Martha Bulloch—Roosevelt's mother—supported the South, and a number of her relatives served in the Confederate army.[14] But his father Theodore Roosevelt Sr. supported the North.[15]

Roosevelt was delighted that the North won. "For the rest of his life," observed biographer Kathleen Dalton, "Theodore expressed powerful emotion when he argued for the constructive effects of the Civil War. He saw it as an apocalyptic battle of the faithful against the forces of evil, which was the view promoted by Protestant clergymen who infused the war with biblical meaning. They taught that from the spilling of blood sins would be remitted."[16]

Roosevelt, however, was ashamed that his father had paid a substitute to fight for him during the Civil War. Although this practice was perfectly legal, young Theodore considered it a blot on the family name, and he resolved to somehow distinguish himself in combat. But he was a frail child who suffered from asthma. Theodore Sr., a businessman and philanthropist managing enterprises his own father had developed, tried many things with his son before he decided that the best bet was vigorous physical exercise. Young

Theodore lifted weights, pursued gymnastics, took wrestling lessons, learned how to swim, rode horses, hiked, and more. His asthma became less of an issue but was never completely eliminated.[17]

At fourteen, Roosevelt found that he enjoyed killing wild animals, and he was given a double-barreled shotgun.[18] The family traveled extensively throughout Europe and the Middle East. In Egypt, for instance, hunting was a highlight. He recalled, "I have had great enjoyment from the shooting here, as I have procured between one and two hundred skins."[19]

An avid reader, particularly of history, Roosevelt favored violent stories with heroes and warfare.[20] In 1876 he entered Harvard College, America's oldest college though not yet the rigorous institution it would later become. At Harvard, Roosevelt met Henry Cabot Lodge, who was teaching history with meager success. When students were no longer forced to take his course, enrollment plunged from fifty to three.[21] While still an undergraduate, Roosevelt began work on his first book, *The Naval War of 1812*. He blamed that war on Thomas Jefferson's failure to build an adequate navy. Roosevelt's writing portrayed fighting as something glorious. Biographer H. W. Brands remarked that the book was "a story of war by one who obviously had never witnessed or experienced the real thing."[22]

In February 1878, Roosevelt was shocked by his father's death, at age forty-six, from cancer.[23] The estate yielded young Theodore an annual income of about $8,000[24]—enough, in those days, for a comfortable life. On his twenty-second birthday he married his neighbor Alice Lee, whom Brands described as "tall and athletic, with wide, pale blue-gray eyes, long golden curls, a pert, slightly upturned nose, a dainty mouth, and a bright, ready smile (friends and relatives called her 'Sunshine')."[25] Six months later, Roosevelt enrolled at Columbia University Law School. He didn't like corporate law, in particular the *caveat emptor* principle ("let the buyer beware"), which applied even more to politicians than to consumer goods.[26] He and Alice traveled to Europe. A highlight of the trip was their visit to Napoleon's tomb. "I do not think there is a more impressive sepulcher on earth than the tomb," he remarked. "It is grandly simple."[27] Already Roosevelt was apparently an admirer of the French dictator and conqueror.

HANGING OUT WITH POLITICIANS

After two years, Roosevelt lost interest in law and dropped out of law school. He began to hang out with local politicians. About once a week, he visited Morton Hall, a Fifty-ninth Street saloon where officeholders and aspiring officeholders discussed schemes for the next election.[28] There he met Joseph Murray, a former functionary in the Democratic Tammany Hall political machine. Murray, who had bolted to the Republicans, needed someone to run for the New York State Assembly from the Twenty-first District. Roosevelt was interested, and in November 1881 he was elected.

In Albany, Roosevelt found himself surrounded by so much corruption that he ought to have learned that government was an unlikely means of doing good. According to Brands, "The worst grafters could be found introducing the most stringent anticorporate regulatory schemes, only to abandon them in committee when the required contributions came in. At other times the same legislators could give the most impassioned speeches against obviously crooked bills, and then, after similar reconsideration by the corporations, attach cosmetically appealing but essentially meaningless amendments and vote in favor."[29]

Ignoring the corruption around him, Roosevelt made a name for himself by joining a campaign to extract more tax revenue from Manhattan Elevated, a mass transit company. He considered higher taxes a "progressive" measure.[30] At first, he had the courage to demand an investigation of Judge Thomas Westbrook, accused of accepting payoffs to support the takeover of Manhattan Elevated by speculator Jay Gould.[31] There was an investigation, but, aided by some bribery, a majority of the Judiciary Committee determined that Westbrook hadn't done anything wrong.[32] Roosevelt later acknowledged that he might have been wrong.[33]

In January 1883 Roosevelt was elected Speaker of the Assembly and soon found himself making compromises. He voted for price controls on subway fares—the "Five Cent Bill" aimed to reduce the fare from 10 cents to a nickel.[34] New York's governor Grover Cleveland, however, believed the bill was unconstitutional and vetoed it. When Cleveland was hailed as a man of principle, Roosevelt acknowledged the error of his ways. Speaker Roosevelt's prestige took another hit when one of his Republican allies, Assemblyman Henry L. Sprague, was accused of corruption, including a charge that he asked legislators to vote on bills not once but a number of times.[35]

Although Roosevelt considered himself a reformer, in 1884 he campaigned for Republican presidential candidate James Blaine, known for giving government jobs to as many of his cronies as possible and for accepting bribes to promote railroad land grants— the opposite of what Roosevelt supposedly stood for. During the presidential campaign, Roosevelt hammered Blaine's opponent Grover Cleveland for belonging to the Democratic Party, which he blamed for the South's seceding from the Union and provoking the Civil War.[36]

Roosevelt ought to have learned that power corrupts and that government could never be counted on to do good, but somehow he reached the opposite conclusion. He ran for mayor of New York City in 1886 and came in third, partly because many Republicans believed the Democratic candidate Abram S. Lee was a better bet to defeat the radical candidate Henry George, who hoped to solve social problems by imposing a single tax on land.[37] Two years later, Roosevelt campaigned for the Republican presidential candidate Benjamin Harrison. Democrat Grover Cleveland won a majority of the votes cast, but Harrison won a majority of electoral votes and therefore the election. Roosevelt wanted a job with the new administration in Washington.[38] His preference was for something in the

State Department, where he could become involved with foreign affairs.[39]

POLITICAL CORRUPTION EVERYWHERE

Harrison offered to name Roosevelt the Civil Service commissioner, responsible for enforcing the Civil Service Act. The act had been passed in 1883 following the assassination of President James A. Garfield two years before by a disgruntled federal bureaucrat. The law was supposed to curb the spoils system—a president's practice of firing competent bureaucrats from rival political parties and hiring people, often incompetent, from his own political party.[40]

Reforming the Civil Service became a political movement of sorts. "The movement's literature has about it all the faded ludicrousness of Moral Rearmament," biographer Edmund Morris observed. "How could intellectuals, politicians, socialites, churchmen, and editors campaign so fervently on behalf of customs clerks, Indian school superintendents, and Fourth-Class postmasters? How could they wax so lyrical about quotas, certifications, political assessments, and lists of eligibles? How, indeed, could one reformer entitle his memoirs *The Romance of the Merit System?*"[41]

But the Civil Service commissioner headed a token agency, responsible for only about 28,000 low-level federal jobs, a quarter of the total. Another 112,000 federal jobs weren't subject to the merit system. Moreover, the power of the commissioner was limited. As Morris explained, "A Commissioner might personally investigate cases of examination fraud in Kansas, or political blackmail in Maine (provided he could find enough money in the budget to get there), but even if the evidence uncovered was flagrant, he could do little more than recommend prosecution to the Cabinet officer responsible."[42] And the recommendations could be rejected.[43]

Roosevelt reported that federal hiring practices, supposedly based on merit, were riddled with fraud.[44] Politically acceptable candidates were given the answers to questions they would be asked on Civil Service examinations.[45] The examination grades of politically unacceptable candidates were lowered.[46] According to biographer Paul Grondahl, "Roosevelt immediately terminated a postmaster in Indiana who had been operating a gambling room at his station. Roosevelt rooted out scores of newspaper editors who had been put on the government payroll for supporting Harrison's favorable editorials and positive coverage. Republican supporters who had been promised jobs were brought in to replace Democratic postmasters at a rate of one every five minutes in the early days of the new administration."[47]

Roosevelt battled with John Wanamaker, the Philadelphia department store entrepreneur who served as Harrison's postmaster general and was a strong defender of the spoils system. Wanamaker was relentless in his efforts to clear Democrats out of the federal government and hire Republicans regardless of merit.[48]

Grondahl suggested that merit hiring would have been throttled by the sluggish pace of the federal bureaucracy: "Politicians and high-ranking government officials lingered over late breakfasts, broke for full-service lunches, closed their offices in late afternoon, made the rounds of lavish society dinners, took extended breaks for major holidays, and essentially shut down the operations of the Capitol during a lengthy summer recess."[49]

In the 1892 presidential election, Cleveland defeated Harrison, and Roosevelt was soon struggling to prevent Democratic officials from hiring incompetents.[50] He decided against running for mayor of New York City in 1894. William L. Strong, a Republican businessman, won and appointed Roosevelt police commissioner.

Grondahl described the corruption Roosevelt faced in New York City: "The streets surrounding Police Headquarters were narrow and cobbled, crowded with grimy tenement buildings, riotous taverns and bustling brothels . . . the gloomy and prisonlike Police Headquarters—where rats roamed the filthy basement and human vermin came and went on the ground floors—was located in a cauldron of crime and vice, peopled with street hustlers and hoodlums, grifters and con men, prostitutes and alcoholics. At the top of this food chain of graft and corruption were the police officers themselves. Although the average patrolman possessed only rudimentary reading and writing skills, he was a highly evolved Tammany species who had perfected the art of intimidation, extortion, and bribery among shopkeepers and merchants." The 1894 Lexow Commission produced a report with some ten thousand pages of documentation about police bribes and kickbacks.[51]

Roosevelt aggressively fought corruption, starting with police chief Thomas F. Byrnes, who extorted money from rich and poor alike, either to provide protection against criminals or to ignore violations of laws. When questioned about the sources of his wealth, Byrnes cited good advice from the Wall Street speculator Jay Gould.[52] Byrnes was forced out. Roosevelt began prowling the streets at night, looking for cops goofing off. He found plenty who, instead of walking their beats, were sleeping, gambling, or whiling away their time in eateries.[53]

Roosevelt became a crusader who tried to enforce rather than repeal bad laws. He earned notoriety enforcing "blue laws" against serving liquor on Sundays or after 1:00 A.M. on any other day. He shut down saloons and arrested the owners. There were vehement protests against Roosevelt's prohibition crusade, especially from German and Irish immigrants. Germans led protest marches involving thousands of people who just wanted to enjoy a Sunday gathering at a beer garden. Newspaper publisher William Randolph Hearst played to the widespread resentment against Roosevelt's arrogant interference with the pleasures of ordinary folks: "East Side, West Side all around the town, yesterday went King Roosevelt I, ruler of New York and patron saint of dry Sundays."[54]

The law applied to saloons but not restaurants. Roosevelt recalled in his autobiography that "a magistrate was found who decided judicially that seventeen beers and one pretzel made a meal—after which decision joy again became unconfined in at least some of the saloons, and the yellow press gleefully announced that my 'tyranny' had been curbed."[55]

Brands added, "A second loophole exempted hotels, presumably on grounds that out-of-staters shouldn't be subjected to New York's peculiar habits. Many saloons therefore reconstituted themselves as hotels, renting out a few rooms above the main body of the premises. Since these weren't honest hotels, they attracted few honest guests; instead they catered to those who preferred to rent beds by the hour. To his dismay Roosevelt discovered that by trying to stamp out the small vice of Sunday imbibing, he had contributed to the larger one of prostitution."[56]

Nevertheless, Roosevelt began to gain a national reputation as a reformer. But the people who knew him best—in New York State—resented him as a nuisance interfering with their pursuit of simple pleasures.

PLAYING COWBOY

At a party in New York City in May 1883, Roosevelt met H. H. Gorringe, who shared his interest in military history and hunting. Gorringe suggested that they go to the Dakota Territory for buffalo hunting. By September, Roosevelt—without Gorringe, as it turned out—said good-bye to his pregnant wife Alice and embarked on what would be the first of many trips to the West.[57] According to biographer Brands, "His primary goal was to add to his life list of animal trophies."[58] He reportedly was so delighted at killing his first bison that he danced a jig around the carcass.[59] The future conservationist was doing his part to push the bison toward extinction.

Roosevelt was captivated by the vast open spaces, spectacular scenery, and hardy people he encountered. More than most affluent easterners who visited the West, Roosevelt enjoyed tough jobs like rounding up cattle.[60] After the deaths of his wife (of Bright's disease) and his mother (of typhoid fever) on the same day, February 14, 1884, Roosevelt spent much time in the West to overcome his grief.

The inheritance from his father gave him the means to become a cattle rancher.[61] He went into the cattle business with a cowboy he had known for only a few hours and gave the man a $14,000 check for initial expenses.[62] Things seemed to be going well until 1886, when the worst winter in a long time hit the Great Plains. It began with a blizzard in early November, more than a month before serious snowfall usually begins. Temperatures reportedly plunged to 70 degrees below zero. The bitter cold persisted, and there was one snowstorm after another through February. Most of Roosevelt's cattle, already weakened by the previous summer's drought, which had reduced the amount of grass they could eat, died. Half of his inheritance was gone.[63] Roosevelt suffered a devastating loss on his investment.

As Brands pointed out, "Those who weathered the winter of 1886–87 and eventually came out ahead would be those who bought land, fenced it, built barns, drilled wells, raised hay, cut and stored it, imported better breeds, and did the thousand things that separated successful farmers—and businessmen—from those who failed."[64] Roosevelt had underestimated how things could go wrong. Biographer Edmund Morris characterized him as a "financial imbecile."[65]

But Roosevelt had made many friends among the ranch hands and others he met in the Dakota Badlands. He won their respect for his willingness to attempt tough jobs and share hardships. They became enthusiastic supporters when he embarked on a career in national politics.[66]

THE GOSPEL OF GOOD INTENTIONS

Meanwhile, Roosevelt had been in touch with journalist and photographer Jacob A. Riis, who was to have considerable influence on

Roosevelt's thinking. Roosevelt wrote that "The man who was closest to me throughout my two years in the Police Department was Jacob Riis[67] . . . my whole life was influenced by my long association with Jacob Riis, whom I am tempted to call the best American I ever knew."[68]

Riis was born in Ribe, Denmark, the third of thirteen children, on May 3, 1849. He found work as a carpenter in Copenhagen and emigrated to the United States in 1870. He slept in filthy police station lodging houses and took whatever jobs he could get before ending up in the news bureau of the *South Brooklyn News*. He subsequently worked as a police reporter for the *New York Tribune* and the *New York Sun*. He was shocked at the crowded, squalid conditions that so many city people endured. He recorded what he saw in photographs as well as in news stories. He did an extended, illustrated report for *Scribner's Magazine* in 1889, and this became a book, *How the Other Half Lives: Studies Among the Tenements of New York,* published in 1890. Roosevelt read the book while he was police commissioner.

Riis presented poverty as a shocking social problem, and it was shocking compared to the living standards many of his contemporaries had achieved. But he didn't ask whether the poor were better off in his time than they had been in the past. Human beings began life on earth without skills or tools. For thousands of years, poverty was universal. There was nothing unusual about it. In 1651, the English political thinker Thomas Hobbes remarked about "the life of man, solitary, poor, nasty, brutish, and short."[69]

The real news was not that there were large numbers of poor people, since all people used to be poor, but that so many people had emerged from poverty. There had been gradual improvement in living standards throughout most of the world and dramatic improvements in the West, particularly the United States.[70] By any measure, the poor in the United States were better off than the poor had been in the past. People were living longer. Moreover, if living conditions were really worse in the United States than in other countries, presumably immigration to the United States would have declined if not stopped altogether. Yet every year during the time of Jacob Riis and Theodore Roosevelt, hundreds of thousands of immigrants came to the United States.[71]

Riis was specifically concerned about how the rising demand for living space drove up the value of land in New York City as increasing numbers of poor immigrants settled there. Single-family homes gave way to multifamily homes and then to apartment buildings whose units were, in turn, subdivided and further subdivided until a number of families lived in a single room with little ventilation or light. "Still the crowds did not abate," Riis remarked.[72] Instead of acknowledging that the situation arose from the need for the cheapest possible space, Riis blamed real estate entrepreneurs for accepting too many people into their buildings. The alternative to such tenements would appear to have been homelessness, for if these immigrants could have afforded the nicer and more spacious apartments Riis envisioned, they would have moved.

Riis's reports about urban slums evoked widespread sympathy, but he wanted more than sympathy. He wanted government to do something about poverty. He held the utopian view that if legislators had good intentions and passed good laws, somehow things would get better. He referred to "the spirit of justice that is the soul of every law."[73] Roosevelt agreed, as he wrote: "I felt that with Jacob Riis's guidance I would be able to put a goodly number of his principles into actual effect."[74]

Perhaps it was because of Riis's influence that Roosevelt began to promote the idea of achieving reform through government and to disparage the profit-seeking entrepreneurs who had done so much to expand the economy, create jobs, and improve living standards. Riis quoted Roosevelt as saying, "There is not in the world a more ignoble character than the mere money-getting American, insensible to every duty, regardless of every principle, bent only on amassing a fortune, and putting his fortune only to the basest uses— whether these uses be to speculate in stocks and wreck railroads himself, or to allow his son to lead a life of foolish and expensive idleness and gross debauchery."[75]

A little reflection about the eons required for human beings to advance as far as they had would have suggested to Riis and Roosevelt that they were hoping for a simplistic solution to a complex problem. The ultimate solution was for poor people to acquire more valuable skills with which to earn more money and afford better housing, but obviously that was a long-term process. If the government demolished tenements, it would just reduce the supply of cheap housing, forcing poor people to make even more intensive use of the housing that remained—and many poor people would have gone homeless.

Sociologist Herbert Spencer reported this was what happened in Great Britain at the time Riis was developing his ideas. Spencer referred to the "Artisans' Dwelling Acts, giving to local authorities powers to pull down bad houses and provide for the building of good ones. What have been the results? A summary of the operations of the Metropolitan Board of Works, dated December 21, 1883, shows that up to last September it had, at a cost of a million and a quarter to ratepayers, unhoused 21,000 persons and provided houses for 12,000—the remaining 9,000 to be hereafter provided for, being, meanwhile, left houseless."[76]

The disastrous results of Great Britain's "Artisans' Dwelling Acts" should have made evident to Roosevelt and Riis that governments had a poor record getting things done, and that the likely results of a government program to build cheap housing would be to (1) increase the burden on taxpayers, (2) increase the amount of middle-income housing—reflecting the influence of people paying for it—and (3) encourage corruption such as occurred when the federal government got involved with the transcontinental railroad. Roosevelt had witnessed more than enough corruption to discourage serious consideration of a big government housing program. Corruption in New York, observed biographer H. W. Brands, "was epidemic and entrenched."[77]

Despite all his firsthand experience with corruption, Roosevelt concluded that government could do good if only *he* had enough power. He was, after all, an impulsive man of action, not a thinker. From journalists he embraced an idea that had begun to catch on after the Civil War: A more powerful government could somehow solve social problems. It seems he never considered the fact that laws often backfire. His main concern was to acquire political power. When Jacob Riis asked Roosevelt why he went into politics, he reportedly replied: "I wanted to belong to the governing class, not to the governed."[78]

At least one contemporary expressed concern about Roosevelt's hunger for power. Henry Adams wrote: "Power is poison. Its effect on Presidents had always been tragic, chiefly as an almost insane excitement at first, and a worse reaction afterwards. . . . Power wielded by abnormal energy is the most serious of facts, and all Roosevelt's friends know that his restless and combative energy was more than abnormal."[79]

CHAPTER TWO

WHY DID ROOSEVELT WANT TO ENTER OTHER PEOPLE'S WARS?

ALTHOUGH THEODORE ROOSEVELT did not add much to territory controlled by the United States, he was the most outspoken advocate of an interventionist foreign policy. Successors including Woodrow Wilson, Franklin D. Roosevelt, Lyndon Johnson, and George W. Bush would embrace his doctrine, enter foreign wars, and otherwise intervene in the affairs of other nations.

Theodore Roosevelt insisted that war was a good thing. He declared, "All the great masterful races have been fighting races, and the minute that a race loses the hard fighting virtues, then, no matter what else it may retain, no matter how skilled in commerce and finance, in science or art, it has lost its proud right to stand as the equal of the best."[1] According to the American philosopher William James, one of Roosevelt's contemporaries, he "gushes over war as the ideal condition of human society for the manly strenuousness which it involves and treats peace as a condition of blubberlike and swollen ignobility, fit only for huckstering weaklings."[2]

Roosevelt was determined to defy limitations on power, especially *his* power. He specifically rejected the Founders' principle that American military actions should be limited to defense, declaring that the United States should assume responsibility for civilizing the world. He wrote, "A nation's first duty is within its own borders, but it is not thereby absolved from facing its duties in the world as a whole; and if it refuses to do so, it merely forfeits its right to struggle for a place among the peoples that shape the destiny of mankind."[3]

Carl Schurz, an abolitionist, diplomat, and general, characterized Roosevelt's view this way: "Everything apt to promote his chances is good and every adverse influence wicked, and that, therefore, those who decide to vote against him . . . are unpatriotic citizens and bad Americans."[4] Roosevelt dismissed the German-born Schurz as a "prattling foreigner."[5]

PRECEDENTS FOR EXPANSION

Roosevelt came along after a succession of expansionist presidents and secretaries of state. James K. Polk was elected because of his commitment to expansion, and during his one term (1845–1849) he added more territory than any other president. He promoted the annexation of Texas, which brought war with Mexico. The United States won and ended up with 1.2 million square miles of territory eventually divided into the states of California, Texas, Arizona, New Mexico, Utah, and parts of Colorado and Wyoming. Polk negotiated with the British to acquire the Oregon territory. In addition, Iowa and Wisconsin joined the Union during his presidency.

Secretary of State William Seward, who served both Abraham Lincoln and Andrew Johnson, explored many possibilities for expansion. Historian Warren Zimmerman explained, "He wanted to push the United States north into Canada, south into Mexico, and west toward Asia. In the Caribbean he sought a coaling station for the U.S. Navy in the Dominican Republic, signed a treaty with Denmark for the purchase of the Virgin Islands, and won the agreement of Colombia for the right to build a canal across the Isthmus of Panama. He also made tentative probes at the Caribbean islands of Cuba, Haiti, Culebra, French Guiana, Puerto Rico, and St. Bartholomew. He courted Denmark for both Iceland and Greenland."[6]

He negotiated the purchase of Alaska from Russia for $7.2 million—roughly 2 cents per acre. Most Americans were skeptical about empire building, and the acquisition of Alaska was ridiculed as "Seward's Folly" and "Seward's Icebox."

Through all these maneuvers, the Monroe Doctrine acquired a new meaning. In his seventh annual address to Congress on December 2, 1823, President James Monroe reaffirmed the traditional American foreign policy of staying out of other people's wars. Monroe declared that the United States would oppose efforts by European countries to establish new colonies in the Americas or to interfere with colonial struggles for independence. The aim of the Monroe Doctrine was defensive: to keep potential adversaries as far away as possible from the United States. By the late nineteenth century, however, the Monroe Doctrine had come to mean that the United States should aim to expel European countries from the Western Hemisphere and reserve for itself the prerogative of intervening in the affairs of Latin American nations. When, in 1886, the United States negotiated with Germany over control of the Pacific island of Samoa, Secretary of State Thomas F. Bayard cited the Monroe Doctrine to bolster American claims. The German Foreign Office replied that Americans seemed to believe the Pacific Ocean should be treated like "an American lake."[7]

When the United States had secured its claims to the Pacific Coast from California to Washington and not much more "free" land was available for homesteading, the historian Frederick Jackson Turner expressed his view that the "closing of the frontier" was a major turning point in American history. He developed his case in a paper presented at a Chicago meeting of the American Historical Association in 1893. He subsequently concluded, "That these energies of expansion will no longer operate would be a rash prediction; and the demands for a vigorous foreign policy, for an interoceanic canal, for a revival of our power upon the seas, and for the extension of American influence to outlying islands and adjoining countries, are indications that the movement will continue."[8]

Expansion had everything to do with imperialist ideology and nothing to do with capitalism. A tiny portion of U.S. output went overseas. In 1900, for instance, exports were only about 5 percent of the estimated U.S. gross national product.[9] The biggest export markets for the United States were Great Britain, Germany, Canada, and France—prosperous Western nations, not colonial territories.[10] U.S. businesses mainly lobbied for high tariffs to keep out imports. Moreover, noted historian Walter McDougall, "U.S. business killed reciprocity treaties with Canada (1865) and Mexico (1883) and blocked annexation of the Hawaiian Islands (1893), for fear of competition."[11]

LODGE AND ROOSEVELT

In 1884, Roosevelt met Henry Cabot Lodge, his former Harvard professor, at Boston's St. Botolph Club.[12] The purpose of the meeting was to discuss how to prevent Maine's James G. Blaine from winning the Republican presidential nomination. Roosevelt and Lodge ultimately decided it was more important to support the Republican Party than to embark on a vain attempt to head off the corrupt Blaine, but out of this meeting would grow a very close political relationship. Later, Lodge would join Roosevelt as an ardent expansionist and would be a key ally in many of the political battles that lay ahead. According to biographer Alden Hatch, "Lodge was fascinated by the sandy-haired, bespectacled young man, eight years his junior, whose enormous energy, reckless courage, high ideals, and volcanic enthusiasm surpassed his own. Roosevelt was a gentleman in the accepted sense of the word—old New York family, Harvard, all that— who had the attribute Lodge so greatly lacked—the ability to mix with men of all kinds and classes, and *enjoy it*. Roosevelt looked up to Lodge because he was older but not ossified, experienced but not cynical, and because Roosevelt, who had literary aspirations and a quick, inquiring mind, recognized Lodge's vastly superior intellect."[13]

Born in Boston May 12, 1850, Lodge graduated from Harvard College and earned a Ph.D. in political science. He revered Abraham Lincoln, who had fought the Civil War not to liberate slaves—he had been willing to compromise on slavery—but to save the Union. Lodge's biographer noted that he "had no use for the Abolitionists."[14] One of Lodge's ancestors, George Cabot, had been a leader of New England Federalists, advocating a strong central government. So it is perhaps no surprise that, like Roosevelt, Lodge was an admirer of Federalist Alexander Hamilton. He wrote a biography of Hamilton, published in 1882.

By 1887, Lodge had given up on teaching and had been elected to Congress. In 1893, he was elected to the U.S. Senate and eventually became chairman of the powerful Senate Foreign Relations Committee. Lodge wasn't interested in foreign policy because of any threat to national security. Nobody seriously threatened the United States. Historian Robert Endicott Osgood observed that "national security was a thin reed for supporting a preparedness movement of the dimensions envisaged by America's most vocal nationalists."[15] Both Lodge and Theodore Roosevelt were among those nationalists.

ROOSEVELT'S "GUIDING LIGHT"

Roosevelt's "guiding light," to cite historian David McCullough's phrase, was Alfred Thayer Mahan (1840–1914)—"a tall, spare, beaked, painfully shy, deadly serious naval officer and scholar, who looked like a predatory bird."[16] Mahan provided crucial intellectual support for Roosevelt and everyone else in the expansionist movement. His 1890 book, *The Influence of Sea Power upon History, 1660–1783*, presented a case that naval supremacy was essential for commercial supremacy. Mahan explained how naval power proved decisive in major battles. He urged that the U.S. navy be expanded so that it could take action anywhere in the world—and help the United States achieve supremacy. Although Mahan had previously opposed imperialism, expanding the navy required establishing coaling stations, if not colonies where ships could be refueled and repaired, so he embraced imperialist views.

In 1864 Mahan joined the faculty of the Naval Academy, which had been transferred from Annapolis, Maryland, to Newport, Rhode Island, because of the Civil War. Nine months later, Mahan was assigned to help manage the Union naval blockade of the South, preventing war materials and other supplies from reaching the Confederacy. Apparently, however, the U.S. navy did not try to spot or develop talent. After a quarter century in the navy, Mahan was assigned to the Brooklyn Navy Yard, where he was given such clerical tasks as flag testing. He started a program for testing thread and lard oil. The navy was a typical bureaucracy—Mahan found that the Navigation Office didn't have navigational charts of New York Harbor or Long Island.[17]

Mahan came to believe that the navy should be bigger, not because of any national security threat but because there were too many officers—a consequence of Civil War expansion. Apparently the government didn't want to cut back or close the Naval Academy, even though the officers it was producing outnumbered the available assignments. According to biographer Robert Seager II, Mahan believed "that a New Navy of modest size would absorb the officer surplus."[18] Seager added that "in his mind, the well-being of the Navy was important without reference to expansion. It had saved the Union during the Civil War. If for no other reason than that it was an institution worth preserving. It also commanded his loyalty because he had given his life to it and because he reluctantly continued to serve in it. It galled his professional ego that it was a laughingstock all over the world."[19]

Mahan soon came to believe there were good reasons for expanding the navy beyond providing jobs for surplus naval officers.

While in Peru in 1883, he discovered the German historian Theodor Mommsen's three-volume *History of Rome*. Mommsen emphasized that Rome's superior navy was crucial to its military success. For example, because Roman ships controlled the Mediterranean during the Second Punic War (third century B.C.), the Carthaginian general Hannibal had taken his army along a hazardous mountain route from Spain to Italy and along the way lost half his men.[20]

Mahan wrote his first book, about the role of the navy during the Civil War, in 1883, but the book contained none of the ideas that later made him famous. He began articulating these views only when he accepted a teaching position at the Naval War College in Newport, where in 1885 he delivered a series of lectures making the case that the United States needed a powerful navy. Mahan first met Roosevelt at the Naval War College, after he invited the young Civil Service commissioner to lecture about the role of the navy during the War of 1812 (Roosevelt's book *The Naval War of 1812* was published in 1882). The two men were drawn together by their passion for naval history.[21]

Mahan's lectures became the basis of his book *The Influence of Sea Power upon History, 1660–1783*.[22] Roosevelt wrote Mahan: "I can say with perfect sincerity that I think it very much the clearest and most instructive general work of the kind with which I am acquainted . . . a naval classic."[23]

Historian Warren Zimmerman pointed out that "*The Influence of Sea Power upon History* was neither an original nor a wholly accurate work. Other writers, from Xenophon to British and American authors, had emphasized the primacy of sea power. Part of Mahan's thesis was undercut by the rise of nonmaritime powers like Germany and Russia. The victor of Waterloo [the Duke of Wellington] might have been surprised at Mahan's assertion that sea power had defeated Napoleon. Anchored in the age of sail, Mahan was singularly insensitive to the technical innovations that accompanied steam and to new technologies like the submarine.

Like most promoters of a single explanation for the complex sweep of history, he was a gross oversimplifier."[24]

Nonetheless, the book was well received. The British were pleased with Mahan's view that they owed their commercial success to their sea power,[25] although they seemed a bit embarrassed that a masterpiece of naval strategy would come from the supposedly unsophisticated Americans, who didn't have a big navy. Germany's Kaiser Wilhelm II, who envisioned a great navy for his country, expressed enthusiasm for the book. It was also translated into Japanese.[26]

The U.S. navy responded to Mahan's newfound influence by granting him a sabbatical year, enabling him to write a sequel, *The Influence of Sea Power upon the French Revolution and Empire, 1793–1812* (1892).[27] Roosevelt reviewed it and urged that the U.S. navy be expanded before an enemy might attack.[28]

When Democrat Grover Cleveland won the 1892 presidential election, Mahan went into print with militant imperialist views opposed by Cleveland. Mahan wrote a letter published in the *New York Times* on February 1, 1893, expressing alarm about the "barbaric" Yellow Tide flowing toward the Sandwich Islands (as the Hawaiian Islands were then called). He demanded annexation by "a great, civilized, maritime power"—the United States.[29] After seeing this blast, Walter Hines Page, editor of *The Forum* magazine, asked Mahan to expand on his views. Mahan wrote an article titled "Hawaii and Our Future Sea Power," in which he said: "The issue [of annexation] cannot be dodged. We can now advance, but, the conditions of the world being what they are, if we do not advance we recede. The Hawaiian group possesses unique importance—not from its intrinsic commercial value, but from its favorable position for maritime and military control [of the Pacific Ocean]."[30]

It was bad form for a navy officer to publicly express views contrary to official administration policies. Pressure intensified to get Mahan out of the country. Many officials believed that the proper place for a naval officer was at sea, not ashore writing books.

Theodore Roosevelt and Henry Cabot Lodge told Mahan they had tried to persuade officials that he would do more good for his country in a library than on a ship.[31] But they had no luck. On May 3, 1893, the navy ordered Mahan to assume command of the 342-foot-long cruiser USS *Chicago*.[32]

When the *Chicago* reached Britain, Mahan was welcomed like a conquering hero. The British viewed *The Influence of Sea Power upon History* as a vindication of the British navy. Mahan dined with Queen Victoria and her guest Kaiser Wilhelm II. He met British admirals, generals, and aristocrats at a succession of banquets.[33] Sales of his books soared.[34] Mahan returned to the United States and retired from the navy in September 1896, after nearly forty years of service—an even more influential spokesman for American expansion than when he had been ordered to sea.

LOBBYING TO SEIZE HAWAII

Spurred on by Mahan's growing influence during the 1890s, Roosevelt, Lodge, and other expansionists focused on Hawaii. Since the islands were between the United States and the Orient, and they had deep harbors, they could serve as a naval base. If Britain or Japan were to gain control of Hawaii, it would be harder for the United States to expand in the Pacific, and—some warned—there might be a security threat to the United States. Lodge, Roosevelt, and Mahan demanded that the United States annex—seize—Hawaii.

Back in 1851, the Hawaiian king Kamehameha III (r. 1825–1854) had suggested that the United States take over the islands to avert a takeover by France.[35] U.S. secretary of state Daniel Webster had told France that American ships were prepared to defend Hawaii, and the French had stayed out. In 1875, the United States and Hawaii negotiated a treaty to facilitate trade between the two countries.[36] Nine years later, revised treaty terms permitted the

United States to establish a naval base at Pearl Harbor.[37] The revised treaty wasn't ready for presidential approval until Grover Cleveland was in the White House.

Cleveland, the former mayor of Buffalo and governor of New York, had distinguished himself as an honest politician. A principled defender of liberty, he believed government should refrain from interfering in the lives of people at home and abroad. He repeatedly vetoed bills to increase taxes and spending. He opposed imperialist schemes to establish American colonies overseas as the British had once established colonies in North America.

Cleveland wanted to maintain American influence in the Hawaiian Islands, but he opposed a forcible takeover. In his second annual message to Congress (December 6, 1886), he remarked: "The Polynesian Island groups have been so absorbed by other and more powerful governments that the Hawaiian Islands are left almost alone in the enjoyment of their autonomy, which it is important for us should be preserved." Less than a year later, on November 9, 1887, the revised treaty went into effect.[38]

Meanwhile, American sugar planters and missionaries successfully pressured King Kalakaua (r. 1874–1891) to accept a constitution that would limit his power and enable resident Americans (who weren't Hawaiian citizens) to play an official role in Hawaiian affairs.[39] This arrangement continued until Kalakaua died while visiting the United States in 1891. His sister, Princess Liliuokalani, became queen. On January 14, 1893, she declared her intention of scrapping the constitution, and she began exercising arbitrary power. She demanded the power to appoint and dismiss ministers at will.[40] She eliminated regulations limiting the right to vote to those with substantial property.[41] She ruled that individuals wishing to vote must become naturalized citizens—she was undoubtedly aware that resident Americans, who accounted for perhaps a quarter of the population,[42] wished to retain their American citizenship.[43] Defenders of the queen claim that she didn't want to deprive Americans of civil liberties, because she wanted Americans to remain in the islands, intermarry, and be absorbed by the Hawaiian people and their culture.[44]

By this time, Grover Cleveland was out of office, and Republican Benjamin Harrison was president. He and his secretary of state, James G. Blaine, were eager expansionists. John S. Stevens was appointed U.S. minister to Hawaii, and he issued a series of statements to the press saying that Hawaii was crucial for American interests. He warned what might happen if another country seized control of the islands.[45]

Sanford Dole, a son of missionaries who became a wealthy sugar and pineapple grower in the islands, served as associate justice on the Hawaiian Supreme Court, and he led a revolution against Liliuokalani. She abandoned her plans for Hawaiian control, but this wasn't enough. Dole and his comrades wanted her out. The USS *Boston* dispatched some 160 marines to help establish a provisional government headed by Dole.[46] He immediately sailed for the United States to present his case that Hawaii should be annexed. By February 15, 1893, President Harrison had sent the Senate an annexation treaty. But his term was nearly over, and senators believed the issue should be handled by the next president—Grover Cleveland, again.

Five days after taking office for the second time, Cleveland asked that the proposed treaty be returned to him so he could study it. He saw no problem with annexation, provided it wasn't being forced on the Hawaiians. He declared, "If a feeble but friendly state is in danger of being robbed of its independence and sovereignty by a misuse of the name and power of the United States, the United States can not fail to vindicate its honor and its sense of justice by an earnest effort to make all possible reparation."[47] Cleveland's secretary of state, Walter Quintin Gresham, emphatically opposed building an American empire. But he was determined to maintain the naval base acquired at Pearl Harbor and to expand commercial dealings with Hawaii.[48]

Cleveland sent former Georgia congressman James H. Blount to

Hawaii to investigate the situation. Blount reported that annexation was a Republican plot. He ordered the marines to return to their ship, and he replaced the flag of the provisional government with the old Hawaiian flag. But Dole and his comrades had armed themselves, and they refused to back down. Cleveland did not want to get into a fight with Americans. Not knowing what else to do, the president asked what Congress might recommend.

The House of Representatives condemned the American-led revolution but refused to help Liliuokalani return to power. Henry Cabot Lodge, who in 1893 won election as U.S. senator from Massachusetts, delivered a series of speeches urging annexation. He warned that British annexation of Hawaii would impair the ability of the United States to defend itself. He expressed concern that some twenty thousand Japanese people were living in Hawaii, and he reported that a Japanese warship was patrolling the islands.[49] Lodge acknowledged the influence of Mahan's writings. He was learning how a senator could generate public support for his policies, and he emerged as the leading advocate of American imperialism. President Cleveland, however, opposed annexation, and no action on the annexation treaty was taken for five years.

PROVOKING WAR WITH SPAIN

Republicans agitated for intervention in Cuba, where Spanish colonial rulers were allegedly committing all sorts of atrocities. Cuba was the last Spanish colony in the Western Hemisphere. Other Spanish colonies had achieved their independence decades earlier. In December 1896, the *New York Herald Tribune* warned that the United States was on "the brink of war."[50] Grover Cleveland, with a few weeks left in his second term, would have none of it, and the war scare subsided.

Cleveland and the Democrats were blamed for the depression of the mid-1890s, and Republicans regained the White House in 1897.

The new president, former Ohio governor William McKinley, was determined to press ahead with an expansionist agenda. McKinley was widely perceived as kind, charming, and agreeable to a fault. He seemed not to have strongly held views. Some associates, however, noted that he was able to prevail by letting others take credit. Secretary of War Elihu Root remarked, "I have been with him again and again before a Cabinet meeting and found that his ideas were fixed and his mind firmly made up. He would then present the subject to the Cabinet in such a way as not to express his own decision, but yet bring about an agreement exactly along the lines of his own original ideas while the members often thought the ideas were theirs."[51]

The expansionist agenda, as expressed in the Republican platform, included the annexation of Hawaii, "enlargement of the Navy," and "everywhere American citizens and American property must be absolutely protected at all hazards and at any costs."[52] American voters, however, didn't seem much interested in overseas military adventures.

McKinley recognized that there was strong opposition— including opposition within his own party—to an aggressive foreign policy.[53] Businessmen generally were opposed to war because war disrupted trade and destroyed capital. Journalism—notably the sensationalist newspapers published by William Randolph Hearst and Joseph Pulitzer—was about the only business that stood to gain from war. Dramatic headlines would sell newspapers. Moreover, a war in Cuba had some obvious risks. During the 1890s, some fifty thousand Spanish soldiers had died in Cuba, and another fifty thousand were casualties as a result of wounds or disease.[54] So McKinley kept his views to himself, and he tried to be as reassuring as he could toward everybody. But his actions made his intentions clear.

He named Ohio senator John Sherman, an advocate of expansion, to be secretary of state. For senators and others wishing to avoid foreign entanglements, there was good news: The seventy-three-year-old Sherman was in declining health, and by accepting this appointment, he opened up a Senate seat for Mark Hanna, who had done much to advance McKinley's political career and who opposed overseas adventures. Then, on April 19, 1897, McKinley named Theodore Roosevelt assistant secretary of the navy. This position was Roosevelt's reward for vigorously promoting McKinley's election. Roosevelt called for more warships to be built, even though the United States faced no military threats. He emerged as a flamboyant advocate of U.S. intervention in the affairs of other nations. He achieved unusual influence for somebody in a junior position because his boss, Navy Secretary John D. Long, a much older man, rarely came to work.[55] Roosevelt soon became exasperated that few voters seemed to share his bellicose views, and he declared, "I wish to heaven we were more jingo about Cuba and Hawaii."[56]

Roosevelt began to meet with like-minded influential friends at the Metropolitan Club in Washington, D.C.—Senator Henry Cabot Lodge, Commodore George Dewey, Captain Alfred Thayer Mahan, Captain Leonard Wood, and author Brooks Adams.[57] Their aims were to expand the U.S. navy, annex Hawaii and thereby secure a naval base in the Pacific Ocean, expel European powers from the Western Hemisphere, and make the United States a world power. At the Naval War College in Newport in 1897, Roosevelt delivered a speech in which he declared that the best way to maintain peace was to prepare for war. This meant expanding the navy. Despite his words about peace, it was apparent that he would love a war. He remarked, "No triumph of peace is quite so great as the supreme triumphs of war."[58]

Cuba looked like fertile ground for American intervention. American investors had committed substantial funds to the Cuban sugar business, and there had been many revolts against the corrupt and inefficient Spanish colonial administration. Some 200,000 Spanish soldiers were in Cuba, struggling to put down a rebellion that had broken out in 1895. Both sides committed atrocities. Business was at a standstill.

On May 4, 1897, Democratic senator John Morgan, a member of the Senate Foreign Relations Committee, which stood to gain power as foreign affairs became more important, announced that American citizens were starving to death in Cuba.[59] A week later, Republican senator Joseph Gallinger proposed that Congress appropriate $50,000 to help feed starving Americans in Cuba. On May 17, President McKinley spoke in support of this measure. Although the plan was to have Americans distribute the money, pro-peace senators failed to realize this could become a prelude to full-scale American intervention in Cuba. Soon a number of Republican senators were suggesting that American soldiers go into Cuba to protect the rights of Americans there.[60]

On June 26, McKinley sent a tough message to Enrique Depuy de Lôme, Spain's minister to the United States. The president demanded that Spain stop its repression and offer reforms that would satisfy the Cuban rebels. Stopping the repression, however, probably would have emboldened the rebels demanding independence and made it less likely they would accept reforms involving continued Spanish colonial rule. McKinley's apparent intention was to prolong the crisis and ensure American military intervention.

Assistant Secretary of the Navy Theodore Roosevelt noted that Spain had a fleet based in Manila, capital city of the Philippines— a Spanish colony. He expressed the view that if the United States intervened in Cuba, it might also consider attacking the Spanish fleet in the Philippines. McKinley encouraged Roosevelt to plan such an attack.[61] Roosevelt convinced the president to name Commodore George Dewey, who displayed aggressive leadership, commander of a U.S. fleet in Asia. McKinley agreed.[62]

On October 6, Spain threw an unexpected obstacle in the way of American expansion. The Liberal Party came to power, ordered an end to repression in Cuba, and announced that Cuba would be granted autonomy comparable to Canada's autonomy from Britain. A gloomy Roosevelt remarked: "Owing mainly to the change in

Spanish policy, it is not possible at the moment to do anything about Cuba."[63]

After some rioting in Havana, the U.S. consul there asked that an American warship come to Cuba and provide some protection. McKinley dispatched the USS *Maine,* a twenty-four-gun battleship, and in an effort to show this was not a hostile move, he told Spain that its ships could visit U.S. ports.

On February 15, 1898, around 9:40 P.M., an explosion ripped through the hull of the *Maine,* and it quickly sank in Havana harbor. Reportedly 252 of the 350 men aboard were killed. Survivors were rescued by the Spanish cruiser *Alfonso XII,* moored at the nearest buoy.

It wasn't known whether the *Maine* had hit a mine, whether it had been hit by a torpedo, or whether there was some kind of accident on the ship. Charles Sigsbee, the *Maine*'s captain, issued a cautious dispatch to Navy Secretary Long, saying, "Public opinion should be suspended until further report."[64] According to historian Walter Millis, the possibility of an accident was considered, "but the Navy early began to show reluctance to make what seemed tantamount to a confession of gross inefficiency."[65]

The tragedy proved to be a bonanza for rival newspaper tycoons Pulitzer and Hearst. Pulitzer's *New York World* seized on the story and, according to Millis, sold 5 million copies in one week, and "before the war was over it was to reach 1,300,000 in a single day." The *World* "tried to send its own divers down to examine the *Maine* wreckage," Millis writes, while Hearst's *New York Journal* "launched a massive subscription campaign among prominent people for a monument to the *Maine*'s dead."[66] Hearst had dispatched famed artist Frederic Remington to Cuba so he could produce dramatic illustrations of the coming war. After a while, Remington telegrammed Hearst: "Everything is quiet. There is no trouble here. There will be no war. I wish to return." Hearst replied: "Please remain. You furnish the pictures and I'll furnish the war."[67]

Day after day, Hearst exploited the sinking of the *Maine*. Although nobody knew the cause of the explosion, the *New York Journal* ran a front-page story on February 17 with this headline: "THE WARSHIP MAINE WAS SPLIT IN TWO BY AN ENEMY'S SECRET INFERNAL MACHINE."[68] The following headline appeared on February 21: "HAVANA POPULACE INSULTS TO THE MEMORY OF THE MAINE VICTIMS."[69] On February 23: "THE MAINE WAS DESTROYED BY TREACHERY."[70] A letter in which Spain's Ambassador de Lôme criticized President McKinley was stolen by Cuban rebels and released to the *New York Journal*. Hearst made it a front-page story under the headline "THE WORST INSULT TO THE UNITED STATES IN ITS HISTORY."[71] The ambassador resigned immediately.

Roosevelt must have feasted on such jingo journalism. He had long been beating the drums for war and was frustrated by efforts to maintain peace. "I have been hoping and working ardently to bring about our interference in Cuba," he declared.[72] Memories of Civil War horrors had receded, and new generations, who had never experienced war, seemed to think only of the opportunities for glory. "Remember the *Maine*!" became a popular slogan. Still, McKinley delayed making a decision.

On February 25, Secretary of the Navy Long had to be away from the office, and he warned Assistant Secretary Roosevelt against "any step affecting the policy of the administration without consulting the President or me."[73] But Roosevelt sent a telegram to Admiral George Dewey, preparing him for war: "Order the squadron . . . to Hong Kong. Keep full of coal. In the event of declaration of war Spain, your duty will be to see that the Spanish squadron does not leave the Asiatic coast, and then offensive operations in Philippine Islands."[74]

On April 11, McKinley asked Congress for a declaration of war.[75] Eight days later, after jingo journalism had whipped up public hysteria for war, the Senate approved by a surprisingly close vote of 42 to 35.[76] If four senators had cast votes for peace, America might have avoided a war. The government began assembling ships and men for an assault on Cuba.

Theodore Roosevelt had his wish.

WHAT TO DO WITH THE PHILIPPINES?

Commodore George Dewey reached Manila Bay on April 30. The next day, his ships began firing and destroyed the Spanish fleet in about an hour. What was Dewey supposed to do next? If he bombarded Manila until the government surrendered, he would have to take over the city and assume responsibility for providing basic services, but he lacked the means to do that. The army could patrol the city, but it wasn't prepared to govern.[77]

Two days later, McKinley asked that soldiers be dispatched to the Philippines. Dewey thought five thousand would be enough.[78] As historian Walter Karp observed, these were "the first American soldiers ever to leave the Western Hemisphere—eleven thousand miles from the cause of humanity [Cuba]."[79]

McKinley ordered General Wesley Merritt to command ground forces in the Philippines. Merritt asked whether McKinley wanted "to subdue and hold all of the Spanish territory in the islands, or merely to seize and hold the capital."[80] A week went by before McKinley offered the vague instruction that Merritt provide "order and security to the islands while in the possession of the United States."[81]

Commodore Dewey and others assumed that the United States would be seeking independence for the Philippines, since that was U.S. policy for Cuba. Accordingly, Dewey provided safe passage back to Manila for Emilio Aguinaldo y Famy, a revolutionary leader against Spanish rule who had been exiled to Hong Kong and Singapore. After his return to the islands, Aguinaldo resumed his struggle for Philippine independence.

When McKinley heard that Dewey had brought Aguinaldo back to the Philippines, he was horrified. He cabled Dewey "not to have political alliances with the insurgents or any faction in the islands that would incur liability to maintain their cause in the future."[82] American diplomats in Hong Kong and Singapore, however, had given Aguinaldo the impression that the United States was fighting for Philippine independence.[83] On June 12, 1898, Filipinos declared independence and announced they were establishing a republic of which Aguinaldo would become president.

Aguinaldo cooperated with American forces as they cornered the Spanish in Manila. His men surrounded the city on three sides while Dewey's ships pounded Spanish positions. General Merritt persuaded Aguinaldo to give up an easily defended position in Manila if Americans provided artillery. Aguinaldo withdrew, but Merritt refused to deliver the artillery.[84]

On August 12, the Spanish surrendered to the Americans in Manila. Aguinaldo learned that American forces were ordered to keep his men out of Manila, and he was not permitted to attend the surrender ceremony. Outraged, he began to prepare for war against the new American rulers.[85]

McKinley claimed the Philippines by right of conquest, even though the Philippines had not been conquered. The U.S. presence was still limited to ships and soldiers in Manila, although the Philippines consisted of some 7,100 islands covering about 115,800 square miles. On December 10, 1898, U.S. and Spanish representatives signed the Treaty of Paris, in which Spain granted the Philippines, Puerto Rico, and Guam to the United States. In return for the Philippines, the United States paid Spain $20 million.

Thousands of Americans volunteered for the Philippine war, perhaps to enjoy the excitement and perhaps to show that they had as much courage as their fathers who had served in the Civil War. But the U.S. government was scandalously unprepared. There weren't enough blankets, tents, food, or weapons for everybody. Conditions on ships bound for the Philippines were unspeakable.

Linn reported, "Bunks were stacked four feet high, some men had to crawl over a half dozen bodies to get to their sweat-soaked, moldy straw mattresses. The transports heaved and pitched, there were too few toilets, and soon the lower decks were almost awash in vomit. The fresh meat spoiled within a week, and thereafter the men received little but fatty canned bacon, potatoes, coffee, and hardtack bread, wretchedly prepared and served so inefficiently that by the time a soldier had made it through the chow line the food had congealed to a cold, slimy, gray mass known as 'slum.' "[86]

What did McKinley imagine the United States might do with the Philippines? Filipinos spoke some seventy languages. Ruled by Spain for 333 years, Filipinos had little experience with Anglo-American ideas of individual rights, religious toleration, and constitutional limits on government power. Since Filipinos were Asian, they would encounter the same prejudice as Chinese and Japanese immigrants to the United States. It was unlikely that McKinley, Roosevelt, or any other expansionist contemplated statehood for the Philippines.

On February 4, 1899, American and Filipino forces began fighting each other. Filipinos suffered early defeats. As the United States increased its military presence in the Philippines—it peaked at about forty thousand soldiers in December 1900—more Filipinos realized they couldn't win head-on.[87] On November 13, 1899, Aguinaldo declared that he would pursue a long-term guerrilla strategy aimed at degrading and discouraging American forces. He urged his men to abandon their uniforms and wear civilian clothing.[88] They would operate in small units to maximize their mobility and minimize their risks; they would attack the Americans at weak points, then disappear into the general population.[89]

THE HEROICS THAT PROPELLED ROOSEVELT
TO THE PRESIDENCY

Roosevelt knew that during a war, military officers in the field, not Washington bureaucrats like himself, would be in the public eye. Seeking fame and relishing the prospect of a fight, he resigned from the Navy Department and, at age thirty-nine, looked for a way to fight in Cuba. He remarked, "It does not seem to me that it would be honorable for a man who has consistently advocated a warlike policy not to be willing himself to bear the brunt of carrying out that policy."[90]

How did Roosevelt plan to claim some glory? He was not interested in lining up like an ordinary recruit. He wanted a leadership role. His opportunity came when Congress authorized the recruiting of special cavalry regiments from the West. Roosevelt received permission from War Secretary Russell Alger to seek recruits from among the cowboys and hunters he had known during his years out west.[91] He was made the colonel of what became known as the First Volunteer Cavalry, or "Rough Riders," as a newspaperman called them.

Roosevelt threw himself into the task. He recruited some 750 men in Arizona, New Mexico, Oklahoma, and the Indian Territory. An additional 250 men came from eastern colleges—Roosevelt stressed the value of their athletic ability. The men gathered near San Antonio, Texas, for what little training they were going to get.

Anticipating that the war with Spain would be brief, Roosevelt worried that it might be over before his regiment arrived in Cuba. He frantically wrote his influential friend Senator Henry Cabot Lodge: "Do not make peace until we get Puerto Rico."[92] Another, even more alarming possibility was that Spain might grant Cuba independence without a war.

Roosevelt and his Rough Riders traveled by train for Tampa, where some thirty thousand American soldiers were to board ships for Cuba. The ship to which the Rough Riders had been assigned was also assigned to two other regiments, and it couldn't accommodate everybody. Desperate to be the first ashore in Cuba, Roosevelt scrambled to get his men on board first but had to leave behind almost all the horses for lack of room. Then Roosevelt and everyone else had to bide their time for a week because the ships were detained in the harbor.

U.S. warships shelled Cuban beaches around Santiago, driving Spanish soldiers away, so the troopships landed the Americans without opposition. They began to march toward Santiago and engaged in a few skirmishes with the retreating Spanish forces. On July 1, Roosevelt's Rough Riders and other American units crossed the San Juan River while dodging bullets from Spanish riflemen atop San Juan Hill and Kettle Hill.

American officers were trying to figure out what to do when Roosevelt seized the initiative. He mounted his horse and dashed back and forth among his Rough Riders, around the base of Kettle Hill, urging them to charge. When some of them hesitated, he shouted that if he could risk being shot off his horse, they could surely run up the hill. His behavior was reckless, but the strategy worked. After a few minutes, the Spanish—outnumbered perhaps fifteen to one—withdrew. By the time Roosevelt and the Rough Riders reached the top, they had the hill to themselves. With nightfall approaching, Roosevelt decided to stay there rather than advance to Santiago. He and his men enjoyed the food left behind by the Spanish.

From Kettle Hill and nearby San Juan Hill, American artillery began to fire on Santiago and on Spanish ships in Santiago Bay. Spanish admiral Pascual Cervera decided to take his fleet to sea, but he encountered American battleships and cruisers, and all six Spanish ships were destroyed. Two weeks later, Spanish forces in Santiago surrendered. Spanish diplomats agreed to a peace settlement on August 12.

The assault on Cuba had been brief but deadly. Of the thousand or so Rough Riders who had joined Roosevelt, 600 were either dead or hospitalized. Another 123 were being attended to by doctors. Reportedly three-quarters of the 1,014 American war dead were killed by tropical diseases like malaria, dysentery, and typhoid fever.[93]

"Many of the wounded," according to historian Walter Millis, "weren't discovered until a day or two after the battle; but already the wagons which had been sent up with ammunition and rations were coming back, loaded with injured men from the advance dressing-station under the bank of the San Juan River. It was a dreadful journey over a rocky and jolting road, and when the agonized bodies were at last turned upon the ground at the field hospital established near [General William] Shafter's headquarters, there were neither the facilities nor the personnel to take care of them."[94] Roosevelt conceded that war was "a grim and fearful thing."[95]

Roosevelt subsequently lobbied aggressively to have himself awarded the Congressional Medal of Honor. But he was denied, perhaps because he had served for only two weeks and his exploits were limited to a single day.[96] More than a century later, Roosevelt was awarded a Medal of Honor posthumously by President Bill Clinton.[97]

McKinley aimed to eliminate the Spanish presence everywhere else in the Caribbean, so after Spanish forces were defeated in Cuba, Major General Nelson Miles sailed to Puerto Rico. His forces landed near Ponce, marched to San Juan, established a military government, and headed the army of occupation in Puerto Rico. McKinley believed that maintaining naval forces there would put the United States in a good position to secure a canal across Panama, if one were built.[98]

On August 12, the day that Spain surrendered, McKinley capped his triumph by seizing Hawaii. "We need Hawaii just as much and a good deal more than we did California," he declared. "It is Manifest Destiny." Congress passed a joint resolution for annexation of the islands, and McKinley signed it.[99] Former president Grover Cleveland reflected: "As I look back upon the first steps in this miserable business, I am ashamed of the whole affair."[100]

ANTI-IMPERIALISTS

Theodore Roosevelt expressed a popular view, but it wasn't the only view. Others passionately opposed the idea of turning the American republic into an empire. The Anti-Imperialist League was established in Boston in November 1898. "Patrician conservatives composed its upper echelons," noted historian Stanley Karnow. "George Boutwell, the president, was a vintage Republican who had been governor of Massachusetts and Grant's secretary of the treasury. Grover Cleveland and Andrew Carnegie figured among its distinguished members, along with numbers of prominent lawyers, educators, editors and clergymen. Many, in their sixties or seventies, yearned to keep America unfettered by foreign entanglements. Several, abolitionists before the Civil War, equated the Filipino quest for independence with the Negro struggle for freedom."[101] Theodore Roosevelt dismissed these people as "men of a bygone age."[102]

One Anti-Imperialist League member who was a bit harder to dismiss than the others was novelist, essayist, and humorist Mark Twain. The *New York Herald* published an interview with him, in which he reflected:

> I left these shores, at Vancouver, a red-hot imperialist. I wanted the American eagle to go screaming into the Pacific. It seemed tiresome and tame for it to content itself with the Rockies. Why not spread its wings over the Philippines, I asked myself? And I thought it would be a real good thing to do.
>
> I said to myself, Here are a people who have suffered for three centuries. We can make them as free as ourselves, give them a government and country of their own, put a miniature of the American constitution afloat in the Pacific, start a brand new republic to take its place among the free nations of the world. It seemed to me a great task to which we had addressed ourselves.

But I have thought some more, since then, and I have read carefully the treaty of Paris, and I have seen that we do not intend to free, but to subjugate the people of the Philippines. We have gone there to conquer, not to redeem. We have also pledged the power of this country to maintain and protect the system established in the Philippines by the Friars.

It should, it seems to me, be our pleasure and duty to make those people free and let them deal with their own domestic questions in their own way. And so I am an anti-imperialist. I am opposed to having the eagle put its talons on any other land.[103]

One of Mark Twain's most famous protest pieces, "The War-Prayer," might have been inspired by Theodore Roosevelt's wild enthusiasm for war. Mark Twain wrote, "O Lord, our God, help us to tear their soldiers to bloody shreds with our shells; help us to cover their smiling field with the pale forms of their patriot dead; help us to drown the thunder of the guns with the shrieks of their wounded, writhing in pain; help us to lay waste their humble homes with a hurricane of fire; help us to wring the hearts of their unoffending widows with unavailing grief; help us to turn them out roofless with their little children to wander unfriended the wastes of their desolated land in rags and hunger and thirst, sport of the sun-flames of summer and the icy winds of winter, broken in spirit, worn with travail, imploring Thee for the refuge of the grave and denied it—for our sakes who adore Thee, Lord, blast their hopes, blight their lives, protract their bitter pilgrimage, make heavy their steps, water their way with their tears, stain the white snow with the blood of their wounded feet! We ask it, in the spirit of love, of Him Who is the Source of Love, and Who is the ever-faithful refuge and friend of all that are sore beset and seek His aid with humble and contrite hearts. Amen."[104]

Another eloquent opponent of American imperialism was Yale sociology professor William Graham Sumner. A champion of laissez-faire, he opposed government intervention in the American economy as well as government intervention in the affairs of other nations. On January 16, 1899, Sumner delivered a talk titled "The Conquest of the United States by Spain" at Yale's College Hall. He declared:

> We have beaten Spain in a military conflict, but we are submitting to be conquered by her on the field of ideas and policies. Expansionism and imperialism are nothing but the old philosophies of national prosperity which have brought Spain to where she now is. Those philosophies appeal to national vanity and national cupidity.
>
> Everywhere you go on the continent of Europe at this hour you see the conflict between militarism and industrialism. You see the expansion of industrial power pushed forward by the energy, hope, and thrift of men, and you see the development arrested, diverted, crippled, and defeated by measures which are dictated by military considerations. . . . It is militarism which is eating up all the products of science and art, defeating the energy of the population and wasting its savings. It is militarism which forbids the people to give their attention to the problems of their own welfare and to give their strength to the education and comfort of their children. . . .
>
> The American people believe that they have a free country, and we are treated to grandiloquent speeches about our flag and our reputation for freedom and enlightenment. . . . Now what will hasten the day when our present advantages will wear out. . . . The answer is: war, debt, taxation, diplomacy, a grand governmental system, pomp, glory, a big army and navy, lavish expenditures, political jobbery—in a word, imperialism.[105]

To such reasoning, Roosevelt never offered much more than a toothy smile and a war whoop. But when the seemingly easily conquered Philippines became a quagmire for the United States, Americans lost their eagerness to pursue a global empire.

DOUBTS ABOUT OVERSEAS CONQUEST

The Spanish-American War concluded with "A Treaty of Peace" negotiated in Paris. It was signed by representatives of the United States and Spain on December 10, 1898. McKinley needed the votes of two-thirds of the Senate for approval, and getting them proved difficult because of doubts about whether the United States should be conquering people who lived thousands of miles away. There were ninety Senate seats, and Republicans held forty-six. Republicans disapproved of the idea of an American empire. Many Democrats were opposed, too. William Jennings Bryan, who hoped to be the Democratic presidential candidate in 1900, persuaded seventeen of the Senate Democrats to vote yes and give McKinley his treaty, because this would give Democrats the opportunity to blame Republicans for the quagmire in the Philippines. A Senate vote was scheduled for February 6, 1899, but McKinley still didn't have enough support. According to historian Stanley Karnow, "[Henry Cabot] Lodge and [Mark] Hanna cornered senators in the cloakrooms, bartering their votes in return for coveted committee slates and funds for projects back home. McKinley, himself playing patronage, promised a federal judgeship to a crony of Louisiana's Samuel McEnery and gave John McLaurin of South Carolina the right to name his state's postmasters. He also won over George Gray, the anti-imperialist Democrat from Delaware who had served on the peace delegation to Paris, with a seat on the circuit court."[106]

After all the jingo journalism, the war whoops by Theodore Roosevelt, and the cloakroom deals in the Senate, the Senate voted 57 to 27—achieving a two-thirds majority by a single vote. *McClure's*, the progressive muckraking magazine that published attacks against Standard Oil and other demonized businesses, officially joined the jingos and blessed the new American empire. In its February 12, 1899, issue, *McClure's* published Rudyard Kipling's poem "White Man's Burden," celebrating imperialism. The poem begins:

Take up the White Man's burden—
Send forth the best ye breed—
Go, bind your sons to exile
To serve your captives' need;
To wait, in heavy harness,
On fluttered folk and wild—
Your new-caught sullen peoples,
Half devil and half child.

Although the treaty was contested, the Cuban adventure propelled Theodore Roosevelt into big-time politics. Suddenly, he became the odds-on favorite for the governorship of New York. He was elected in November 1898. Other than promoting "good government," though, he had no specific program.[107] To get rid of him, Thomas Platt, the Republican Party boss in New York State, promoted Roosevelt as William McKinley's vice presidential candidate for the 1900 election. McKinley and Roosevelt won.

On September 6, 1901, anarchist Leon Czolgosz, twenty-eight, waited in line to shake hands with McKinley in the Temple of Music at the Pan-American Exposition in Buffalo, New York. When it was Czolgosz's turn to meet the president, he pulled out a .32-caliber revolver and fired twice, perforating McKinley's stomach.[108] McKinley died from gangrene eight days later. Roosevelt, who had been summoned from a vacation in the Adirondack Mountains, was sworn in as president. He was forty-two.

Upon taking office, he affirmed his solidarity with other imperialist powers: "It is infinitely better for the whole world that Russia should have taken Turkestan, that France should have taken Algiers, and that England should have taken India."[109] He declared that the United States must rule the Philippines with a firm hand: "we must treat them with firmness and courage. They must be made to realize . . . that we are the masters."[110]

QUAGMIRE IN THE PHILIPPINES

Theodore Roosevelt enthusiastically defended the American conquest of the Philippines. He viewed Filipinos as "Tagal bandits," "Malay bandits," "Chinese halfbreeds," or "savages, barbarians, a wild and ignorant people." Roosevelt believed that "the most ultimately righteous of all wars is a war with savages."[111]

The situation in the Philippines, however, became increasingly confused. "Even as the United States stood on the threshold of a great leap toward Pacific empire," observed historian Brian McAllister Linn, "no one knew what the agents of empire were supposed to be doing. Not the soldiers speeding toward San Francisco, not the harried staff officers at the port, not Brigadier General Thomas M. Anderson, appointed to command the first expeditionary brigade, not the 8th Corps commander [Wesley] Merritt, not the commanding general, Miles, not even the commander in chief."[112]

Because of the Filipinos' guerrilla strategy and the difficulty of communicating with units scattered on many islands, local guerrilla leaders made most of the command decisions. Emilio Aguinaldo issued orders, but often they either never got through or took so long to get through that their relevance had been overtaken by events. The guerrilla strategy actually undermined Aguinaldo's power and made him more of a symbolic leader.

How much popular support was there for the guerrillas? They must have had some, because they were able to gather excellent intelligence about the locations and movements of American forces, which required cooperation from local people. But the guerrillas frequently seized what they needed, inflicting about as much harm on Filipino civilians as bandits or tax collectors.

The United States had important military advantages. The navy blockaded the Philippines, stopping shipments of weapons to the guerrillas and limiting guerrilla movements among the islands. U.S. soldiers had superior rifles and field artillery and were better trained than guerrilla recruits.[113] The willingness of U.S. soldiers to help build roads, schools, and other things led many Filipinos to conclude that life would be better under American rule.[114]

The Americans, however, did much that alienated local populations. They supported local officials who were inclined to give government jobs to their friends and relatives. The army conscripted Filipinos to build roads.[115] It became increasingly strict about enforcing General Order 100, originally issued during the U.S. Civil War, which authorized harsh measures against anyone who resisted the army's efforts to restore order. Many army officers believed that if they cracked down on Filipinos backing the guerrillas—by suspending civil liberties and executing offenders—the war might soon be over. "A few killings under G. O. 100 will aid very much in making the enemy stop these assassinations," remarked Brigadier General Jacob H. Smith.[116]

Relentlessly harassed by Filipino guerrillas, Brigadier General Arthur MacArthur approved a "new and more stringent policy" in an effort to prevent supplies from reaching guerrillas. MacArthur announced that leading Filipinos who had not publicly sworn their loyalty to the United States would be treated as backers of the guerrillas. He recommended that "whenever action is necessary the more drastic the application the better."[117]

Torture became an accepted method of prompting Filipino villagers to disclose what they knew about the identity of guerrilla leaders and the location of their supplies. One witness described the method known as the "water cure": "The victim is laid flat on his back and held down by his tormenters. Then a bamboo tube is thrust into his mouth and some dirty water, the filthier the better, is poured down his unwilling throat."[118]

Martin Delgado, guerrilla leader on Panay, surrendered on January 10, 1901. Nicolas Capistrano, guerrilla leader in northern Mindanao, surrendered in March. In the spring of 1901, Americans captured a letter from Aguinaldo to his brother asking for reinforcements.

The job of tracking down Aguinaldo fell to Frederick Funston, who was responsible for military operations in northern Luzon. Funston had a dim view of the people he was supposed to be liberating. He remarked, "A Filipino is chronically tired; he is born tired; he stays tired and he dies tired. If you hire him he will labor a few days, and then he goes out of the work business for about a week, while he attends a fiesta or two."[119] Funston believed the best policy was to "rawhide these bullet-headed Asians until they yell for mercy."[120]

Funston recruited Macabebes, an indigenous people cooperating with the Americans, to dress like insurgents and pose as the reinforcements for which Aguinaldo had asked. Funston played the part of an American prisoner. He led these men from Casiguran Bay to Palanan—a trek of almost one hundred miles through malarial jungles, across rivers infested with crocodiles, up steep mountains, through territory populated by guerrillas and hostile aborigines—and captured Aguinaldo on March 23, 1901. The guerrilla leader was weary of constantly retreating to evade Americans as well as hostile natives. The combination of frequent movements and poor communications left him substantially out of touch with what remained of the guerrilla movement. His men were debilitated by malaria and other tropical diseases, and adequate food was hard to come by. Aguinaldo agreed to retire and accept a pension. He publicly urged an end to Filipino resistance, which had been winding down anyway as a consequence of repressive measures, but his announcement probably made surrender more acceptable.

All this so that the United States could play an international power game. Historian Walter Karp observed, "The transformation of the United States, already an imperial republic, into an active world power had been the [Republican] party's goal since the onset of the political crisis. With jingoism rampant in the country, with American troops stationed five hundred miles from Hong Kong, the means for doing so for the first time lay at hand. To imperialists and anti-imperialists alike it was obvious that the annexation of the Philippines could give America a major voice in the affairs of China, the then-current cockpit of European greed and ambition. It was obvious, too, that any American intervention in China meant embroilment in European rivalries—'connections with European complications'—as McKinley had rightly put it. Therein lay the advantage of intervening in Chinese affairs. A direct plunge into Europe was still politically impossible; entanglement with Europe violated a still-binding American tradition. That tradition, so crippling to any large foreign policy, McKinley and the Republican oligarchy were determined to breach."[121]

ROOSEVELT TWISTS THE MONROE DOCTRINE

As president, Roosevelt turned his attention to Venezuela, where Cipriano Castro with his provincial army had seized power in 1899. Castro spent his time putting down revolts, spending money, and defaulting on debts owed to British, German, and Italian citizens. He packed Venezuelan courts with men who could be counted on to rule against foreigners. Roosevelt told British, German, and Italian diplomats that the Monroe Doctrine did not mean that a Latin American country could get away with "misbehavior" against a European nation.[122]

Roosevelt was nonetheless concerned about a possible occupation of Venezuela that would establish a European presence in the Western Hemisphere. He ordered the mobilization of the U.S. fleet in the Caribbean and appointed Admiral George Dewey, who had conquered the Philippines, to command it.[123] On December 8, 1902, British, German, and Italian ships blockaded Venezuela's five major ports, demanding that the government fulfill its obligations to creditors. Roosevelt's secretary of state, John Hay, warned a German diplomat that Congress might demand that Roosevelt enforce the Monroe Doctrine and keep Europeans out of Latin

America. At the same time, the German ambassador to the United States, Theodor von Holleben, warned the German king—Kaiser Wilhelm II—that a German occupation of Venezuela would jeopardize relations with the United States.[124] Castro asked Roosevelt to act as an intermediary and transmit a request for arbitration with the European powers, and international commissions were set up to handle the disputes.

In his December 3, 1901, message to Congress, Roosevelt declared: "We do not guarantee any state against punishment if it misconducts itself, provided that punishment does not take the form of the acquisition of territory by any non-American power." Roosevelt remarked that if a Latin American nation misbehaved, a European nation would be within its rights to "spank" it.[125] Enough Americans, however, were concerned about European intervention that Britain, Germany, and Italy backed off. The British didn't want to risk undermining relations with the United States, and the Germans apparently feared being the only European power in the Caribbean and having to deal with the United States, whose ships were stationed in Cuba under Admiral Dewey.[126]

In July 1903, four months after the Venezuelan situation had been resolved, Roosevelt faced a crisis in the Dominican Republic, another deadbeat with European creditors. Representatives of the German, Italian, and Spanish governments pressured Dominican officials to sign an agreement for repaying Dominican debts to foreign nationals. A Dominican government official asked Washington to get them out of the mess by taking over the island nation's finances. In February 1904, Roosevelt ordered Admiral Dewey to Santo Domingo. In a rare show of restraint, Roosevelt declined to have U.S. forces occupy the Dominican Republic.

On May 20, 1904, the president explained what came to be known as the Roosevelt Corollary to the Monroe Doctrine. He wrote his former secretary of war, Elihu Root: "If a nation shows that it knows how to act with decency in industrial and political matters, if it keeps order and pays its obligations, then it need fear no interference from the United States. Brutal wrongdoing, or an impotence which results in the general loosening of the ties of civilized society, may finally require general intervention by some civilized nation; and in the Western Hemisphere the United States cannot ignore this duty."[127] In December 1904, Roosevelt made the same declaration in his annual message to Congress, thus formalizing this aggressive new policy.

Then the situation in the Dominican Republic deteriorated. The easiest solution to the country's foreign debt problem was for the United States to administer Dominican customs revenues and ensure that the money was used to pay off debts.[128] Roosevelt ordered this on February 7, 1905. In the short term, Roosevelt's policy worked. As historian William Henry Harbaugh related, "For some years thereafter the islanders enjoyed such a financial stability as they had never before experienced. Roads were built, schools established, and a revenue service created. The foreign debt was drastically scaled down, and the Dominican share of customs collections soared beyond all previous totals. Moreover, the threat of European intervention was dissipated."[129]

The Roosevelt Corollary, however, would have far-reaching consequences. Roosevelt's predecessors had interpreted the Monroe Doctrine to be more than simply a defensive measure, but no one had made such a bold departure from American tradition. With the Roosevelt Corollary, the United States was no longer saying to Europe, "Stay away from the Western Hemisphere." Theodore Roosevelt had twisted the Monroe Doctrine to justify intervening in the affairs of America's neighbors. No longer would the United States be fighting wars only when its own national security was at stake. Roosevelt had changed everything.

SEIZING PANAMA

Theodore Roosevelt's scheme to enlarge the U.S. Navy and achieve global power for the United States required a canal across Central America, so that naval ships could more quickly move from the Atlantic to the Pacific Ocean as needed. A canal would shorten voyages by some 8,000 miles, making it unnecessary to sail down the east coast of South America, around Cape Horn, then up the west coast of South America in order to reach the Pacific Ocean. Roosevelt clearly anticipated U.S. intervention in the affairs of Asian nations. He later wrote in his autobiography, "It was essential that we should have it clearly understood, by our own people especially, but also by other peoples, that the Pacific was as much our home waters as the Atlantic."[130]

Back in 1850, the United States and Britain had signed the Clayton-Bulwer Treaty, in which they agreed that neither country would attempt to build such a canal without the other, and that such a canal would be open to ships from all nations during both war and peace. Others were also interested in a canal that would link the Atlantic and Pacific oceans, especially after the completion of the Suez Canal in 1869. In 1879, Ferdinand de Lesseps, the Frenchman who had managed construction of the Suez Canal, established the Compagnie Universelle du Canal Interocéanique to build a canal across the Isthmus of Panama. He was able to raise only 30 million of the 400 million francs he believed he needed.

Because of changes in elevation, the construction of the canal required a tremendous amount of digging and the building of a series of locks to raise and lower ships from one level to the next as they moved east or west. The route was blocked by a mountain range some 550 feet high and nine miles wide. Engineers had to deal with the raging Chagres River. Costs skyrocketed, tropical diseases devastated the workers, and in 1889 Lesseps's company was liquidated.

In 1894, the company was reorganized but gave up on the project four years later. To recoup some of the investors' losses by selling canal-building rights and company assets, Philippe Bunau-Varilla, the former chief project engineer and a major shareholder of the company, tried without success to interest the Russian government in the canal. Then he approached the British government, but Britain was preoccupied with fighting the Boers in South Africa.[131]

By this time, Mahan, Lodge, Roosevelt, and others believed it was essential for the United States to control a Panama canal. The Clayton-Bulwer Treaty with Britain had to be disposed of. John Hay, McKinley's secretary of state, negotiated the Hay-Pauncefote Treaty (1900) with Britain. The treaty authorized the United States to build the canal but bowed to British insistence that it be open to ships of all nations during war and peace. Roosevelt, then governor of New York, was adamant that the United States control the canal.[132] He declared, "This seems to me vital, from the standpoint of our sea power, no less than from the standpoint of the Monroe Doctrine."[133]

Hay told Roosevelt to mind his own business and to let the president and Congress handle the treaty, but Roosevelt reaffirmed his concern. Lodge, a member of the Senate Foreign Relations Committee, urged an amendment to the treaty, giving the United States the right to build military fortifications so that the canal could be defended and access could be controlled. The Senate voted for the treaty with this amendment on December 20, 1900. By then, Roosevelt had become president, and he believed the urgent need for the canal had been demonstrated during the Spanish-American War. After the sinking of the *Maine* in Havana harbor, President McKinley had ordered America's first battleship, the *Oregon*, then in San Francisco, to get to Cuba as quickly as possible. The voyage took sixty-seven days.[134]

Meanwhile, the French had suggested that the value of their property in Panama—their improvements, their equipment, and other assets—was about $109 million, which was viewed as their asking price for a buyout. Then in January 1902 the French let it be known they would consider selling for $40 million.[135] Despite congressional votes to authorize building a canal through Nicaragua, President Roosevelt told influential congressmen that he strongly favored Panama. According to historian David McCullough, self-made engineer George Morison was probably the person who convinced Roosevelt that the obstacles in Panama could be overcome.[136]

In 1902, Iowa senator William Hepburn introduced a bill authorizing a canal through Nicaragua, but Wisconsin senator John Spooner introduced an amendment authorizing the purchase of the assets of the New French Canal Company in Panama for $40 million if the United States could negotiate a treaty with Colombia, which controlled Panama.[137] If a treaty could not be negotiated, the Spooner Amendment authorized the president to proceed with a canal through Nicaragua.

Philippe Bunau-Varilla stepped up his lobbying for a buyout, establishing his headquarters at New York's Waldorf-Astoria Hotel. He warned that volcanic eruptions in Nicaragua could damage a canal built there. On May 2, as if on cue, Martinique's long-dormant Mount Pelée erupted, killing some thirty thousand people. Less than two weeks later, Nicaragua's own Mount Momotombo erupted. The ever resourceful Bunau-Varilla jumped on the news, and suddenly Panama became the preferred location for a canal. On June 19, the Senate passed the Spooner Amendment, 42 to 34. A week later, the House passed it, 259 to 8, and Roosevelt signed it into law on June 28.

Colombia, in the throes of civil war, refused to approve a canal treaty. Colombian politicians objected to granting sovereign power to the United States in the proposed six-mile-wide Canal Zone, but undoubtedly they wanted some of the $40 million. Without consulting any Colombian officials, Roosevelt sent the U.S. marines to secure the Panama Railroad. Of course, this action aggravated relations with Colombia.

On January 21, 1903, Secretary of State John Hay issued an ultimatum to Colombia: If the canal treaty were not signed soon, the United States would open negotiations with Nicaragua. The Hay-Herran treaty was signed, then ratified by the U.S. Senate on March 17. What would the Colombian government do?

The prevailing view in Colombia was that the treaty was one-sided and ought to be rejected. Hay warned that rejecting the treaty would force the United States to take some kind of retaliatory action. White House sources released information to the *New York World*, which on June 13 ran a story saying, "President Roosevelt is determined to have the Panama canal route. He has no intention of beginning negotiations for the Nicaragua route."[138] The writer added ominously, "The State of Panama, which embraces all the proposed Canal Zone, stands ready to secede from Colombia and enter into a canal treaty with the United States. The State of Panama will secede if the Colombian Congress fails to ratify the canal treaty. A republican form of government will be organized. This plan is said to be easy of execution, as not more than 100 Colombian soldiers are stationed in the State of Panama."[139]

To generate public support in the United States, the Roosevelt administration portrayed Colombian officials as a bunch of thieves. Roosevelt himself denounced them as "those bandits in Bogotá."[140] Meanwhile, the State Department conveyed the impression that the money Colombians wanted would come from the United States, although it actually would have come from the French. As historian McCullough pointed out, Roosevelt and his associates grossly misrepresented Colombia: "Colombian regard for the political ideals of the United States was enormous. The country's federal and state system had been modeled after that of the United States. Bolívar, the Liberator, was known as the 'George Washington of South America.' Wealthy and educated Colombians sent their sons to be educated in the United States. By no means did the leading political figures fit the portrayal Theodore Roosevelt was to provide."[141]

Roosevelt did not have to wait long for an opportunity to take military action. Dr. Manuel Amador Guerrero conspired with several friends to lead a revolution against Colombia, for local control of the proposed Panama Canal Zone. He needed money, so he traveled to New York and met with Bunau-Varilla, who agreed to fund the revolution with $100,000—after independence was declared. Bunau-Varilla had met with President Roosevelt, who suggested that U.S. naval ships might help prevent Colombia from landing soldiers needed to suppress revolution. Bunau-Varilla provided Guerrero with a code for revolutionary communications, a military plan for defending Colón and Panama City, and a draft declaration of independence and constitution. Bunau-Varilla even came up with a flag for Panama.

Roosevelt dispatched two army officers to Panama so they could provide him with a personal report on the situation there. They indicated that revolutionary units were forming and guns were being smuggled into Panama. Bunau-Varilla met with Secretary of State John Hay, who advised, "Orders have been given to naval forces on the Pacific to sail towards the Isthmus."[142] Bunau-Varilla told Guerrero that when the revolution occurred, he wanted to be the one to negotiate the canal treaty with Hay.[143]

After Guerrero returned to Panama, he cabled Bunau-Varilla, demanding that he arrange to have a U.S. naval ship appear at Colón. He wanted his coconspirators to see that the United States would be providing needed support before they committed themselves and put their lives on the line. Bunau-Varilla contacted Assistant Secretary of State Francis B. Loomis. The USS *Nashville*, then at Kingston, Jamaica, began sailing 500 miles toward Colón.

On November 2, the Colombian naval ship *Cartagena* arrived soon after the *Nashville*, and the next morning it unloaded some five hundred Colombian soldiers. Generals Juan Tobar and Ramón Amaya were persuaded to board a special train—a locomotive and a single passenger car—for Panama City. Their soldiers were supposed to follow. But the soldiers were detained, the generals were arrested, and the conspirators proceeded to form a new government. Captain John Hubbard of the *Nashville* issued an order forbidding the Panama Railroad to transport either Colombian or Panamanian soldiers, effectively preventing the Colombian soldiers from disrupting efforts to secure the new government. The *Cartagena* sailed away, leaving the *Nashville* in command of Colón—and all troop movements in Panama.

Because the revolution occurred on the U.S. election day, election results rather than the Panama revolution dominated newspaper coverage for several days. But when Panama coverage increased, Roosevelt was widely criticized. He denied having anything to do with events in Panama: "It is reported we have made a revolution, it is not so."[144] Roosevelt asked his attorney general, Philander C. Knox, to assist in developing a defense of his policy toward Panama, and Knox reportedly remarked, "Oh, Mr. President, do not let so great an achievement suffer from any taint of legality."[145] At a Cabinet meeting, Roosevelt asked Secretary of War Elihu Root how well he was defending his Panama policy, and Root remarked: "You have shown that you were accused of seduction, and you have conclusively proved that you were guilty of rape."[146]

In his *Autobiography,* Roosevelt asserted, "No one connected with the American Government had any part in preparing, inciting, or encouraging the revolution, and except for the reports of our military and naval officers, which I forwarded to Congress, no one connected with the Government had any previous knowledge concerning the proposed revolution, except such as was accessible to any person who read the newspapers and kept abreast of current questions and current affairs."[147] He attacked Colombia for blocking construction of a canal.

Roosevelt compared his action toward Panama with Thomas Jefferson's acquisition of the Louisiana territory. But Roosevelt glossed over the fact that the United States paid France $15 million for Louisiana but seized land from Colombia.

Not until after Roosevelt died did the United States concede that it owed Colombia anything. In 1921, the U.S. Senate ratified the Thompson-Urrutia Treaty, agreeing to pay Colombia $25 million for Panama. Two decades later, the historian Samuel Flagg Bemis expressed the view of many that Roosevelt's seizure of Panama was a "really black mark in the Latin American policy of the United States, and a great big black mark, too. It has been rubbed off, after much grief, by the reparations treaty of 1921. We may now hope that all the rancor of a generation of Yankeephobia that followed Roosevelt's rash and lawless act has been buried in the grave of the impulsive statesman who perpetrated it."[148]

AN OVERLOOKED YET MOST INFLUENTIAL PRESIDENT

Theodore Roosevelt's foreign policy has never commanded as much attention from historians as the foreign policy of war presidents such as Abraham Lincoln, Woodrow Wilson, and Franklin Delano Roosevelt. But Theodore Roosevelt articulated the doctrine of global interventionism that revolutionized U.S. foreign policy. Traditional policy had been to stay out of other people's wars. Roosevelt believed in entering other people's wars to seek glory and maybe do good. He believed in trying to build other people's nations, whether or not other people wanted America to do so. He insisted that U.S. military action wasn't limited to protecting U.S. national security. By hammering away at traditional limitations on the conduct of U.S. foreign policy, Theodore Roosevelt laid the groundwork for the vast expansion of executive power that occurred in the twentieth century.

CHAPTER THREE

WHY DID ROOSEVELT BRAG ABOUT "TRUST-BUSTING" THAT HARMED THE AMERICAN CONSUMER?

THEODORE ROOSEVELT bragged about wielding a "big stick" against the "mighty industrial overlords."[1] He denounced free markets as "a riot of individualistic materialism."[2] He declared that "individualism proved to be both futile and mischievous."[3] He criticized the courts, which he called "agents of reaction . . . hostile to the interests of the people . . . impotent to deal with the great business combinations."[4]

How did businesses harm consumers? Did they charge high prices? Did they cut back output? Did they sell shoddy products? Did they drive down wages and make Americans poorer? Roosevelt never made any such charges, although he spoke ominously about "the evil done by the big combinations."[5] His only specific charge was that entrepreneurs "demanded for themselves an immunity from governmental control which, if granted, would have been as wicked and as foolish as immunity to the barons of the twelfth century."[6] In his most outrageous rhetorical outburst, he said that "of all the forms of tyranny the least attractive and the most vulgar is the tyranny of mere wealth, the tyranny of a plutocracy."[7]

It is curious indeed that Roosevelt claimed the moral high ground to attack alleged private monopolists when the government itself was the principal source of monopolies in America. There were government school monopolies in every state, for which millions of people were forced to pay taxes whether they used the schools or not. The federal government enforced its monopoly on handling first-class mail. Theodore Roosevelt promoted a federal dam-building monopoly, and he supported the progressive movement to establish a government power-generating monopoly. The federal government acted in restraint of international trade by enforcing tariffs that forced consumers to pay as much as 100 percent more for essentials like clothing. Roosevelt repeatedly threatened to push for lower tariffs, but then traded away the threat when he sought political support for expanding government intervention in the economy, as was the case with the 1906 Hepburn Act. According to historian John Morton Blum, Roosevelt "had strongly endorsed the principle of protection [high tariffs], chastised his Secretary of War for favoring tariff reduction in a campaign speech, and denounced the Democrats for their insistence that protection was robbery."[8]

AN ERA OF INTENSE COMPETITION

Roosevelt had it all wrong when it came to the American economy. Far from being riddled with terrible problems caused by irresponsible, self-serving capitalists, the American economy was among the wonders of the world, a major reason why millions of people left their homes and traveled thousands of miles to pursue the American dream.

Many authors since the time of the English economist Thomas Malthus (1766–1834) have blamed poverty on overpopulation. But while America's population increased rapidly during the late nineteenth century, its economy boomed and living standards improved. The population grew 85 percent from 25.5 million in 1880 to 47.3 million in 1910,[9] thanks in part to surging levels of immigration. By 1910, about 16 percent of Americans were foreign-born.[10] More people meant more customers, more workers, and bigger markets.

Many of the greatest late-nineteenth- and early-twentieth-century entrepreneurs were immigrants, including Maximilian Delphinius Berlitz (language schools), Jacob Henry Schiff (banking), Meyer Guggenheim (smelting), Levi Strauss (apparel), Claus Spreckels (sugar), John Jacob Bausch (optics), Frederick Weyerhaeuser (timber), Augustus Busch (beer), Andrew Carnegie (steel), Joseph Pulitzer (publishing), William Fox (movies), Jack Warner (movies), and Louis B. Mayer (movies). The U.S. gross national product grew from an estimated $11 billion in 1880 to $18.7 billion in 1900 and $35.3 billion in 1910.[11] The United States, which a few decades earlier had been an undeveloped country, was soon to surpass Europe.

This was an era of intense competition, not monopoly. Whereas monopolies try to curtail output and put upward pressure on prices, output soared, putting downward pressure on prices. For example, steel production soared from 1.3 million tons in 1880 to 11.2 million tons in 1900—the year the United States Steel Corporation was established—and 28.3 million tons a decade later.[12] Crude petroleum production advanced from 152 trillion British thermal units in 1880 to 369 trillion in 1900 and 1,215 trillion in 1910, the year before Standard Oil was broken up.[13] Although sugar refining was reported to be in the hands of monopolists, output expanded from 1.9 billion pounds in 1880 to 4.8 billion pounds in 1900 and 7.3 billion pounds in 1910.[14] A Census Bureau index of the value of food products advanced from about 1,679.4 in 1880 to 3,333 in 1900 and 6,129.6 in 1910[15]; the bureau's index for clothing went from 358.2 in 1880 to 817.4 in 1900 and 1,408.3 in 1910.[16]

The late nineteenth century and early twentieth century was a period of dramatic innovation, which made it increasingly difficult for anyone to sustain a monopoly. The number of patents issued annually by the U.S. Patent Office increased from 12,903 in 1880 to 24,644 in 1900 and 35,141 in 1910,[17] the year the one millionth U.S. patent was issued.[18] This period was the heyday of inventors such as Thomas Alva Edison, Alexander Graham Bell, George

Westinghouse, Gottlieb Daimler, George Eastman, Lee De Forest, George Washington Carver, Charles Steinmetz, and Orville and Wilbur Wright. Old businesses based on one technology were continuously challenged by new businesses with new technologies that made possible greater capabilities, better quality, and lower costs.

Traditional manufacturing and financial centers in the Northeast faced competition in the Midwest and West. Economic historians Ernest L. Bogart and Donald L. Kemmerer wrote: "The tendency was for a growing proportion of agricultural machinery and farm implements, of building and construction materials, of wood manufactures, especially furniture, of foods and drinks, of railway supplies, and of the iron and steel industry, including automobiles, to concentrate in the Middle West."[19] Great fortunes also were made in the West, providing further competition with the East. Merchants Mark Hopkins (1813–1878), Collis P. Huntington (1821–1900), and Charles Crocker (1822–1888) joined lawyer-politician Leland Stanford (1824–1893) and made their fortunes with the Central Pacific Railroad, Southern Pacific Railroad, and many other business ventures. Irish-born John William Mackay (1831–1902) made his fortune in Nevada silver mines, which he used to start the Bank of Nevada and finance the laying of transatlantic cables. George Hearst (1820–1891) amassed wealth from silver mining in Nevada and Utah, gold mining in South Dakota, and copper mining in Montana, leaving his son William Randolph Hearst with the means to buy newspapers and myriad other things.

New financial sources competed with Wall Street. The capital needed for westward business expansion came overwhelmingly from retained corporate earnings and from local sources. Meatpacker Philip D. Armour stressed in a letter to his sons "how necessary it is for Armour & Co., and the Armour Packing Co., to have more money in their business. I don't want any one to draw out personal money, but keep it in the business as more money is needed badly."[20] Historian Gabriel Kolko reported, "The activities of the Chicago and St. Louis banking clearing houses grew four times during the two decades after the ending of the Civil War, while New York's remained constant. Because Wall Street would not and could not supply necessary funds to Midwestern manufacturers, some local industrialists created and dominated their own banks for those occasions when self-financing was insufficient, and access to cheaper capital was decisive to the successes of the Rockefeller and Carnegie empires."[21]

PRICES GO DOWN, DOWN, DOWN

Theodore Roosevelt's speeches and writings contain many references to monopolies, but it's hard to find any mention of price trends—even though outrageous prices have long been viewed as a principal sin of monopolies. Similarly, most accounts of the American economy stress the attempts to establish monopolies. For instance, Columbia University historian Stuart Bruchey in *Enterprise: The Dynamic Economy of a Free People* (1990) went on for pages about pooling, trusts, gentlemen's agreements, and communities of interest and other efforts to limit competition, creating the impression that these efforts were typically successful.[22] Elsewhere, Bruchey discussed persistent price competition, but inexplicably he didn't make an obvious connection and acknowledge that efforts to sustain monopolies were *generally unsuccessful*. That the authors of hundreds of similarly dysfunctional books bemoaned "ruthless" price-cutting and "cutthroat competition" means one of two things: Either there were not many monopolies, or monopolies were not having the effects that they were presumed to have—namely, high prices. A few extraordinarily superficial accounts ignored evidence of price-cutting altogether. Joy Hakim's ten-volume children's *History of US* has reportedly sold over 4 million copies, and it was condensed into a single volume, *Freedom: A History of US*. In her account of late-nineteenth-century industrial development titled "An Age of Extremes," Hakim tossed around clichés like "robber baron," "merchant princes," and "the greatest, wisest and meanest monopoly known to history." She described Andrew Carnegie as a "lord" intent on "keeping wages low and profits high." Nowhere did she say a word about what happened to prices during this seemingly terrible period.[23]

Well, prices declined during the last three decades of the nineteenth century. As the economist Stanley Lebergott pointed out, "Crude oil sold for $12 to $16 a barrel in 1860, but for less than $1 in each year from 1879 to 1900. The simple explanation of this immense depression in prices was that the industry, which had pumped less than 1 million barrels in 1860, was flooding the markets by 1900 with 63 million barrels annually."[24] Most attempted monopolies were flops. As Lebergott continued: "Unfortunately for all these would-be cartel operators the inevitable happened. The high price led to the drilling, and completion, of some 418 new wells in the same period. . . . These inevitably produced still more oil, and drove the price back down."[25] Writing about the period 1866 to 1896, Lebergott observed that "interest rates were actually cut in half during these decades. . . . What money monopolists in their right mind would have squeezed their profits by cutting the rates they charged? The record suggests no monopoly."[26]

The cost of shipping goods by river, canal, wagon, and railroad also declined during this time.[27] Nobel laureate George J. Stigler reported that "average railroad freight charges per ton mile had fallen by 1887 to 54 percent of the 1873 level, with all lines in both the eastern and western regions showing similar declines."[28] The costs of shipping goods overseas also fell dramatically.[29] As a consequence, producers were able to enter distant markets, *undermining local monopolies*. Furthermore, falling prices intensified pressure on inefficient, high-cost producers. According to Bogart and Kemmerer, "The burden of the testimony by business men before the Industrial Commission in 1899 was that a strong impelling force to industrial combination was 'competition so vigorous that profits of nearly all competing establishments were destroyed.'"[30] Although there were continuing efforts to establish monopolies and a "great merger wave" occurred in the late 1890s, the U.S. Census Bureau reported that the number of commercial and industrial firms in the United States increased from 1.11 million in 1890 to 1.17 million in 1900 and 1.51 million in 1910. Among commercial and industrial firms, the business failure rate and the average liability per failure actually declined between 1890 and 1910.[31] And as prices declined, the quality of goods improved. Technology led to better and more consistent quality.

Moreover, companies prospered when they were able to develop good brand names, because people became repeat buyers of products they had confidence in. Marketing goods to repeat buyers was much cheaper than finding new customers, so companies had an incentive to keep repeat buyers satisfied by offering quality products. Department stores such as Macy's (New York), John Wanamaker's (Philadelphia), and Marshall Field's (Chicago) prospered by establishing themselves as sellers of brand names. Customers who were satisfied with one of a store's products were likely to be good prospects for the store's other offerings. The value of a satisfied customer far exceeded the value of a single purchase, giving stores incentives to offer consistent quality at competitive prices. Chain stores, too, competed by offering more value for a customer's money. The Atlantic & Pacific Tea Company began business in 1859 and by 1870 had opened many grocery stores, becoming the first major chain. Nine years later, Frank W. Woolworth pioneered "5 and 10 cent" stores offering a wide range of inexpensive items.

As Montgomery Ward, Sears, Roebuck, and other mail-order businesses found out, consumers would send their money to people they had never met and wait for delivery only if there was a money-back guarantee. Because handling returned goods was costly, mail-order businesses had incentives to stock good-quality products that seldom had to be returned. The development of mail-order businesses undermined local monopolies and helped give people in rural areas more choices than they ever had before.

FARMERS AND MERCHANTS LOBBY
FOR HIGHER PRICES

There didn't seem to be much, if any, complaining from consumers, because entrepreneurs were making it possible to enjoy a growing abundance of modern conveniences at lower and lower prices. During this period of peacetime prosperity, millions of ordinary people were beginning to live like kings. Harvard Law School antitrust law professor Phillip Areeda acknowledged, "The record proves neither the overwhelming public clamor often asserted nor the indifferent public attitudes asserted by a few."[32]

Unsuccessful competitors, however, were complaining. In the 1870s and 1880s, owners of small farms and small businesses had a hard time competing against larger, more efficient competitors selling goods at discount prices. Small farmers who shipped goods short distances resented bigger shippers who got better deals from the railroads. The railroads charged bigger shippers less per mile than smaller shippers had to pay, because bigger shippers were often sending goods longer distances. Keep in mind that everybody's railroad rates were falling, and bigger shippers offered the railroads genuine economies of scale.

Lobbyists for farmers and small businessmen launched a lobbying campaign against consumers, demanding government action to stop low-cost large competitors. The principal lobbying organizations were the National Grange, National Farmers Alliance, and the National Anti-Monopoly Cheap Freight Railway League.[33] Farmers were probably the most vocal adversaries of big businesses.[34] "The farmers' organizations," wrote economist Thomas DiLorenzo, "claimed that trusts and combinations were monopolies so that the things they bought (from the trusts) were becoming increasingly expensive relative to the prices of farm products. Thus the trusts were allegedly 'exploiting' the farm population. But the facts do not support this interpretation. From 1865 to 1900 agricultural terms of trade improved from the farmers' perspective. While there was a declining general price level during much of this period, farm prices fell less than all other prices, producing real gains for farmers. Also, the quality of many manufactured goods was improving because of technological changes in the manufacturing sector so that the agricultural terms of trade were even better for farmers."[35]

The Chicago meatpackers encountered tough resistance as they tried to expand into local markets. According to Stuart Bruchey, "From the beginning Swift had to contend with prejudice against eating meat killed more than a thousand miles away and many weeks earlier. He did so by advertising. He also had to combat boycotts of local butchers and the concerted efforts of the National Butchers' Protective Association to prevent the sale of his meat in local markets. The association was confident it could do this by inducing various state legislatures to pass a law prohibiting the sale of dressed beef, mutton, or pork unless it had been inspected by state officials twenty-four hours before slaughter. The requirement would effectively banish the Big Four from all but the Chicago market. In 1884 the association persuaded lawmakers in Minnesota, Indiana, and Colorado to enact such a law."[36]

Muckraking journalists like Henry Demarest Lloyd and Ida M. Tarbell, joined by "yellow journalism" moguls Joseph Pulitzer and William Randolph Hearst, sided with the high-cost small producers lobbying against consumers. These journalists implicitly confirmed that prices were falling by portraying discounting as an evil. Newspaper stories featured vicious personal attacks on low-cost producers. The muckrakers promoted hysteria about the large size of many businesses, ignoring the rapid expansion of huge, dynamically competitive markets during the late nineteenth and early twentieth centuries.

Perhaps no muckraker was more melodramatic than Lloyd, in his book *Wealth Against Commonwealth* (1894). "Between this plenty ripening on the boughs of our civilization and the people hungering for it," he wrote, "step the 'cornerers,' the syndicates, trusts, combinations. . . . Holding back the riches of earth, sea, and sky from their fellows who famish and freeze in the dark, they declare to them that there is too much light and warmth and food. They assert the right, for their private profit, to regulate the consumption by the people of the necessaries of life, and to control production, not by the needs of humanity, but by the decisions of a few for dividends."[37]

Low-cost producers undoubtedly engaged in some unsavory business practices, but they weren't alone. High-cost producers did everything they could to survive. There was plenty of "muck" on both sides.

One clear mistake made by the low-cost producers was to remain silent when savaged by the muckrakers. John D. Rockefeller's policy, for instance, was to ignore the criticism. No one, certainly none of the entrepreneurs, spoke out to defend the enterprises that had so dramatically improved Americans' lives by expanding output and cutting prices.

A SMOKE SCREEN TO ENACT
HIGHER TARIFFS

The 1888 elections gave Republicans control of the White House and both houses of Congress. Strongly influenced by big business, this became known as the "Billion Dollar Congress." William McKinley, then a Republican congressman from Ohio, introduced a bill to raise tariffs—taxes on imports that force consumers to pay more for imported goods. Protected behind a tariff wall, goods made by inefficient and high-cost domestic producers become price-competitive with imports. Tariffs subsidize inefficiency and allow inefficiency to continue and, often, worsen—at consumers' expense.

The Republicans wanted to raise tariffs not because the Federal government needed money. In 1888–1889, the federal budget showed a $53 million surplus—13.4 percent over tax revenues. Re-publicans were the high-tariff party and they did what they wanted when they had an opportunity. The tariff bill—the *New York Times* called it "the Campaign Contributors' Tariff Bill"[38]—was a monument for the farm lobby. It raised tariffs on imported wool, including coarse carpet wool, which wasn't even produced in the United States.[39] Particularly odious to tariff boosters were surging imports of cheap wool and cotton textiles, used in making inexpensive clothing for poor people, and such imports were hit with tariffs exceeding 100 percent. Cotton stockings faced a 70 percent tariff; linen goods, 50 percent.[40] A 70 percent tariff was imposed on imported tin plates. Overall, the average tariff was 48 percent.[41] "The most important measure adopted during this Congress was what was popularly known as the McKinley Tariff Law," recalled John Sherman, a Republican senator from Ohio.[42]

Theodore Roosevelt never seriously challenged these tariff rip-offs. "For him," observed John Morton Blum, "the tariff was a matter of expediency. The prospect of revision [lower tariffs], even of a tariff debate, alarmed the standpatters sufficiently to provide an effective disciplinary tool." Later, he would abandon any effort to reduce tariffs if he could get enough support for his schemes to interfere with the economy.[43]

Washington politicians seem to have felt vulnerable to criticism for forcing up consumer prices. They posed as consumer champions by supporting an antitrust bill against big businesses, to be enacted before the tariff. During the antitrust debates, Senator John Sherman—who was on the finance committee, which deliberated on tariffs—received a number of politically persuasive letters. Most of the letters came from small businesses, primarily oil refineries, that hoped to limit the market-share gains of bigger and lower-cost competitors. Sherman never heard from farmers or consumers. Farm organizations lobbied aggressively for antitrust restrictions on more cost-competitive big businesses, so the absence of letters from farmers probably didn't mean much. The absence of letters from consumers is more revealing, because for decades many people have assumed that the antitrust bill was enacted to help consumers.

Rhode Island's Senator Nelson Aldrich proposed legislative language exempting from antitrust prosecution any business combination that would "lessen the cost of production or reduce the price of any of the necessaries of life."[44] This proposal was resisted by farmers and businesses eager to raise prices, particularly when higher tariffs prevented consumers from buying cheaper goods made overseas. Connecticut's Senator Orville Platt protested, "I am entirely sick of this idea that the lower the prices are the better for the country, and that any effort to advance prices, no matter how low they may be, and that any arrangement between persons engaged in business to advance prices, is a wrong and ought to be redressed and punished."[45] Sherman himself gave away the game by attacking big businesses that "subverted the tariff system; they undermined the policy of government to protect American industries by levying duties on imported goods."[46]

If the bill had contained language about monopoly prices, that might have suggested its purpose was to help protect consumers, but the Senate Judiciary Committee omitted any such language. The bill, 897 words, was notably vague. It would outlaw "Every contract, combination in the form of trust or otherwise, or conspiracy, in restraint of trade or commerce among the several States, or with foreign nations," and any attempt to "monopolize any part of the trade or commerce." There would be decades of legislative and courtroom debates about the meaning of these words.

Economist Christopher Grandy pointed out that the antitrust bill seemed consistent with common law principles about monopoly.[47] Traditionally, the focus had been on barriers to entry in a business—for example, government-granted monopoly franchises to suppliers of water and electricity, tariffs and other government limitations on trade, and licensing restrictions that limited entry. Such restrictions had always been the principal source of monopoly, and in their absence profit-seeking entrepreneurs could be counted on to enter poorly served markets. With freedom of entry, attempted monopolies were unstable and invariably failed.

Senator Sherman and others claimed that monopolies controlled seventeen industries: castor oil, bituminous coal, cotton-seed oil, iron and iron nuts and washers, jute, lead, leather, linseed oil, liquor, matches, petroleum, salt, steel, steel rails, sugar, twine, and zinc. Thomas DiLorenzo cited the government's own data, principally the Census Bureau's *Historical Statistics of the United States,* to discredit that claim. "Real GNP increased by approximately 24 percent from 1880 to 1890," DiLorenzo reported, "while those allegedly monopolized industries for which some measure of real output is available grew on average by 175 per cent—seven times the rate of growth of the economy as a whole . . . some of the industries grew more than ten times faster than real GNP. These included steel (258 per cent), zinc (156 per cent), coal (153 per cent), steel rails (142 per cent), petroleum (79 per cent) and sugar (75 per cent).

"These trends continued to the turn of the century," DiLorenzo continued. "Output expanded in each industry except castor oil, and, on average, output in these industries grew at a faster rate than the rest of the economy. Those industries for which nominal output data were available expanded by 99 per cent compared to a 43 per cent increase in nominal GNP, while the other industries increased real output by 76 per cent compared to a 46 per cent rise in real GNP from 1890 to 1900."[48]

DiLorenzo also points out that prices fell dramatically in the years leading up to passage of the antitrust bill: "For example, the average price of steel rails fell from $68 to $32 between 1880 and 1890, or by 53 per cent. The price of refined sugar fell by 22 per cent, from 9 cents per pound in 1880 to 7 cents in 1890. It fell further to 4.5 cents by 1900. The price of lead dropped by 12 per cent, from $5.04 per pound in 1880 to $4.41 in 1890. The price of zinc declined by 20 per cent, from $5.51 to $4.40 per pound from 1880 to

1890, and the price of bituminous coal remained steady at about $3.10 per pound, although it fell by 29 per cent, to $2.20 from 1890 to 1900. Although the consumer price index fell by 7 per cent from 1890 to 1890, this was proportionately less than all of these items except coal."[49]

Nonetheless, the Senate drafted and on April 8, 1890, passed by a 51-to-1 vote legislation that became known as the Sherman Anti-Trust Act. The House vote, on June 20, 1890, was unanimous. On July 2, President Benjamin Harrison signed it into law.

According to economist Thomas W. Hazlett, "among those congressmen who voted 'Yes' or 'No' on both bills (i.e. excluding those who abstained on either), 142 members voted identically on the bills, while only 17 crossed over (i.e. voted 'Yes' on one and 'No' on the other. The hypothesis that the votes on these laws were independent of each other can be dismissed at the 99.9 percent confidence level. . . . A similar pattern does not evidence itself in the Senate, where there was only one 'No' vote on Sherman, and a close party line vote on the tariff. (This distribution is without proconsumer implications. The proconsumer thesis would be suggested by a high correlation between 'Yes' votes on Sherman and 'No' votes on the tariff.) Still, the clear pattern exhibited by Republican members of the Senate and by both parties in the House suggests that those who voted for the Sherman Act were likely to abandon the consumer welfare clause on the tariff, while those who promoted consumer welfare by opposing the tariff were highly likely to oppose the Sherman Act."[50]

The *New York Times* reported, "That so-called Anti-Trust law was passed to deceive the people and to clear the way for the enactment of this . . . law relating to the tariff. It was projected in order that the party organs might say to the opponents of tariff extortion and protected combinations, 'Behold! We have attacked the Trusts.'"[51]

Although the link between high tariffs and monopolies was missed by the muckraking journalists, it was widely understood. In

The Tariff and the Trusts (1907), New York lawyer Franklin Pierce fumed: "We legalize conditions out of which an evil arises and then attempt to suppress the evil by penal statutes. We provide for high duties upon foreign imports for the protection of home industries, and when a monopoly controlling the home market results therefrom, then pass penal laws punishing the monopoly. In this way our politicians prove to the great combinations who furnish campaign disbursements for political parties their fidelity to monopolistic interests, while, by the penal statute, they assure the people that they are against trusts. . . .

"Our protective tariff is the genesis of the trust. The trust comes out of it as naturally as fruit from blossom. Obviously the control of a market by a combination or trust is facilitated where the field of competition is artificially limited to one country since it is easier to combine the producers of one country than those of all countries, and to the extent all must concede that the tariff encourages trusts."[52]

Between 1890 and 1900, the federal government filed eighteen antitrust cases, only three of them against major industrial companies.[53] One of the cases, *United States v. E. C. Knight Co.* (1895), resulted in a key Supreme Court decision. The E. C. Knight Company was a Philadelphia-based importer and refiner of sugar. Knight and three other sugar producers contracted to sell their operations to the American Sugar Refining Company, which controlled most of the sugar business in the United States. Chief Justice Melville Weston Fuller, a Democrat appointed by President Grover Cleveland because he shared the president's belief in free enterprise, low taxes, and free trade,[54] wrote the majority opinion. Fuller believed it was prudent to limit central government power by maintaining a separation of powers between federal and state governments. Accordingly, he expressed a strict interpretation of the Constitution's commerce clause (Article I, Section 8): A company that did not engage in interstate commerce was not subject to federal regulation even if it established, say, a manufacturing monopoly.

Fuller explained, "if the national power extends to all contracts and combinations in manufacture, agriculture, mining, and other productive industries, whose ultimate result may affect external commerce, comparatively little of business operations and affairs would be left for state control."[55] The Supreme Court thus upheld the circuit court ruling and rejected the Justice Department's antitrust case.

Ironically, the Justice Department's antitrust lawyers had charged that "American Sugar Refining Company might obtain complete control of the price of sugar in the United States."[56] *But sugar prices were falling.* As economist Dominick T. Armentano noted, "Refined sugar sold at retail for more than 9 cents in 1880; 6.9 cents in 1890; 5.3 cents in 1895; 6.1 cents in 1900; 6.0 cents in 1905; and 6.0 cents in 1910. Wholesale prices per pound were 9.602 cents in 1880; 6.171 cents in 1890; 4.152 cents in 1895; 5.320 cents in 1900; 5.256 cents in 1905; and 4.972 cents in 1910. The theoretical margin between raw and refined sugar, out of which the refiner must make his profits, fluctuated from a high of 1.437 cents in 1882 (well before the 'monopoly') to .720 cents in 1890; .882 cents in 1895; .500 cents in 1899; .978 cents in 1905; and .784 cents in 1910. The margin was lower in 1895 (when American Sugar did 95 percent of the sugar refining) than it was in 1910 (when they did less than 62 percent). . . . The failure of antitrust law to divest the Sugar Trust did not produce the all embracing, exploitative monopoly envisioned by economic theory, and any restraint of trade that did occur in sugar was due more to U.S. tariff policy than to free market monopoly power."[57]

The Supreme Court's ruling established that the federal government should not interfere with corporate mergers. In an effort to deal with the consequences of falling prices, more and more corporate executives sought to consolidate operations with other companies. A merger wave during the late 1890s involved companies accounting for an estimated 50 percent of U.S. manufacturing capacity.[58] Among the companies that merged or reorganized were

American Tobacco, International Harvester, International Paper, and Republic Steel. The biggest of the mergers was United States Steel.

After 1900, concern about these mergers faded because most had not worked. In 1913, Yale University economics professor Arthur S. Dewing reported, "The failure of the National Salt Company affords one of the best examples of the results of an effort to raise prices through an attempt to control the total production of the country. The National Cordage failure was due to manipulation in all directions, the raw material, the finished product, and the market for the company's securities. The failure of the American Bicycle Company is a conspicuous instance of the collapse of a financial structure. The somewhat unfortunate history of the American Malting Company turns chiefly upon the fact that the enterprise had less earning capacity than it promoters had expected. The long continued failure of the Cotton Duck Consolidation attests in clear language to the extreme—perhaps unsurmountable—difficulty of obtaining a man with skill of management sufficient to manage a large and scattered group of mills as efficiently and as economically as the man of ordinary ability can manage a single mill. The failure of the Corn Products, the American Malting, the United States Realty, and the New England Cotton Yarn Company were the result of payment of dividends on stock which, in each of these cases, was unwarranted. Petty jealousy sprung up where before there was only mutual confidence, and as the ties of organization became less personal, the Asphalt Consolidation crumbled to pieces."[59]

Historian Gabriel Kolko observed, "The decline of mergers was due to the collapse of the promises of stability, profits, and industrial cooperation. Save for the outside promoter who took his profit immediately and then broke his ties with the consolidation, the larger part of the mergers brought neither profits nor less competition. Quite the opposite occurred. There was more competition, and profits, if anything, declined. Most contemporary economists and many small business entrepreneurs failed to appreciate this fact, and historians have probably failed to recognize it altogether. This phenomenon, I maintain, is a vital key to understanding the political history of the period of reform preceding World War I."[60]

ROOSEVELT'S FIRST BIG ANTITRUST CASE

Theodore Roosevelt's first important antitrust case involved the railroad industry—an odd choice because the federal government had lavished land grants and other subsidies on the railroad companies. The most notorious financial scandal of the nineteenth century—Crédit Mobilier—occurred as a direct consequence of government intervention in the railroad business. Another irony was that Roosevelt's first big antitrust case targeted men who had saved collapsing railroads and cut railroad rates.

When President McKinley was shot on September 6, 1901, the stock market plunged and continued to fall after his death, probably anticipating the succession by Vice President Theodore Roosevelt, who, as New York governor, had made clear his determination to pursue "trust-busting." As president, Roosevelt denounced successful entrepreneurs as "malefactors of great wealth," giving investors good reason to be wary of taking political risks.

From 1900 to 1905, the Justice Department filed eleven antitrust cases, including two against major industrial companies.[61] Most important were the cases against Northern Securities (filed in March 1902) and Swift (May 1902). Roosevelt aimed to overturn the Supreme Court's *Knight* decision and open the way to wideranging government interference in the economy.

The Northern Securities case involved two outstanding American railroad entrepreneurs—James J. Hill (1838–1916), who built the Great Northern Railway, and his chief competitor, Edward H. Harriman (1848–1909).

Hill started his career as a freight agent, arranging the efficient transfer of goods between boats and local railroads—there weren't yet any rail connections to Chicago or other distant points.[62] He prospered as the Milwaukee & St. Paul and the St. Paul & Pacific railroads handled an increasing volume of hard wheat shipments.[63] He developed a steamboat business serving farmers in the fertile valley of the Red River of the North, which flows north through Minnesota, North Dakota, and into Canada.[64] He expanded his business to become a broker in wood, the principal fuel.[65] He recognized that if sufficient operating efficiencies were achieved, railroads could supply people with coal.[66]

Hill spent years observing the railroads he dealt with. According to historian Albro Martin, Hill gained "a practical knowledge of the physical side of railroading which was seldom found in one with neither formal engineering training nor long years of experience and operation. He had long since come to understand the most important fact about railroading: the combination of the self-propelled vehicle and the iron rail roadway was a unique and virtually universal solution to the problem of inland transportation, because a locomotive pulling a train of loaded cars on a low-friction track was far cheaper than any other form of land transportation, and the rails could go almost anywhere."[67]

The most impressive railroad in the region was the Northern Pacific, which was chartered by Congress in 1864, given land grants and other subsidies, and further financed by the Philadelphia-based banker Jay Cooke. But the Northern Pacific's managers believed that the best way to make money was to sell off land grant properties rather than work to operate their railroad efficiently.[68] Cooke, financially overextended, went bankrupt during the panic of 1873. The St. Paul & Pacific went bankrupt, too, and six years later,[69] Hill acquired its assets with three partners and backing from the Bank of Montreal.[70] The business was reorganized as the St. Paul, Minneapolis & Manitoba Railway Company.[71] None of this was easy. "Eighteen months before," Martin notes, "the associates had stood alone, their scheme spurned by a shrewd English banking firm and by the knowledgeable railroad specialist who had investigated it. When they decided to go ahead it had been fully understood on all sides that they were risking all they possessed."[72] Hill, as general manager,[73] sold his other businesses and focused on making the best railroad in the Northwest.[74]

Each year brought more competition. The Milwaukee & St. Paul established a Chicago connection and became the Chicago, Milwaukee & St. Paul, convincing Hill that he had to maintain his competitive position with a Chicago connection.[75] That railroad also established a line into the Red River of the North valley, which Hill viewed as his territory.[76] The Chicago, Burlington & Quincy planned a line to the Twin Cities.[77] The Northern Pacific continued operating and seemed to get a boost when, in 1883, the German-born, New York–based journalist and financier Henry Villard took over and combined it with his Oregon Railway & Navigation Company.[78] The Northern Pacific was close enough to the St. Paul, Minneapolis & Manitoba lines that Hill saw there was always a potential threat to build feeder lines that would draw business away from him. When the Northern Pacific proceeded to build a transcontinental line, Hill knew it would take away some of his freight business.[79] He discussed a joint venture with the struggling[80] Canadian Pacific, but the Canadians' insistence that the entire length of a transcontinental line would have to go through Canada killed the deal.[81] During the mid-1880s, a new railroad was built to transport flour eastward from Minneapolis to Sault Ste. Marie, from which point it could be shipped across the Great Lakes.[82] All this meant farmers had more and more options for getting their crops to market.

Railroad rates declined faster than most other prices, squeezing profit margins of the St. Paul, Minneapolis & Manitoba.[83] Hill maintained his program of continuous improvement. He replaced all major wooden trestles and bridges.[84] In addition to ongoing outlays for construction, Hill needed more rolling stock. According to Martin, "There would never, it seemed, be enough boxcars, gondolas, and flats to carry the freight; they seldom seemed to be in the right place; and division superintendents never seemed to think they had locomotives enough to move them about."[85]

When, in 1884, a British bank asked Hill what comments he might offer investors, he replied: "During the past two years we have spent a great deal of money for steel rails, ballasting track, transfer yards, terminal facilities, new equipment, new shops, and in fact we have put the road in better condition than any railway similarly situated that I know of in the west. . . . We have now over one thousand miles with a 26-foot maximum grade and only 220 miles with over a 30-foot maximum grade. The latter we expect to reduce to 26-foot maximum within the next two years. When this is done no railway in the world of one thousand miles or more will have the same low gradients."[86]

On September 18, 1889, Hill reorganized his operations to form the Great Northern. His engineers built a transcontinental line, boring through mountains, crossing rivers, dealing with floods and mudslides.[87] Hill directed his engineers "to make the work permanent and good in every respect so that it will not have to be done over again."[88] The Great Northern's tracks crossed the Rockies and the Cascades to Seattle. The last spike was pounded in on January 6, 1893.[89] Hill relentlessly cut costs and boosted freight volume, achieving an average payload of 300 tons per train—a billion tons per year.[90] He pioneered the idea of a low-cost, high-volume railroad.[91] The Great Northern prospered even during the panic of 1893, which triggered another bankruptcy for his rival, the Northern Pacific, weakened by poor management.[92] "No railroad," wrote historian Martin, "ever enjoyed more trust, or was given the benefit of more doubts, and betrayed them more, than the Northern Pacific under Henry Villard. 'Under Villard' is perhaps unfair, for the brilliant publicist and financial arranger was a poor builder and manager of railroads, and made little show of actually running the Northern Pacific from his headquarters in New York. Men like Hill knew that Villard, at best, was closing his eyes to conflicts of interest between the railroad and its operating executives . . . the need for physical improvements was ignored."[93]

Hill was very proud that the Great Northern "was built without any government aid, even the right of way, through hundreds of miles of public lands, being paid for in cash."[94] Hill spent his time running a railroad, not lobbying politicians for favors. He mainly wanted to be left alone.[95] Hill's success was proof that neither government land grants nor subsidies were needed to build successful railroads. Indeed, the experience of the Northern Pacific, Union Pacific, Sante Fe, and other railroads seemed to suggest that subsidies undermined incentives for railroads to root out incompetence and corruption.

Hill feared that in bankruptcy, relieved for a while of the obligation to pay interest on its bonds, the Northern Pacific might cut rates, imperiling the Great Northern.[96] He met with European creditors to discuss the possibility of acquiring the Northern Pacific.[97] Financier J. P. Morgan, who had reorganized many a bankrupt railroad, agreed to underwrite securities on behalf of a reorganized Northern Pacific.[98]

There was some competition between these railroads. Northern Pacific went from Duluth to St. Paul, Everett, Seattle, and Portland, and there was a branch line to Helena. Great Northern went from Duluth to St. Paul, Helena, Spokane, Seattle, Tacoma, and Portland. In 1893, though, the Northern Pacific became insolvent, and control passed to receivers appointed by U.S. courts. Before foreclosure, J. P. Morgan and other Northern Pacific bondholders arranged for the railroad to be taken over by Hill's Great Northern.

Minnesota's attorney general got involved, claiming that the acquisition would be illegal. After a frustrating legal battle, Hill and Morgan abandoned the idea of acquiring the Northern Pacific. They decided to pursue acquisition of the Chicago, Burlington & Quincy Railroad. But this plan brought them head-to-head with Edward H. Harriman, a railroad entrepreneur who had an extraordinary talent for turnarounds, saving companies that were losing money and in danger of going out of business. Typically, Harriman confronted struggles among incompetent managers, equity investors, bondholders, bank lenders, and other creditors. His challenge was to figure out what was worth salvaging, what had to be eliminated, how to do both, and how to get additional funding after all the obvious sources of funds had dried up. To manage turnarounds successfully, one had to be smart, decisive, and tough, and Harriman was all three.

Harriman, according to historian Maury Klein, "was intense and combative—the forerunner of an age when speed and efficiency would replace grace and charm. On duty he was a human computer, his mind racing so quickly over data to conclusions that others could hardly follow him. Coming late to railroads, the oldest and most hidebound of major industries, he looked at its hoary traditions with fresh eyes and with startling speed literally reinvented the business. In one decade his innovations shoved an industry made moribund and dispirited by the depression of 1893–97 into the twentieth century. The railroads under his control became models for others to emulate. He modernized not only their physical plant but their organizations, business practices, financing, and safety records."[99]

Born in 1848 in Hempstead, New York, the son of an Episcopal clergyman, Harriman began his career as a Wall Street stock clerk. He did so well trading for himself that he was able to buy a seat on the New York Stock Exchange. In 1879, he married Mary Averell, daughter of the owner of the Ogdensburg & Lake Champlain Railroad. He acquired the Sodus Bay & Southern Railroad, which went inland from Lake Ontario, achieved operating efficiencies, then sold it at a profit to the Pennsylvania Railroad.

Harriman bought an interest in the Illinois Central Railroad, which had been chartered in 1851 to lay track from Cairo, Illinois (where the Ohio and Mississippi rivers come together), to Galena (in northwestern Illinois). The Illinois Central had been the first railroad to receive a federal land grant, under an act signed by President

Millard Fillmore. The Illinois Central made acquisitions and extended its lines south to New Orleans. Harriman secured a position on the board, helped strengthen the company's finances, and helped the railroad expand westward.

Harriman set his sights on the Union Pacific Railroad, which had received huge subsidies to build the eastern segment of the first transcontinental railroad. The Union Pacific had become embroiled in the biggest U.S. financial scandal of the century, involving the crooked contracting firm Crédit Mobilier. For a while, the Union Pacific was owned by Wall Street operator Jay Gould, who kept it going by juggling finances. Then came the panic of 1893. Traffic in copper, iron, and silver fell 46 percent between 1892 and 1894. Coal traffic fell 18 percent. Brick and stone, 54 percent. Lumber, 45 percent. Salt, 30 percent. Wheat, 74 percent. Corn, 47 percent. Barley and other grains, 74 percent.[100] Lacking effective leadership, the railroad went bankrupt.

Reorganizing the Union Pacific involved dealing with Congress, because of debts owed the federal government, and would be a nightmare. The Union Pacific had a hodgepodge of properties in separate receiverships, so a potential acquirer almost certainly faced multiple legal proceedings. For example, explained historian Klein, the Union Pacific's Gulf Line "was a hybrid created by merging the Denver, Texas & Fort Worth (or Panhandle road, as it was called) with a smattering of Union Pacific branches. But the Panhandle was itself a hybrid bred from two incompatible strains."[101]

What talents were available to attempt a reorganization of the Union Pacific? The three strongest executives on Union Pacific's board—Jay Gould, Sidney Dillon (a former president of the railroad), and Frederick L. Ames (whose family helped found the railroad)—had died by 1893.[102] J. P. Morgan, who made his formidable reputation reorganizing troubled railroads, tried to do something with the Union Pacific but gave up. He encouraged the small and dapper Jacob Schiff, the leading partner at rival Kuhn, Loeb & Company, to explore possibilities.[103] Schiff waited to see what might happen as a result of McKinley's victory in the 1896 presidential election.[104]

In 1897, Harriman, working with Schiff, acquired Union Pacific properties from Omaha, Nebraska, to Ogden, Utah. He paid $110 million, then spent millions more upgrading the operation by double-tracking single-track lines, reducing grades, eliminating curves, replacing wooden bridges, expanding train yards, and purchasing better locomotives and cars. Harriman financed these improvements and paid off debt with backing from James Stillman's National City Bank and from the Rockefellers.

In 1901, Harriman tried to acquire a route into Chicago by gaining control of the Chicago, Burlington & Quincy Railroad. He was again backed by Jacob Schiff of Kuhn, Loeb. But James Hill wanted to buy the railroad for its Chicago connection. Thwarted in his efforts to buy the Burlington directly, Harriman began buying stock of the Northern Pacific, which owned a substantial amount of Burlington stock. There was about $80 million of Northern Pacific common stock and $75 million of preferred stock. J. P. Morgan controlled no more than $40 million, which he thought would be enough to ensure control. By April, Harriman, through Schiff, managed to buy $27 million of common stock and $25 million of preferred stock.[105] Soon there were speculative frenzies in the stock of both Northern Pacific and Union Pacific. Harriman acquired more shares of Northern Pacific but wasn't sure he had gained control.

On November 12, 1901, J. P. Morgan and James Hill formed the Northern Securities Company as a New Jersey holding company. It had $400 million of capital—only United States Steel Corporation had a larger capitalization.[106] Hill and his associated stockholders turned their Great Northern shares over to Northern Securities Company. Morgan and his associated stockholders turned their Northern Pacific shares over to Northern Securities. In return, Hill and Morgan received Northern Securities shares. Harriman and Hill resolved their differences, and Harriman joined Hill and Morgan as a principal in the Northern Securities Company.

"The idea of a holding company," explained Maury Klein, "was to control several roads with a minimum of capital, but Harriman and his banker friends had something more in mind: to impose order on the chaotic rail industry. Large profits required a steady flow of capital from Europe, but the bankers could sell American securities to their overseas clients only if the emerging rail systems were efficient, well-managed, and free from the strife that had bled them to death earlier. Achieving this stability was the goal of community of interest, the voting trusts, the advisory boards, and every other device of the era."[107]

Gains for the Northern Securities investors were most likely to come from overhauling the Northern Pacific, which had long been managed poorly. Either Hill or Harriman could have worked wonders. They would have insisted on higher standards for management, construction, service, and myriad other matters vital to the successful operation of a railroad. Roosevelt biographer Edmund Morris acknowledged that Hill, Harriman, and Morgan were "Decent, driven men [who] had enriched themselves beyond imagination by anonymous deals in railroad stocks. They had built up great transportation systems, stimulated interstate commerce, and improved life for uncounted millions of people. Their philanthropies were legion, their senses of social responsibility sincere."[108]

Roosevelt, however, despised Morgan and was spoiling for a fight. According to H. W. Brands, "Northern Securities wasn't the worst trust in America . . . but Roosevelt realized he had to start somewhere, and the railroad giant appeared as good a place as any. If Roosevelt had simply been interested in reforming the railroad, he might reasonably have cut a deal with Morgan. But Morgan and the railroad represented a whole category of corporate wrongdoing."[109] On February 19, 1902, Theodore Roosevelt's attorney general Philander Knox announced that the government was filing an antitrust lawsuit against the company.[110]

On August 23, Roosevelt visited city hall in Providence, Rhode Island, and spoke ominously about trusts: "The great corporations which we have grown to speak of rather loosely as trusts are the creatures of the State, and the State not only has the right to control them, but it is in duty bound to control them."[111] In April 1903, a district court ruled that the Northern Securities deal violated the Sherman Anti-Trust Act, and during the next three months the stock market fell about 10 percent.[112] For a moment, Roosevelt took this decline as a warning about the dangers of government meddling in the economy.

The Supreme Court upheld the case against Northern Securities on March 14, 1904.[113] The majority opinion was written by Justice John Marshall Harlan, a Kentucky Republican who was nominated to the Supreme Court by President Rutherford B. Hayes in 1877. Because the Northern Securities Company had been in existence for less than four years, it hardly had had time to do anything wrong. Harlan objected to the *potential* for harm. "The mere existence of such a combination," he wrote, "and the power acquired by the holding company as its trustee, constitute a menace to, and a restraint upon, that freedom of commerce which Congress intended to recognize and protect, and which the public is entitled to have protected."[114]

Harlan continued, "if the combination [Northern Securities Company] was held not to be in violation of the act of Congress, then all efforts of the national government to preserve to the people the benefits of free competition among carriers engaged in interstate commerce will be wholly unavailing, and all transcontinental lines, indeed, the entire railway systems of the country, may be absorbed, merged, and consolidated, thus placing the public at the absolute mercy of the holding corporation."[115]

Harlan's view was utterly unrelated to the facts. Because of the dramatic expansion of railroad mileage, more markets had more railroad connections, which meant more competition among railroads as well as with water routes. Pools, gentlemen's agreements, and other efforts to thwart competition had repeatedly failed, and railroad rates continued to decline. The Northern Pacific had gone bankrupt twice. Was the public likely to be better served with the Northern Pacific run by mediocre managers or by superior managers?

In his dissent, Justice Oliver Wendell Holmes explained that the phrase "restraint of trade," which appeared in common law cases as well as in the Sherman Anti-Trust Act, traditionally meant barriers to entry preventing firms from entering a business. "Restraint of trade" did not apply to a merger involving people already in a business.[116] Holmes went on to say that the word *monopoly* had been so indiscriminately used as to become meaningless. "According to popular speech," he wrote, "every concern monopolizes whatever business it does, and if that business is trade between two states it monopolizes a part of the trade among the states. Of course, the statute does not forbid that. It does not mean that all business must cease. A single railroad down a narrow valley or through a mountain gorge monopolizes all the railroad transportation through that valley or gorge. Indeed, every railroad monopolizes, in a popular sense, the trade of some area. Yet I suppose no one would say that the statute forbids a combination of men into a corporation to build and run such a railroad between the states. The act of Congress will not be construed to mean the universal disintegration of society into single men, each at war with all the rest, or even the prevention of all further combinations for a common end."[117]

Holmes's dissenting opinion infuriated Roosevelt. Holmes wrote Frederick Pollock, the English legal scholar: "It broke up our incipient friendship, as he looked on my dissent to the *Northern Securities* case as a political departure (or, I suspect, more truly, couldn't forgive anyone who stood in his way)."[118]

There was more than a little hypocrisy in the Roosevelt administration's professed concern to protect consumers from monopoly prices, since the government itself ripped off consumers by maintaining tariffs. Since the Civil War, the federal government had forced consumers to pay 40 percent, 50 percent, even 60 percent above market levels for imported goods.[119] Theodore Roosevelt backed continued high tariffs, so he didn't have much moral standing as a consumer advocate.

Moreover, tariffs were highly discriminatory and disruptive. As the social critic and economist Henry George explained, a tariff "that raises prices for the encouragement of one industry must operate to discourage all other industries into which the products of that industry enter. Thus a duty that raises the price of lumber necessarily discourages the industries which make use of lumber, from those connected with the building of houses and ships to those engaged in the making of matches and wooden toothpicks; a duty that raises the price of iron discourages the innumerable industries into which iron enters; a duty that raises the price of salt discourages the dairyman and the fisherman; a duty that raises the price of sugar discourages the fruit-preserver, the maker of syrups and cordials, and so on."[120]

Roosevelt's 1904 win at the Supreme Court no doubt encouraged the president to continue his antibusiness talk, particularly when financial markets were nervous. Many businessmen feared more aggressive government intervention in the economy.[121] According to Henry Pringle, whose biography of Roosevelt was published in 1931, "One rumor in Wall Street in February, 1907, was that freight and passenger rates would be reduced. Every corporation capitalized at more than $1,000,000 would soon suffer from the Rooseveltian Reign of Terror. So carefully edited a journal as the *New York Times* carried, in the most prominent position on its front page, a dispatch from Washington which said that Roosevelt intended to 'break' Harriman, that the Harriman railroad lines would be declared in restraint of trade, and somehow dissolved. Not long afterwards, Roosevelt had his famous, and all too public, quarrel with E. H. Harriman, a controversy that reflected discredit on both men. The $29,000,000 Standard Oil file was viewed as the final indication that the President proposed to wreck American industry."[122]

From May to September 1907, there was a contraction in the

money supply, apparently due to an outflow of gold from the United States.[123] Gold was a traditional barometer of investor confidence, and the United States was on a gold standard. The contraction put banks under financial pressure, and there was a banking panic in October. Five New York banks failed.[124] J. P. Morgan raised $35 million for banks that he judged were capable of being saved.[125] New York City, however, could find no buyers for its bonds.[126]

For a while, Roosevelt backed off. He let it be known that he would not interfere with United States Steel's plans to acquire Tennessee Coal and Iron Company.[127] He asked Attorney General Charles J. Bonaparte not to file an antitrust lawsuit against International Harvester Company.[128] "Roosevelt was a badly frightened Chief Executive toward the end of 1907," Pringle observed.[129]

Even if it were true that Roosevelt's antibusiness talk and policies weren't the only factors responsible for the panic of 1907, why would a politician deliberately disrupt the economy—particularly in light of the suffering of millions of Americans during the depression of 1893? What was the point of denouncing entrepreneurs who had done so much to make the economy grow, create jobs, lower consumer prices, and raise living standards? Given the evidence surrounding him and contradicting his "trust-busting" attitude, it's difficult not to conclude that Theodore Roosevelt was a petty, power-grubbing politician with a big mouth.

THE STRANGE CASE OF STANDARD OIL

Theodore Roosevelt's most famous, and strangest, antitrust lawsuit was against John D. Rockefeller's Standard Oil companies. Although the federal government had been a principal culprit responsible for forcing up consumer prices through corruption, tariffs, taxes, and wars, Roosevelt claimed the government had moral standing to assert control over the private sector—and Standard Oil made for an ideal scapegoat.

Roosevelt's attorney general William H. Moody filed a 170-page "bill" on November 15, 1906.[130] It charged that Standard Oil was a monopoly acting "in restraint of trade." Roosevelt called Standard Oil's directors "the biggest criminals in the country."[131] Yet the number of oil refineries was increasing, the price of Standard Oil's principal product, kerosene, was falling, and kerosene accounted for a declining share of the market for petroleum products.[132] Moreover, Standard Oil had not tried to get the government to restrict barriers to entry by means of regulations, tariffs, or other measures. Standard Oil competed aggressively in a marketplace relatively free from political interference.[133]

For years, John D. Rockefeller (1839–1937) and Standard Oil Company had been among the progressives' favorite targets. Rockefeller was born on a Richford, New York, farm, started his career working in a small wholesale firm earning $3.57 per week, and grew his oil business through careful management. While his partner, Samuel Andrews, figured out how to extract as much kerosene as possible from oil, Rockefeller built up the company's capital reserves in an attempt to finance growth as much as possible without having to bring in outside lenders or investors. Instead of buying oil from "jobbers," Rockefeller sent his own purchasing agents into the oil fields. He kept detailed records and was always looking for ways to improve operations and cut costs. Cutting costs was essential, because kerosene prices were falling.

Rockefeller's greatest critic was muckraker Ida M. Tarbell, whose reports on the history of Standard Oil were published each month in *McClure's* magazine from November 1902 to October 1904 and appeared in book form in 1904. Tarbell acknowledged that frugality was a key to Rockefeller's success: "He had the frugal man's hatred of waste and disorder, of middlemen and unnecessary manipulation, and he began a vigorous elimination of these from his business. The residuum that other refiners let run into the ground, he sold. Old iron found its way to the junk shop. He bought his oil directly from the wells. He made his own barrels.

He watched and saved and contrived. Low-voiced, soft-footed, humble, knowing every point in every man's business, he never tired until he got his wares at the lowest possible figure. To drive a good bargain was the joy of his life. He could borrow as well as bargain. The firm's capital was limited; growing as they were, they often needed money, and had none. Borrow they must. Rarely if ever did Mr. Rockefeller fail."[134]

In 1870, Rockefeller persuaded his brother William to join his oil refining business.[135] Henry M. Flagler and S. V. Harkness also became partners, and the Standard Oil Company came into being with $1 million in capital. The name "Standard" was intended to assure consumers that they could rely on the company for consistent quality. (Kerosene varied considerably at that time, and people could be hurt or killed when lighting kerosene that contained too much gasoline or naptha.) Flagler, still in his twenties, already had made a fortune distilling whiskey, then lost it in the salt business. He was an aggressive negotiator who handled Standard Oil's business with railroads, securing rate discounts that helped the company sell its products for lower prices. Standard Oil had an estimated 4 percent of the kerosene refining business, in an industry with perhaps 250 firms.[136] Falling kerosene prices led Rockefeller and other refiners to discuss ways to cut one of their major costs—the rates railroads charged for shipping oil to markets.

Deeply offended by Rockefeller's aggressive pursuit of railroad rate discounts, Tarbell insinuated that discounting was a sin. "In 1868 or 1869, a rival in the business," she wrote, "went to the Atlantic and Great Western road, then under the Erie management, and complained, 'You are giving others better rates than you are us,' said Mr. Alexander, the representative of the firm. 'We cannot compete if you do that.' The railroad agent did not attempt to deny it—he simply agreed to give Mr. Alexander a rebate also. The arrangement was interesting. Mr. Alexander was to pay the open, or regular, rate on oil from the Oil Regions to Cleveland, which was then forty cents a barrel. At the end of each month he was to send to the railroad vouchers for the amount of oil shipped and paid for at forty cents, and was to get back from the railroad, in money, fifteen cents on each barrel."[137]

Tarbell proceeded to report "a still more important bit of testimony" from Lake Shore Railroad vice president J. H. Devereux. This railroad desperately needed to ship a lot of oil from Cleveland, where it had established lines. A number of Cleveland refiners considered moving their business to Titusville, Pennsylvania, where they could take advantage of cheap shipping rates offered by the Pennsylvania Railroad. The question for Devereux, in 1868, was "whether he could meet the [low] rates the Pennsylvania were giving and increase the oil freight for the Lake Shore."[138] Rockefeller and his partners decided to keep their business in Cleveland, and they got the railroad rate discounts they needed. This upset Alexander. Tarbell reported, "The railroad took the position with him that if he could ship as much oil as the Standard he could have as low a rate, but not otherwise."[139]

Tarbell's hostility to discounting reflected her view "that the railroad being a common carrier had no right to discriminate between its patrons."[140] But the costs of serving different shippers varied considerably. As historian Ron Chernow explained, "Rockefeller and Flagler didn't simply try to squeeze the railroads—they were much too shrewd and subtle for that—but offered compelling incentives. For instance, they agreed to assume legal liability for fire or other accidents and stop using water transport during the summer months. The biggest plum they dangled before Devereux was a promise to supply the Lake Shore with an astonishing sixty carloads of refined oil daily. Since Rockefeller lacked the refining capacity to fulfill this ambitious pledge, he was evidently prepared to coordinate shipments with other Cleveland refiners. For any railroad, the prospect of steady shipments was irresistible, for they could dispatch trains composed solely of oil-tank cars instead of a motley assortment of freight cars picking up different products at different places. By consolidating many small shippers into one big shipper making regular, uniform shipments in massive quantities, the railroads could reduce the average round-trip time of their trains to New York from thirty days to ten and operate a fleet of 600 cars instead of 1,800."[141]

Chernow continued: "Rockefeller's firm invested heavily in warehouses, terminals, loading platforms, and other railroad facilities so that the roads probably derived more profit from his shipments than from those of rivals who paid higher rates. Small, irregular shipments were the bane of railroads for the simple, mechanical reason that they forced the trains to stop repeatedly to pick up single carloads of oil. Rockefeller had to run his refineries at full capacity even when kerosene demand slackened. He therefore paid a price for his rebates and felt that equal rates for all shippers would have unfairly penalized his firm."[142]

Tarbell's journalistic "scoop" was reporting the inside story of the secret scheme known as the South Improvement Company, an agreement among Standard Oil and three principal railroads in the region—the Pennsylvania, New York Central, and Erie—which specified that (1) each railroad would get a share of Standard Oil's shipping business—45 percent for the Pennsylvania, 27.5 percent for the New York Central, and 27.5 percent for the Erie; (2) other refiners would be charged higher rates and Standard Oil would receive rebates; (3) Standard Oil would receive a "drawback" fee on every barrel of oil shipped by other refiners; and (4) the three railroads would share with Standard Oil information they had about what other refiners were doing.[143]

Small refiners were outraged at the scheme, and Tarbell embraced their views. She objected to volume discounts as unfair, wrong, outrageous, immoral. She lashed out at "the vicious system of rebates practiced by the railway."[144] She portrayed opponents of discounting as heroic white knights and the South Improvement Company as the villain in a morality tale: "no triumph could stifle the suspicion and the bitterness which had been sown broadcast through the region. Every particle of independent manhood in these men whose very life was independent action had been outraged. Their sense of fair play, the saving force of the region in the days before law and order had been established, had been violated. These were things which could not be forgotten. There henceforth could be no trust in those who had devised a scheme which, the producers believed, was intended to rob them of their property."[145]

Who was the primary offender in this tale? The "Mephistopheles of the Cleveland company," Tarbell wrote—"John D. Rockefeller."[146] She snarled: "He was willing to array himself against the combined sentiment of a whole industry, to oppose a popular movement aimed at righting an injustice, so revolting to one's sense of fair play as that of railroad discriminations."[147] His company was "blackened by commercial sin."[148]

Blinded by her belief that discounting was sinful, Tarbell failed to recognize that the South Improvement Company was a desperate effort to deal with excess capacity in the railroad business and in the oil refining business. The big news was not that the scheme was attempted, because many cartels were attempted in many industries during this era of falling prices. The big news was that the scheme failed. Despite the clout of the participants who were alleged to be monopolists, railroad rates and kerosene prices continued to fall.

Tarbell repeatedly suggested that Rockefeller controlled the price of oil, forced it up, and charged whatever he liked. She referred to the "Petroleum Plot."[149] She said, "Mr. Rockefeller still held to his theory that to make oil dear was worthy of public approval."[150] She wrote, "refined oil went up steadily with crude."[151] In her conclusion, she declared that "the purpose of the Standard Oil Company is the purpose of the South Improvement Company—the regulation of the price of crude and refined oil by the control of output."[152] One might never know from reading *The History of Standard Oil* that oil prices were actually falling.

Standard Oil prospered, in part, because Rockefeller was able to continue cutting costs quickly enough that the company could make money even as kerosene prices fell from 30 cents per gallon in 1869 to 11 cents a gallon by 1874[153] and 8 cents per gallon in 1885.[154] As kerosene prices fell, high-cost refiners could be expected to drop out of the business. Tarbell sniped at Rockefeller for wanting to continue growing his company and creating jobs: "Certainly Mr. Rockefeller should have been satisfied in 1870. But Mr. Rockefeller was far from satisfied. He was a brooding, cautious, secretive man, seeing all the possible dangers as well as all the possible opportunities in things."[155]

During the 1870s, Standard Oil began buying up oil refiners and rapidly expanded its market share. By 1880, Standard Oil had acquired fourteen firms and held stock in twenty-five others.[156] An oil producer named Lewis Emery prospered by building oil refineries to sell to Standard Oil. He acquired the Octave Oil Company and Refinery, then sold it to Standard for $45,000 in 1876.[157] Three years later, he helped establish Logan, Emery & Weaver, a firm that built a refinery and sold it to Standard in 1887.[158] Emery became president of United States Pipeline; Standard Oil eventually purchased most of its stock.[159] "Emery clearly had a successful career," noted economist John McGee, "an important part of which consisted of selling companies to Standard and others."[160] Tarbell acknowledged in her autobiography that Emery "was a rich man, and he was making the most of his money."[161] Despite all the money Emery made selling refineries to Standard Oil, he gulled Ida Tarbell with his self-serving complaints: "I had and have as much brains as John D. Rockefeller, but I have never had his cunning nor his ability to use unscrupulous means or unscrupulous men to carry out a programme."[162]

McGee pored through some eleven thousand pages of trial testimony on Standard Oil's practices and refuted the widely asserted claim that Standard Oil engaged in "predatory" price-cutting, which generally meant pricing products below cost. McGee could identify no Standard Oil acquisitions that involved "predatory" price cutting. What he did find were plenty of straightforward acquisitions. Many of the best managers of the acquired companies became millionaires as Standard Oil partners.

Rockefeller undoubtedly bought many refineries for less than what the sellers hoped to realize, but falling oil prices reduced the value of the refineries. Those built in the early stages of an oil boom lost worth after large numbers of refineries were built, producing more oil than could be easily absorbed by the market.

McGee explained that because Standard Oil was the largest refining company, it would have incurred the largest losses by pricing its products below cost or by practicing "predatory" price-cutting. In addition, if a competitor had been driven out of business by Standard Oil's "predatory" price-cutting, the refinery itself would not have vanished. If, after a competitor shut down, Standard Oil tried to push up prices to recoup its losses and make profits, another entrepreneur would have been able to acquire and reopen the shuttered refinery with more competitive pricing, and Standard Oil would have incurred the biggest losses without reducing the number of competitors. The surest method was to simply acquire competitors and continue their operation, which is what Standard Oil did. McGee's report was published in 1959, and when economist Randall Mariger revisited the issue in 1978, he confirmed McGee's findings.[163]

The acquisitions raised legal issues, because Standard Oil was incorporated in Ohio and state corporation charters didn't permit the acquisition of stock in out-of-state companies. The solution was to set up Standard Oil as a "trust": Forty-two investors with an ownership interest in the thirty-nine Standard Oil companies gave their shares to a group of nine "trustees," and in exchange the investors received trustee certificates reflecting their ownership. This was the beginning of holding companies.[164] A decade later, the Ohio Supreme Court ruled that the trustee arrangement was illegal. New Jersey, however, enacted a law that made it possible for companies to hold shares in other companies, and in 1897 Standard Oil was incorporated in New Jersey as a holding company.[165]

These legal complications certainly weren't the fault of Rockefeller and Standard Oil. They were trying to serve a national market, working with laws enacted when few businesses served customers beyond their local area. Why, indeed, should corporation laws restrict the world's largest free-trade area, a key to the phenomenal prosperity of the American economy? Such legal restrictions made no more sense than the medieval trade restrictions, river tolls, and other barriers to trade that stifled the growth of enterprises in France, Germany, Russia, and elsewhere in Europe. These large territories remained poor, in part, because of laws that restricted the size of their markets.

Standard Oil continued to invest heavily in cost-cutting innovations. Economist Dominick T. Armentano mentioned "machines that turned out 24,000 five-gallon tin cans daily by 1890."[166] There were seventeen Standard Oil manufacturing plants in Europe, five thousand tank wagons, 150 tank cars, plus leased warehouse and depot facilities.[167] Standard Oil's share of the refining market was about 88 percent in 1890, when the price of refined oil fell to 5.91 cents per gallon.[168] Armentano observed, "at the very pinnacle of Standard's industry 'control,' the costs and the prices for refined oil reached their lowest levels in the history of the petroleum industry."[169]

Still, Tarbell insisted on portraying Rockefeller as an unstoppable monster, warning that "It was only a matter of time, then, when all remaining outside [non-Standard] refiners must come into his fold or die."[170] But that didn't happen. Instead, competition intensified. Oil was discovered in Kansas, Louisiana, Oklahoma, Texas, and California. The number of U.S. oil refiners increased each year; there were 147 in 1911.[171] Most important, among them were a number of solid, growing companies that became large enough to serve large markets: Tide-Water Pipeline Company (c. 1880), Sun Oil (1890),[172] Union Oil Company of California (1890),[173] Pure Oil (1895), Associated Oil of California (1901), Texaco (1902), and Gulf Oil (1907).[174]

In their 1955 history of Standard Oil of New Jersey, Ralph and Muriel Hidy reported that "competition in selling kerosene was more intense in cities where electricity and gas had cut into the market and where Standard Oil's biggest rivals also wanted to have a large volume of sales in order to reduce the per unit overhead costs. All major competitors adopted bulk distribution . . . price wars occurred in New York, Philadelphia, Jersey City, Newark, Des Moines, Indianapolis, and other cities."[175] Standard Oil executives complained that "excessive" production was responsible for "depressed" prices.[176]

Increasingly, as Standard Oil expanded abroad, it encountered new competitors arising from new oil fields developed by some of the world's wealthiest people. During the 1870s, the Nobel brothers, from Sweden, and the Rothschilds, based in London, began developing the rich Russian oil fields in Baku. Marcus Samuel, who started his career selling seashells in London, made a colossal leap and conceived of building tankers that could ship Russian oil safely through the Suez Canal to Bangkok and Singapore, undercutting Standard Oil, and he later helped take advantage of oil discoveries in Sumatra to build the Shell Oil Company. Sumatran oil also helped launch the Royal Dutch oil company. At the dawn of the twentieth century, international oil price wars limited profits, and Standard Oil was losing market share abroad as well as at home.[177]

Expanding markets required the financial and managerial resources of larger companies than had been the case when markets were small. With or without Standard Oil, small and high-cost independent oil companies would have had a tough time. But they successfully lobbied for political support to have the government take action against Standard Oil—despite the fact that millions of consumers were better off because Standard Oil had done much to expand the supply of oil, improve quality, and cut prices. Several states filed lawsuits against Standard Oil, its founders, and its officers.

By the time Tarbell's *History of Standard Oil* was published in book form, in 1904, Tarbell herself was said to be the most famous woman in America, and magazine publisher Samuel McClure wanted more articles from her. She agreed to do a two-part personal profile of Rockefeller and abandoned all pretense of objective journalism. "She found him guilty of baldness, bumps, and being the son of a snake oil dealer," wrote biographer Kathleen Brady. "She took his appearance, affected by a stomach ailment and the alopecia which rendered him hairless, as a moral sign."[178]

Tarbell's research associate John Siddell, a former cub reporter for the *Cleveland Plain Dealer*, learned that Rockefeller's father, William Avery Rockefeller, was still alive. Son John had not seen him in years and had said little about him, so everyone thought he was dead. "Devil Bill" was reputed to be a bigamist and scam artist who had been indicted for rape, and Tarbell frantically began to search for him and for photos of him. She obtained a photo but never did find him. When she reported that he was still alive, scandalmongering newspaper publisher William Randolph Hearst joined the hunt, and Joseph Pulitzer, publisher of the *New York World*, offered $8,000 to anyone who provided information that would help track down "Devil Bill." Pulitzer thought he had a deal to publish Frank Rockefeller's diatribes against both his brother John and their father, but Frank backed out. "If you publish that, I'll kill you," he snapped.[179] John D. Rockefeller had bailed out Frank with loans, and Frank probably didn't want to do anything to shut off the money supply. Pulitzer broke the story in 1908, two years after "Devil Bill's" death at age ninety-eight. A Freeport, Illinois, druggist reported selling medicines to somebody going by the name of Dr. William Levingston who resembled the published photo. This turned out to be William Avery Rockefeller, a vagabond peddler and confidence man who had married devout Baptist Eliza Davison in 1837, and had five children with her and with his mistress Nancy Brown in Richford, New York. He eventually disappeared, changed his name to Levingston, claimed to be an eye and ear doctor, and in 1855 married Margaret Allen, with whom he spent most of the rest of his life.[180]

Of course, all this had nothing to do with the good things or bad things done by John D. Rockefeller, but the muckrackers loved to focus on his personal life while failing to appreciate that in free markets, people are led by their self-interest to serve the public. John D. Rockefeller may have done things he ought not to have done, but he could not force people to buy his products, so he improved the quality of his product and cut prices.

Several years passed before the federal antitrust case against Standard Oil, filed during the Roosevelt administration, was resolved. Frank Kellogg, head of the federal Bureau of Corporations, conducted an investigation.[181] There were twenty-three volumes—some twelve thousand pages—of often conflicting testimony.[182] On January 9, 1909, four judges serving on the U.S. Court of Appeals for the Eighth Circuit—Elmer Bragg Adams, William C. Hook, John B. Sanborn, and Willis VanDevanter—ruled that Standard Oil violated the Sherman Act because it had many subsidiaries that could compete with each other but didn't.[183] Notably absent from the court of appeals' decision was any allegation of "predatory" price-cutting. Nor was there a finding of guilt because of railroad rebates. Nor was any effort made to prove that Standard Oil had restricted output and raised prices, for the facts would have proved that output had been increasing and prices falling. The alleged crime was operating a holding company, and the legal remedy was to break up the holding company into its component parts.

The case was appealed to the U.S. Supreme Court. President William Howard Taft's attorney general George Wickersham argued there. Chief Justice Edward Douglass White, a Louisiana Democrat appointed by Grover Cleveland, wrote the majority opinion, issued on May 15, 1911. It was a muddle of contradictory ideas. White admitted that not all monopolies were bad and recommended a "rule of reason" to distinguish between good and bad monopolies. But he did not apply any such "rule of reason" to analyze how Standard

Oil had expanded the output of petroleum products, improved distribution, and cut both costs and prices. Nor did he use a "rule of reason" to discuss how Standard Oil had lost market share as the market expanded rapidly. He did not use a "rule of reason" to comment on the increasing number of companies competing with Standard Oil in the United States and overseas. In White's opinion, the crime was that businesses ceased to compete with one another when they were acquired by the Standard Oil holding company. He wrote, "Because the unification of power and control over petroleum and its products which was the inevitable result of the combining in the New Jersey corporation by the increase of its stock and the transfer to it of the stocks of so many other corporations, aggregating so vast a capital, gives rise, in and of itself, in the absence of countervailing circumstances . . . to the prima facie presumption of intent and purpose to maintain the dominancy over the oil industry, not as a result of normal methods of industrial development, but by new means of combination."[184]

The Supreme Court upheld the court of appeals' order to break up Standard Oil's New Jersey holding company.[185] The independent Standard Oil of New Jersey, which accounted for about half the value of the holding company, later became Exxon. Standard Oil of New York developed into Mobil Oil. Standard Oil of Indiana became Amoco. Standard Oil of California became Chevron. Continental Oil became Conoco. Atlantic became ARCO, then Sun. "These new entities," noted historian Daniel Yergin, "though separated and with no overlapping boards of management, nonetheless generally respected one another's markets and carried on their old commercial relationships."[186]

THE ANTITRUST DELUSION

Antitrust policy was a snare and a delusion. In their book *The Rise of the Corporate Commonwealth* (1988), Louis Galambos and

Joseph Pratt observed that "Neither the presidents, the regulatory agencies, nor the courts put forward an effective measure of concentration that could be understood by potential offenders and used as the lynchpin of antitrust policy."[187]

If the aim had been to promote consumer welfare, progressives would have focused on significantly reducing tariffs, if not eliminating them altogether. But Theodore Roosevelt accepted and promoted high tariffs. His antitrust lawyers thwarted consumer welfare by filing lawsuits against companies that expanded output, cut prices, and benefited millions of consumers. Roosevelt recklessly disrupted the economy by suing or otherwise intimidating employers that created millions of jobs. His "trust-busting" policies involved giving politicians more power on the assumption that they would work for the greater good of the people. But many politicians only caused harm to the American consumer, and these politicians were much harder to control than even the biggest businesses.

CHAPTER FOUR

WHY DID ROOSEVELT CRIPPLE AMERICA'S BIGGEST INDUSTRY?

WHEN THEODORE ROOSEVELT became president, he denounced the railroad industry—America's biggest business. In 1900, over a million Americans worked on the railroads.[1] There were more than 258,000 miles of operating track.[2] All this was hugely expensive, financed from retained earnings and from outside sources. It was no wonder that railroad stocks and bonds accounted for most of the turnover on U.S. securities markets. Altogether, the book value of railroad investments was an estimated $10 billion.[3]

Railroads made it possible for the American economy to function efficiently by gathering bulky resources like iron ore and coal from distant locations so that new industries like steel could develop and deliver their products all across the United States. Without railroads, the cost of shipping agricultural commodities would have been double what it was.[4]

Nobel laureate Robert W. Fogel estimated that without railroads the American economy overall might have been about 5 percent smaller than it was.[5] The tremendous wealth that the railroads generated meant higher living standards for millions of Americans and attracted millions of immigrants to the United States.

These achievements required heroic efforts, and politicians were no help. When they became involved with railroads, the result usually was corruption and collapse. Many different railroads, with track gauges ranging from three to six feet,[6] had to be consolidated and the gauges standardized. Railroads had to be continuously up-graded to accommodate ever-increasing traffic and loads. Efficient railroad systems were the work of extraordinarily talented private entrepreneurs such as Edward H. Harriman and James J. Hill. Dis-counting the vital role they played, Theodore Roosevelt threw ob-stacles in their way.

Like other progressives, he adopted the view that railroads were evil monopolies charging the public too much money—even though railroad rates were declining. He sided with farmers who com-plained that railroads were discriminating against them, although these farmers probably would have gone bankrupt if the railroads hadn't been around to get their produce to market. Without the railroads, midwestern farmers especially would have suffered losses on the value of their land.[7]

Roosevelt knew little about business, as his disastrous ranching losses made clear, and he certainly never seems to have thought about the function of prices in an economy. Nobody could possibly agree on millions of railroad rates, but Roosevelt imagined govern-ment bureaucrats could somehow determine how much the rail-roads should charge when shipping iron ore from Minnesota or anthracite coal from Virginia or corn from Iowa or dressed beef from Chicago or thousands of other products in either new cars that required less handling or older cars that required more han-dling, via the slowest route or the fastest route, to the least efficient or most efficient port. Roosevelt believed that the government could manipulate prices without consequences. He had what historian Albro Martin called "the exhilarating notion that men who lacked the experience, the economic power, and the enlightened self-interest of the leaders of big business could nevertheless establish the pat-terns by which great aggregates of property fitted into the nation's economy."[8]

During his years as Civil Service commissioner and New York City police commissioner, Roosevelt had seen that incompetence and corruption were commonplace in government, and his reform efforts had been thwarted. As president, he should have had no illusions about what to expect from government bureaucracy. Yet biographer Nathan Miller described government control of railroads as a "keystone" of Roosevelt's legislative program.[9] And biographer Edmund Morris believed that government control "was the greatest challenge handed to Congress in forty years"[10] and that "the president had started something very big."[11]

GOVERNMENT-RUN RAILROADS GO BUST

Theodore Roosevelt—a Harvard man—actually assumed that politicians and bureaucrats were capable of running an industry. He was naive to think that they could interfere without serious consequences. He certainly knew that many government-run projects had become scandals during the nineteenth century.

In the 1810s and 1820s, many lobbyists promoted the idea that governments should provide "public" goods such as banks, roads, canals, and railroads. Governments did the planning, financed the projects out of general tax revenues, and managed the projects.

From 1817 to 1825, the state of New York financed and built the Erie Canal, which went 364 miles[12] from Albany—on the Hudson River—to Buffalo, thereby linking New York City and Lake Erie. The Erie Canal was hailed as a big success, credited with cutting the cost of shipments, stimulating the growth of towns like Syracuse, Rochester, and Utica,[13] and bringing to New York City business that otherwise might have gone to Boston or Philadelphia.[14] New York State began building the Champlain Canal, Blackstone Canal, Oswego Canal, Chemung Canal, Chenango Canal, Genessee Canal, and Black River Canal.[15] Altogether, New York incurred $13.3 million in debt for canals.[16]

Fearing business losses, merchants in other states lobbied their state governments to build canals with taxpayers' money. The state of Indiana built the White Water Canal and Illinois & Michigan

Canal.[17] Pennsylvania built the Penn Canal–Main, Penn Canal–Main–Juniata Division, and several others.[18] Ohio built the Ohio & Erie Canal, Ohio & Pennsylvania Canal, Miami & Erie Canal, Sandy & Beaver Canal, Wabash & Erie Canal, Walhonding Branch Canal, and Hocking Branch Canal.[19] Maryland built the Chesapeake & Ohio Canal.[20] Virginia built the James River & Kanawha Canal.[21] In every state, it was claimed that the projects were urgently needed and required more money than could be raised from market sources. Politicians were hailed for having more vision than private entrepreneurs.[22]

States also went into debt to build railroads, which in many places made canals obsolete. By the mid-1830s, Kentucky's railroad debts were $350,000, South Carolina's $2 million, Indiana's $2.6 million, Michigan's $2.6 million, Alabama's $3 million, New York's $3.7 million, Tennessee's $3.7 million, Massachusetts' $4.2 million, Pennsylvania's $4.9 million, and Maryland's $5.5 million.[23] No state attempted more than Illinois, which incurred debts of $7.4 million to build railroads.[24] "With a population of some 300,000 people," explained historian George H. Miller, "she committed herself to a liability of approximately $20,000,000 to obtain a system of railroads, turnpikes, and river improvements that had little relation to the transportation needs of the time and could never have proven successful even if completed. The plan was the result of logrolling on a magnificent scale and contemplated about 1,300 miles of railroad, confined almost entirely to the southern half of the state. The system of finance was to be the same as that developed by New York State for the construction of the Erie Canal, and it provided for the payment of all obligations out of general income from taxes and not merely from revenue derived from the works themselves."[25]

Government involvement in the railroads meant key decisions were made not for sound business reasons but for political reasons. This is especially clear in the case of the New York & Erie Railroad, which railroad historian Albro Martin called "the most poorly planned of the antebellum lines."[26] Its charter, approved on April 24,

1832, was subject to restrictions demanded by pro-canal legislators. The western end of the line reached Lake Erie at the village of Dunkirk (rather than the city of Buffalo)—as far as possible from the Erie Canal. The eastern end of the line was in the village of Piermont, on the west bank of the Hudson River, across from Tarrytown (rather than someplace across from Manhattan). "As if to top those mistakes," Martin writes, "it selected a broad gauge in the mistaken notion that it would not have to share its traffic with standard gauge roads."[27]

State revenues plunged after the panic of 1837, and it became apparent that most of these government-run projects were a bust. They lost money, and the hard-pressed states could not afford to cover the losses. "Many of the enterprises were premature and unnecessary," observed economic historians Ernest L. Bogart and Donald L. Kemmerer. "Most of them were extravagantly, if not corruptly, managed."[28]

According to economic historian Clifford F. Thies, who analyzed the total costs of the Erie Canal, "The canal did in fact generate substantial revenue, and it is true—as it is often said—that the canal soon generated enough in revenue to cover its cost of construction. Yet this statement ignores operating expenses, the cost of 'reconstructing' the canal and of various 'improvements' to the canal, and the time value of funds invested in the canal. Taking these costs into account, the Erie Canal only recovered its full cost toward the end of its revenue-generating lifetime . . . it achieved an internal rate of return of 6.24 percent, which barely exceeds the interest rate (6 percent) New York paid on the first canal bonds it issued."[29] Thies also found that the New York State "turnpikes were also money-losers. The Erie Railroad went bankrupt, forcing the state to assume its bonds. Eight of the banks participating in the Safety Fund failed, in case after case due to 'reckless banking,' causing the Safety Fund itself to fail. New York was pushed to the brink of default, and only avoided doing so by raising taxes."[30]

These government failures were embarrassing, and they forced governments to raise taxes. Ironically, reported Thies, "states that spent themselves into debt did not advance the development of their railroad networks . . . [but] those that adopted amendments to their state constitutions restricting borrowing, investment, loan guarantees, and the like did."[31] Desperate to stop the losses and balance their budgets, states unloaded assets as quickly as they could. Privatization brought relief to overtaxed voters. In Illinois, Miller reported, "The reaction against public ownership was greater . . . , perhaps, than in any other state in the nation. Having attempted one of the most ambitious programs of railroad construction, she had also tasted the most bitter defeat, and was now ready to abolish all her proprietary interests in industrial undertakings."[32]

Nine state governments defaulted on their debts because they spent large sums on banks, turnpikes, canals, and railroads during the 1840s. Economists Arthur Grinath III, John Joseph Wallis, and Richard E. Sylla reported, "By 1841, the combined debt of state governments stood at $193 million, of which roughly 60 percent was for canals and railroads and 30 percent for banks. In 1841 and 1842, Florida, Mississippi, Arkansas, Indiana, Illinois, Maryland, Michigan, Pennsylvania, and Louisiana defaulted on their interest payments. Other states, including Alabama, New York, Ohio, and Tennessee, narrowly avoided default. Mississippi, Florida, Arkansas, and Michigan ultimately repudiated approximately $13,770,000 of their debts."[33]

A major problem with government-run projects was that people generally didn't spend other people's money as carefully as they spent their own. Private individuals had incentives both to (1) take advantage of opportunities that could generate profits and (2) be wary of high-risk situations in which they could lose their own money. There was bound to be much more carelessness in a government project than in a privately run project.

Moreover, private individuals were more likely to make decisions based on merit rather than decisions based on political considerations. Politicians insisted that a railroad go through certain towns for political reasons, even though the towns were not likely to generate enough freight or passenger traffic to justify the cost of construction. Politicians made sure that their political supporters were hired for government projects, despite any lack of competence. Politically connected contractors were hired for construction. When cost overruns occurred, governments imposed little financial discipline, perhaps because they were spending taxpayers' money and not their own. Government-run projects abounded with incompetence and corruption.

The economic growth often credited to the turnpikes, canals, and railroads turns out to have been artificial and illusory. The projects lost money and were kept going only by the transfer of resources from taxpayers elsewhere in the state. Apparent gains in a region served by a canal were offset by losses in a region paying taxes that covered the losses of the canal. Historians have celebrated what they could see—the turnpikes, canals, and railroads—and ignored what they could not see—namely, the things people were unable to do because they had less money in their pockets after paying taxes to cover the losses on government-run projects.

It became obvious that state governments could not be trusted to handle large projects, and as a result, many state constitutions were amended to make sure such disasters never happened again. In 1853, Illinois governor Joel A. Matteson declared, "this state has wisely abandoned the policy of embarrassing the treasury by engaging in works of internal improvement . . . [we have] granted [incorporation] charters with a liberal hand and afforded ever proper encouragement."[34]

GOVERNMENT INTERFERENCE
BREEDS CORRUPTION

Sobered up by the panic of 1837, states aggressively sought to promote railroad construction by offering entrepreneurs charters for limited-liability corporations. If a chartered company failed, creditors could try to collect what they were owed from the company, not from the individual owners. The owners' liability was limited to the money they had invested in the company; their personal assets, such as a bank account or house, were not at risk. This policy led to a tremendous boom in railroad construction during the 1840s and 1850s.

Whenever politicians interfered in the railroad business, however, corruption and inefficiency inevitably occurred. The most dramatic case involved construction of the first transcontinental railroad. Railroad lawyer Abraham Lincoln supported the project, and he made it a priority after he became president in 1861. He believed that recently acquired western territory would be vulnerable to encroachment by a foreign power if the United States were incapable of defending it. The West was hard to defend because of the difficulty of moving soldiers and guns to the West Coast. There were two options. First, sailing to Panama, marching across the disease-infested Isthmus of Panama, and then sailing up the Pacific coast. Second, sail around the stormy tip of South America and then head north. It is not clear, however, who posed a threat. Japan, which was isolated from the rest of the world? Spain, which had lost its South American colonies? Russia, which had hardly any forces in East Asia?

Stephen Ambrose and other historians have faulted private markets for lacking the capital or the imagination to build the transcontinental railroad. Certainly it was true that private entrepreneurs and financiers did not see the point of risking huge sums to build a railroad across a vast, empty, and sometimes mountainous terrain. Private entrepreneurs and financiers *added value* by developing the rail network bit by bit, supporting the expanding freight business. The process was gradual. Grandiose schemes like the transcontinental railroad drained resources from some regions to benefit special interests.

There was no money to be made from operating a railroad

through a desolate wasteland, yet the federal government rewarded railroad contractors with big subsidies: a thirty-year loan at below-market interest rates; twenty sections (12,800 acres) of government-owned land for every mile of track; and an additional subsidy of $48,000 for every mile of track laid in mountainous regions. Thomas Durant, Oakes Ames, and other officers of the Union Pacific Railroad, which went a thousand miles west from Council Bluffs, Nebraska, started the Crédit Mobilier company in 1867 and retained it to do the construction. Crédit Mobilier distributed to shareholders profits estimated at between $7 million and $23 million, depleting the Union Pacific's resources. In an effort to stop congressional investigations, the officers bribed Speaker of the House James G. Blaine and other congressmen with Crédit Mobilier stock. Seldom modest about their thievery, congressmen voted themselves a 50 percent pay raise.[35] The Union Pacific Railroad fell deep in debt, without enough revenue from passengers or shippers, and went bankrupt in 1893.

Mark Twain and his friend Charles Dudley Warner, a lawyer, editor, and publisher, scrambled to write a story based on the Crédit Mobilier scandal while it was still hot. "Oh, I have gathered enough material for a whole book!" Mark Twain wrote his wife Livy. "This is a perfect gold mine." He added that were was "no law against making offensive remarks about U.S. Senators."[36] The resulting book, *The Gilded Age* (1873), featured a railroad-related swindle with characters adapted from the scandal, and it reportedly sold some forty thousand copies. Theodore Roosevelt was of course aware of the scandal and the book.[37]

There was somewhat less government involvement in the construction of the Central Pacific Railroad, which started in Sacramento and went about 1,800 miles east, meeting the Union Pacific at Promontory Point, Utah. The Central Pacific had been started by four California merchants—Collis P. Huntington, Leland Stanford, Mark Hopkins, and Charles Crocker. Like the principals of the Union Pacific, the "Big Four" benefited from government land grants and subsidies. They formed their own construction company to build the railroad, and the construction company prospered while the railroad struggled with debt.

RAILROADS UNDERMINE MONOPOLIES

Far from being evil monopolies, as Theodore Roosevelt claimed, railroads actually undermined monopolies. They provided faster transportation than was available with wagons or barges. They made it possible for farmers to sell to distant markets and for consumers to buy goods from far away and not be limited to locally produced goods.

Before the coming of the railroad, millions of Americans had to deal with all sorts of local monopolies. Economic historian Stanley Lebergott noted that "The United States had been pock-marked by local monopolies of blacksmiths, wheelwrights, millers, retail grocers, cigar workers, physicians, cobblers. Outsiders could not profitably ship their goods, or bring their services in, to compete with these monopolistic craftsmen and handicraft workers. Railroads introduced competing products from a dozen states into every county along or near their lines. They carried the products of new competitors into every region in the nation."[38] Writing in 1909, University of Chicago economist Hugo Richard Meyer observed, "The railways brought about a revolution in transportation by introducing refrigerated cars—which enabled them to carry the surplus butter and other dairy products of Iowa and Illinois into the very market of the New York dairy farmer. The railroads leading to the north, from Georgia, Florida and other South Atlantic states, soon brought north garden truck and fruits in such quantity as to establish an entirely new level of prices for vegetables and fruits."[39]

Between 1850 and 1900, operating railroad track mileage soared 28-fold.[40] In 1886, noted historian Jean Strouse, railroads "settled on a national standard track gauge of 4 feet 8½ inches, which meant that they no longer had to transfer freight to new cars at each new stretch of track. Furthermore, steel rails were replacing iron, and better signals, brakes, and couplers were improving safety. Steadily decreasing transport costs combined with intense competition for traffic and an overall decline in prices to bring passenger rates down 50 percent between 1850 and 1900. Freight charges fell even further—railroad freight revenue went from 1.88 cents per ton mile in 1870 to .73 cents by 1900."[41]

According to historian George H. Miller, in the upper Mississippi River valley (Illinois, Iowa, Wisconsin, and Minnesota), one of the world's richest grain-producing regions, "between 1860 and 1873 over ten thousand miles of railroad were laid. . . . By the latter year, three-fourths of all the land in Illinois was within five miles of a railway; only 1½ percent of its land was over fifteen miles distant. . . . average rail rates on western roads were gradually declining."[42]

"The main line of commerce," Miller continued, "ran down the [Great] Lakes to Buffalo and through the Erie Canal to New York City, but the path of commerce broadened with each year. Improvements in the Welland Canal let larger ships through to Oswego, Ogdensburg, and Canadian ports; railroads in New York State established rivals to Buffalo at Dunkirk and Suspension Bridge. By 1852 there were railroads paralleling the lake route over its full length, for in that year both the Michigan Central and the Michigan Southern completed their connections with Chicago. . . . Although bulk grain shipments continued to use the lakes, higher priced items including . . . flour could bear the cost of rail freight all the way to the East Coast."[43]

Because most commercial centers developed along waterways, and most railroads connected commercial centers, waterways offered alternatives for shippers. Miller noted, "Rivalry among the [Great Lakes] ports must be viewed in the same light. Each port had its own market area resulting from the development of its own hinterland, but the pattern of railroad construction created extensive overlapping. Although each city enjoyed a steady growth in trade, the relative strength of the different markets was constantly changing. Milwaukee was the leading primary wheat market in the world in 1862, but Chicago assumed leadership in the postwar years, and in 1871 Duluth began to claim a share of the trade that might otherwise have gone to one of the Lake Michigan ports. Rivalry among the lake ports, when added to that between the river and the lakes, created a competitive situation of unusual intensity."[44]

Economic historian Fogel reported that there were 4,000 miles of canals and 26,000 miles of navigable streams.[45] "A glance at a map," he wrote, "shows that all of the primary market [producing area] cities were on navigable waterways. Duluth, Milwaukee, Chicago, Toledo, and Detroit were on the Great Lakes; Omaha and Kansas City were on the Missouri; Minneapolis and St. Louis were on the Mississippi; Cincinnati was on the Ohio; and Peoria was on the Illinois River, midway between the Mississippi and Lake Michigan. The lakes, inland rivers, canals, and coastal waters directly linked the primary market cities to most of the secondary market [consuming] cities . . . [and] on a per ton-mile basis, water rates were lower than railroad rates."[46]

Despite the dramatic expansion of the railroad network, the most valuable farmland was near navigable waterways.[47] According to Fogel, "The 1890 report of the Chicago Board of Trade, reveals that 43 per cent of the flour shipped out of that emporium, 58 per cent of the wheat, 63 per cent of the corn, 26 per cent of the oats, 30 per cent of the rye, and 20 per cent of the barley went by water. The statistics of shipments from Duluth, Milwaukee, and other important primary markets tell a similar story. It was on the basis of such data that the Industrial Commission of 1900 concluded that water was the dominant transportation service in the movement of agricultural commodities from the Midwest to the East Coast."[48]

Railroads generally enhanced real estate values, particularly the value of land that was not near a navigable waterway. The closer to railroad stations a farm was, the easier it was for a farmer to ship crops to market, and the more valuable was the farmer's land. Cheap land tended to be remote, at some distance from water or rail transportation.

RAILROADS HELP CUT LAND
TRANSPORTATION COSTS IN HALF

Economists Harold F. Williamson and Arnold R. Daum explained, "In competition with water routes, the railroads could not help but compete with one another, particularly since each trunk line was trying to consolidate its route and increase its market share in the long-haul traffic. After the rates had been driven sometimes as low as 12 cents per hundredweight, a truce was generally called, agreements were signed, and railroad men declared they had learned the folly of their ways. But as soon as the water routes re-opened, or one of the lines—usually the obstreperous Erie—sought to alter the balance of power, the cycle was repeated."[49]

Railroad profits, however, proved to be elusive. Railroad rates fell everywhere, reflecting the general decline of prices during the last two decades of the nineteenth century. Railroad rates fell dramatically between New York and Chicago, and they fell across the South, too. For instance, according to Stanley Lebergott, "the rate for shipping cotton across South Carolina fell 85 percent between 1870 and 1897."[50]

Railroad operators desperately tried to prop up rates by forming "pools"—cartels—whose members agreed not to offer discount prices. The Southern Steamship and Railway Association, the "Iowa Pool," and the "Chicago Eastbound Dead Freight Pool" were among the most active ones, but they didn't last long.[51] It was in the self-interest of each member to secretly offer discounts, hoping to gain a greater share of business while other members charged the agreed-upon rate. Small railroads had stronger incentives than larger railroads to discount their rates, for small railroads had more to gain. Large railroads wanted to maximize revenues from their dominant market shares. Obviously, railroads would have made more money if they could have dispensed with the discounts, but there was so much competition that often the alternatives were to get discounted business or no business.

In 1874, economist Paul W. MacAvoy reported, "There were accusations by the Pennsylvania Railroad that the Baltimore railroad continued to depart from the official rate."[52] A couple years later, the Baltimore & Ohio Railroad charged, "it is positively stated in Chicago and believed by railroad men that the Lake Shore and New York Central made contracts with large shippers for 1,000 cars grain at 15 cents."[53] In 1876, the Erie was discounting its rates. The following year, the Baltimore & Ohio accused the New York Central of discounting. In 1878 and 1879, there was a round of rate discounting in which the Pennsylvania Railroad appeared to be the principal player. A railroad cartel agreement, aimed to prop up rates, collapsed in a year, and pervasive rate discounting continued through 1886. Persistent discounting by a single independent railroad—the Erie—was enough to disrupt attempted cartels. Overall, according to economic historians John M. Peterson and Ralph Gray, "land transportation costs were cut in half between 1860 and 1900."[54]

LOCAL INTERESTS FIGHT
LONG-DISTANCE COMPETITION

Theodore Roosevelt seemed to believe that setting railroad rates was a simple matter of doing right or wrong—and federal bureaucrats could be counted on to do right. He seemed not to understand that bad things would happen when markets were disrupted. For example, setting railroad rates below market levels would depress railroad profits and make it harder to attract capital and make investments where they were needed. For markets to function properly, railroad rates had to reflect the complex interplay among competing ship-pers and competing railroads, among shippers that provided special-ized railcars and those that did not, among high-cost centers and low-cost centers, among long-distance, local, and export markets, and so on. Federal bureaucrats had no way of determining which among thousands of rates needed to be changed, and they lacked incentives to make timely changes. Federal bureaucrats responded to political pressures and set rates that were economically irra-tional, reflecting the clout of powerful lobbyists.

Just consider the complexity of the markets that politicans were interfering with. Railroads competed with canals, and the financial backers of canals opposed railroads at every turn. In New York State, for instance, backers of the Erie Canal led the lobbying ef-forts against railroads.[55] Merchants in Boston and New York City competed for business with merchants in the Midwest.[56] New York City merchants, who dominated the export business, stood to lose if railroad rate discounting was reduced or eliminated on ship-ments from the Midwest.[57] Cities that generated substantial rail-road freight volume and had major rail terminals supported railroad rate discounting, while cities without such volume resented the discounts.[58] State legislatures generally tried to protect politi-cally connected local businesses from out-of-state competition.[59]

Small-town merchants, too, resented having to compete with out-of-state rivals. Lumber was shipped by rail from Chicago direct to Iowa communities, and Iowa grain was shipped by rail to Chi-cago, bypassing Mississippi River ports. Businesses in Iowa port cities such as Burlington, Davenport, and Dubuque lost market share to Chicago. St. Louis, previously the principal market for Iowa grain, also was displaced by Chicago.[60]

Meanwhile, there were complaints that railroads charged higher rates for short-haul shipments than for long-haul shipments. Stan-dard Oil, Armour Packing Company, and other long-haul shippers secured rate breaks because they offered railroads steady business and had invested in special railcars and facilities that yielded greater economies of scale. Small oil refiners resented railroads for quoting lower rates to ship Standard Oil's products. But there was a good reason for the disparity: Standard Oil shipped oil in rail tank cars, and small refiners shipped oil in barrels. Historian Werner Troesken explained, "Barrels leaked and allowed much of the oil to evaporate; tank cars allowed roughly 50 percent less oil to evaporate. Barrels had to be repaired and replaced constantly, which meant refiners typically had to hire a team of coopers to maintain an adequate stock of barrels; tank cars required much less maintenance. Barrels were costly to load and unload from railroad cars; tank cars were not. When shipping oil in barrels, there was a significant risk of accidental explosion; tank cars reduced that risk. In addition, because tank cars required much less handling by railroad workers—railroads offered refiners who shipped their oil in refiner-owned tank cars significant rate reductions relative to those who continued to use barrels."[61]

Outlawing discounted rates would have adversely affected companies besides Standard Oil that had invested in the more efficient railcars. W. C. Warner, secretary of National Oil Company in Titusville, Pennsylvania, claimed that companies that owned some twenty-one hundred rail tank cars and had nothing to do with Standard Oil would be unfairly denied the benefit of their investments in those railcars if the federal government banned the setting of rail rates that reflected the differing costs of various shipping methods. Nonetheless, Ohio senator John Sherman introduced just such a ban—it ended up as a proposed amendment to the Interstate Commerce Act—using language recommended by Great Western Works, a small refiner that shipped oil in barrels.[62] The proposal was defeated.

Small shippers wanted the low rates that large shippers enjoyed—but without having to invest in new technology or offer steady business. In addition, hoping to protect their local businesses from competition, many people objected to the standardization of railroad tracks, which helped to make goods from distant suppliers available to consumers.[63] Railroads ended up extending discounted rates much more than they would have preferred. As much as half of the New York Central's business involved discounted rates.[64]

Farmers complained loudly about railroad rates. In 1867, Oliver H. Kelley, a former farmer who got a job as a clerk in the U.S. Department of Agriculture, started the Order of Patrons of Husbandry, otherwise known as the Grange. It was a group of local associations that aimed to help farmers improve their lives. After the 1873 depression, when farm prices crashed, membership in the Grange grew to around 800,000.[65] There were some three thousand local Granges, two-thirds of them in the four states of the upper Mississippi Valley—Illinois, Iowa, Wisconsin, and Minnesota.[66] Increasingly, local Granges agitated for state price control laws to set maximum railroad rates. Eventually, the issue reached the U.S. Supreme Court.

Initially, the Supreme Court upheld state price control laws. In *Munn v. Illinois* (1877), a case involving a grain storehouse, Chief Justice Morrison R. Waite delivered the majority opinion.[67] He wrote that state-enforced maximum rates didn't deny the grain warehouse and elevator owners equal protection and due process under the Fourteenth Amendment to the Constitution. Justice Stephen J. Field, a Democrat appointed by Abraham Lincoln, offered a forceful dissent: "The principle upon which the opinion of the majority proceeds is subversive of the rights of private property." Nine years later, in *Wabash, St. Louis & Pacific Railway Co. v. Illinois* (1886), the Supreme Court ruled that state railroad price controls conflicted with the federal government's jurisdiction over interstate commerce.[68] Justice Samuel F. Miller, a Kentucky lawyer also appointed by Lincoln, wrote the majority opinion.

Despite all the complaints, railroads were not the main problem for farmers. The main problem was that millions of people, including large numbers of immigrants as well as soldiers demobilized from the Union and Confederate armies, decided to become farmers. According to the Census Bureau, between 1850 and 1900, the number of U.S. farms soared from 1.4 million to 5.7 million.[69] In 1850, there were a reported 293.5 million acres of farmland; in 1900, 841.2 million acres. These dramatic increases in the number of farmers and the number of farms led to increasing supplies of agricultural commodities and downward pressure on farm prices. Moreover, many farmers seem to have underestimated the total cost of earning a living in remote locations. The low cost of land in the most distant places reachable by railroad was offset by high shipping costs—levied both on tools and other manufactured goods that farmers ordered from businesses in major markets and on the agricultural commodities that farmers shipped to major markets.

While farmers in the upper Mississippi Valley insisted that railroad rates were too high, eastern farmers insisted that they were not high enough. They objected to competing with agricultural commodities from the upper Mississippi Valley. They wanted railroad rates to be strictly proportional to distance, so that farmers hundreds of miles away would be priced out of eastern markets. Such objections suggest that farmers in the upper Mississippi Valley actually benefited from discounted railroad rates.[70]

All this goes to show that few people seemed to understand that railroad rates were determined by supply and demand. Rates were likely to be lower between two points where shippers had more choices, regardless of the distance between the points. A combination of routes was likely to be chosen because it achieved the fastest delivery to the most desirable markets at the lowest cost.

Should railroad rates have been based on shipping costs? The principal costs of a railroad were the fixed costs of laying track and acquiring rolling stock. The marginal costs of having a train go one more mile were low. It wasn't easy to say how rapidly a railroad should try to recover its fixed costs. Moreover, during the harvest season, there was a big demand for railcar capacity heading east but not much demand for westbound railcars. If the cars had remained in the East until there were westbound shippers willing to pay what the eastbound shippers paid, there wouldn't have been any cars to handle eastbound shipments. Railroad companies decided that it was better to accept discounted rates than no rates at all for westbound railcars.[71] As Miller pointed out, "Practical men and theorists alike realized that it was impossible to determine the cost of each individual service performed. Due to the intricacies of the problem the unit expense per ton mile of any given commodity was simply beyond measurement."[72]

Was the discounting of long-haul rates really unjust? Literature on the subject reads like medieval efforts to determine a "just" price—an impossible task. There are many reasons why long-haul discounting was perfectly reasonable. First, railroads incurred the costs of loading and unloading goods no matter how far the goods were shipped, so a railroad's costs were not directly proportional to distance. Loading and unloading accounted for a higher proportion of the total cost of a short haul and a lower proportion of the total cost of a long haul.

Second, railroad rates—like any market prices—provided vital incentives to suppliers and customers. If demand for railroad services went up and railroad rates went up with it, there would be two important consequences: All shippers would have an incentive to minimize their use of railroad services, thereby making services available for those with the greatest need; and at the same time, the railroads would have an incentive to make more services available. The more promptly they responded to market signals, the more money they could make. However, if rates were kept below market levels, shippers would have no incentive to conserve scarce railroad services, and railroads would have no incentive to make them more available. Enforcing rates below market levels would prolong and intensify the shortage of railroad services.

THE ICC TRIES TO LIMIT
THE NATIONAL MARKET

On February 4, 1887, the U.S. Congress enacted the Act to Regulate Commerce, which was substantially devoted to establishing the Interstate Commerce Commission, the first federal agency whose purpose was to regulate business.[73] The railroads had helped establish the ICC because limiting the railroads' ability to set prices for their services would end competitors' discounts that eroded their bottom line. As president, Theodore Roosevelt would find in the ICC the perfect tool with which to enact his progressive ideas.

The ICC was in an impossible position. It tried to deal with shippers' complaints, but it also relied on the expertise of the railroads, which for many years meant it had to cater to the railroads' views. As a vast national market developed in the United States during the late nineteenth century, the most intense political battles involved regional interests lobbying the ICC to limit competition from other regions. Local firms in one region—many of them monopolies—objected to discounted long-haul rates because they made it possible for firms in other regions to compete with them for market share.

The ICC responded to such political pressures by serving as an agent of domestic protectionism. It pushed for higher railroad long-haul rates that would help shield local firms from competitors in other regions. It outlawed discounting from published railroad rates.[74] According to Stanley Lebergott, the ICC "early, and openly, wrote to the chairman of the Western Freight Association—an industry group—objecting that 'Complaints still reach us of alleged rate cutting from Missouri River points.' Such prices were costs to farmers, to shippers, and eventually to the American consumer. Yet the new agency described these reductions in a chilling pejorative phrase as 'rate cutting.'"[75] As MacAvoy concluded, "the general trend was to order higher rates."[76]

Had it not been for the U.S. Supreme Court, the ICC would have done even more to protect local interests and obstruct the development of a national market. The Court insisted that regulatory rulings were subject to judicial review. In *Chicago, Milwaukee & St. Paul Railway Co. v. Minnesota* (1890), Justice Samuel Blatchford, a New York City lawyer appointed by Republican Chester A. Arthur, issued the majority opinion: "If the company is deprived of the power of charging reasonable rates for the use of its property, and such deprivation takes place in the absence of an investigation by judicial machinery, it is deprived of the lawful use of its property, and thus, in substance and effect, of the property itself, without due process of law, and in violation of the constitution of the United States; and, in so far as it is thus deprived, while other persons are permitted to receive reasonable profits upon their invested capital, the company is deprived of the equal protection of the laws."[77] Many other ICC decisions were appealed and struck down, effectively limiting the agency's power.

Focused on the alleged unfairness of particular railroad rates, Theodore Roosevelt didn't seem to have appreciated how railroads integrated U.S. regions into a national market and even helped integrate the U.S. market with world markets. Eager for business opportunities and flexible as only private enterprises could be, railroads responded to changing situations beyond the comprehension of ICC bureaucrats or progressive intellectuals.

Hugo Richard Meyer, among the most perceptive of all authors on railroads, made the following observation in 1905: "the Great Northern Railroad has built up, since 1890 or thereabouts, a lumber traffic which now amounts to four train-loads a day across the Cascade Mountains. And because that east-bound lumber traffic is of such proportions that the Great Northern Railroad is absolutely certain of a return load of lumber for every car that reaches the Pacific coast laden with freight carried westward from Duluth and St. Paul, the Great Northern Railroad for some years past has been making rates on American manufactures going to the Orient—in competition with British, Belgian and German manufactures—that are only 50 per cent . . . of what they would be, were it not for the existence of a back-load in lumber. In other words, the success with which the American manufacturer competes in Asiatic markets with the British, Belgian and German manufacturers is due to the existence of a lumber trade between the Pacific coast and the territory east of the Cascade Mountains—a trade that exists only by virtue of daily violation of the doctrine laid down by the Interstate Commerce Commission in *Anthony Salt Co. v. Missouri Pacific Railway Co.*, and in numerous other cases, that no one may be deprived of advantages accruing to him by virtue of geographical position."[78]

Some progressives imagined that controversies would be resolved if U.S. railroads were government-run. Meyer pointed out that European railroads were government-run, yet European governments took even stronger measures than the ICC to protect regional interests and prevent the development of national markets. "Such has been the paralysis of the [Prussian] railways under government-made railway rates," Meyer wrote, "that the grain, timber and beet sugar producers of eastern Germany, as well as the iron and steel manufacturers of the Ruhr district, have had to resuscitate river and canal transportation, which, under the *régime* of private ownership of the railways, had promised in Germany to go the way of the stagecoach, as it has done in the United States."[79] Meyer made similar observations about how government regulations and government-run railroads in France, Austria-Hungary, Russia, and Australia restricted the development of national markets while protecting local interest groups. Yet Theodore Roosevelt, as educated in world affairs as he was, would go on to sign legislation that granted the government more control over the railroads and severely limited the growth of America's biggest industry.

THE GOVERNMENT MAKES RAILROADS
LESS ATTRACTIVE TO INVESTORS

Shippers continued to complain about the alleged unfairness of rebates, and railroads still hoped to stop them. In 1903, Stephen B. Elkins, chairman of the Senate Committee on Interstate Commerce—and a supporter of railroad interests—sponsored a bill to outlaw rebating. Roosevelt signed it. Despite the Elkins Act, though, competitive pressures led to more rebating.[80]

Politically, this was the high-water mark for American railroads. They had gone to the government for benefits they could not secure in open markets. Twice, in 1887 and 1903, antirebating laws had been passed to serve railroad interests. The railroads didn't know it, but they were playing with fire. Although they had failed to stop rebating, they had helped to establish the principle that the government ought to have power over prices. They assumed that government regulatory power could be limited and that they would be the dominant influence on how power was exercised. They missed the trend that was beginning to gather momentum against them—and that Theodore Roosevelt would soon begin promoting.

When Theodore Roosevelt was preparing for the 1904 presidential election campaign, he asked railroad tycoon Edward H. Harriman to help raise $250,000. In return, he reportedly promised to make Harriman's friend Chauncey Depew ambassador to France. In 1904, Depew was a lawyer for New York Central founder Cornelius Vanderbilt, chairman of the board of New York Central Railroad and a U.S. senator from New York. Harriman contributed $50,000 and recruited a number of his friends, including J. P. Morgan, who contributed $150,000, and Morgan's associate, George Perkins, who kicked in a total of $450,000 from himself, the House of Morgan, and New York Life Insurance Company.[81] Depew himself added $100,000, but Roosevelt never made him an ambassador. This was only the beginning of Roosevelt's hostility toward the very railroad men whose money he accepted for his presidential campaign.[82]

Shippers continued to complain about railroad rates even though their net after inflation—about 2½ percent per year[83]—was actually falling.[84] After the 1904 presidential elections, the Senate Committee on Interstate Commerce held hearings on the Hepburn bill to expand the power of the Interstate Commerce Commission. Both railroad men and shippers testified. Roosevelt declared, "The government must in increasing degree supervise and regulate the workings of the railways engaged in interstate commerce. In my judgment, the most important legislative act now needed as regards the regulation of corporations is this act to confer on the Interstate Commerce Commission the power to revise rates and regulations."[85] Given the inflationary trend, setting maximum rates might amount to the same thing as setting specific rates.

On June 29, 1906, Roosevelt signed the Hepburn Act. It increased the ICC from five to seven members, enabling Roosevelt to appoint two more people sharing his views. The law delegated to the ICC the power to set maximum rates, enabled shippers to challenge railroad rates before the ICC,[86] and expanded the ICC's power to regulate railroad terminals, storage facilities, pipelines, and ferries. The law declared that ICC decisions would take effect immediately and that the burden of showing that any decision was unreasonable would fall on the railroads.

That last point signaled an ominous turn. Before passage of the Hepburn Act, if a railroad wished to appeal an ICC decision, the decision did not take effect until the after the appeals process had run its course, perhaps all the way to the U.S. Supreme Court. That process could take several years. The Hepburn Act increased the risk of appealing an ICC decision.[87] The law made ICC decisions effective immediately. Fines (if any) began accumulating right away and could become substantial by the time an appeal was resolved.

"The president was no mere bystander during this lengthy debate," reported biographer Nathan Miller. "He not only worked in bipartisan harmony with a coalition of Republicans and Democrats favoring reform, but tried to influence public opinion with speeches."[88] Roosevelt hailed the Hepburn Act as "a fine piece of legislation, and all that has been done tends toward carrying out the principles I have been preaching."[89]

Compounding this federal action were state laws hostile to railroads and escalating demands from railroad labor unions. Clearly, there was a trend toward more political interference. Seeing that both Congress and the president were hostile to railroads, railroad executives realized that future efforts to raise rates to keep up with inflation were likely to encounter regulatory delay, litigation, and probably more laws. Rate restrictions plus inflation meant that railroads would have a tougher time handling higher traffic loads. "One could stand at a certain point on the main line between Harrisburg and Pittsburgh and see 28 passenger trains and 140 freight trains, hauling 7,000 cars, pass by in 24 hours," noted Martin. "The increase in traffic had outstripped facilities at virtually every point on the system."[90] The greater the traffic congestion became, the greater the amounts of time men were being paid to wait around for their turn to load or unload freight.[91]

By 1906, the railroad network was substantially complete in terms of route mileage, but much more intensive development was needed. A single track connected a substantial number of places. Increasing traffic volume required two or more tracks—as many as six between major points. In some areas, new routes were developed to reduce grades and curves.[92] Iron rails had to be replaced with steel rails, which could bear heavier loads. Wooden bridges and trestles had to be replaced.[93] In urban areas with a lot of street traffic, tracks had to be elevated so that trains could continue moving safely. More industrial sidings, passing tracks, freight yards, and warehouses had to be built. Bigger shipments led to longer trains, and more powerful locomotives were needed to pull them. Steam engines were vulnerable to deadly accidents in tunnels because engineers couldn't see warning signals through the steam, so there was a need to electrify tracks.

To make connections more convenient, "union" stations were built to link several railroads. Perhaps the first of these was Union Depot, Indianapolis, under construction in 1852, to connect seven railroads. St. Louis's Union Station opened in 1894 to facilitate connections among twenty different railroads, and at one time it was reported to be the world's busiest passenger rail terminal. It inspired construction of Union Station in Washington, D.C., which originally occupied some 200 acres and had 75 miles of track. Union stations were built in Kansas City (1914), Chicago (1925), Los Angeles (1939), and other cities.

Even with all these costly improvements, labor costs accounted for 64 percent of total railroad expenses in 1898, declined to 61 percent by 1910, then rose again to 64 percent by 1914.[94] Between 1897 and 1914, prices in the United States rose between 40 and 50 percent.[95] This inflation generated pressure for higher wages and made it more difficult for railroads and other businesses to maintain profits as a source of investment funds.

Theodore Roosevelt overlooked a critical issue: the ability of the railroads to handle the needs of the rapidly growing American economy. There was a serious risk that inadequate railroad capacity would create a massive bottleneck in transportation. Even critics of the railroads like University of Michigan economist I. Leo Sharfman conceded that the "increase in mileage fell far short of the growth in traffic. Between 1895 and 1905, for example, ton mileage increased 118 per cent and passenger mileage increased 95 per cent; during the same period, however, the increase in railway mileage was only 21 percent." Sharfman, writing in 1921, went on to say, "in part, this retardation in physical growth of railway plant was due to impaired railway credit and to the increase of [other] profitable opportunities for industrial development."[96] If railroad investment was urgently needed, and railroads were having trouble financing it, then why did Theodore Roosevelt lead the charge to throw more obstacles in their way?

The flow of capital into the railroad business was adequate for only about a year after the Hepburn Act became law, peaking in 1907. According to Albro Martin, "In the nine years of feverish economic growth from 1898 to 1906, $4.2 billion of fresh capital flowed into the nation's railroads. During this period the annual level of investment, considered as a trendline, was rising in relationship to the trendline for demands on the system. By contrast, in the period 1905–1907 the investment peak was reached and the curve turned downward. Because of the special events which occurred in 1906 in respect to the railroads' ability to increase their revenues on their own initiative, the level of investment in relation to demand for their services that was reached in 1905–1907 was never bettered."[97]

As a result of the government-sanctioned rate restrictions and rising costs, railroad profits fell. Less investment capital came from retained earnings. After 1907, retained earnings never equaled the levels reached from 1904 to 1907.[98] The railroads had to depend increasingly on outside funding sources by issuing more stocks and bonds.[99] Increasingly, these securities were bought by foreign investors. French investors, for instance, became interested in American railroads after the Russian Revolution of 1905 scared them away from further investments in Russia.[100] Moreover, even conservative railroad managements started setting up equipment trusts, using rolling stock as collateral for asset-based financing.[101] This strategy was one favored by companies with weak balance sheets that could not raise enough capital based on their general creditworthiness. Thanks to Roosevelt, this is what the nation's biggest industry had become.

THE MANN-ELKINS ACT INTENSIFIES
THE RAILROADS' FINANCIAL PROBLEMS

Despite inflation and higher railroad costs, some stemming from new labor agreements, railroad rates remained frozen after passage of the Hepburn Act. In 1908 there was talk about increasing rates, but Roosevelt pressured railroad executives not to boost rates before the presidential election, and they backed off. The assault on the railroads did not end with Roosevelt's term in 1909. The anti-railroad, pro-government trend accelerated by Theodore Roosevelt continued long after he left office.

In real terms, railroad rates declined, but some shippers continued to do as the railroads had done—lobby politicians for special privileges. There was support for an amendment to the Hepburn Act allowing old rates to remain in effect while shippers challenged them and ICC officials reviewed the challenges.[102] This would mean that railroads, not shippers, would bear the risk of bureaucratic delays.

On January 7, 1910, President William Taft, who shared Roosevelt's opinion of the railroads, sent a message to Congress about further expanding the ICC's power over them. He urged that the ICC be authorized to initiate rate reductions.[103] He favored establishing a five-judge Commerce Court to hear appeals of ICC decisions.

Taft's attorney general George Wickersham drafted a bill. It was sponsored in the House by Illinois congressman James Mann, who had introduced the Pure Food Act (1906), and in the Senate by West Virginia's Stephen Benton Elkins. The proposal gave the Interstate Commerce Commission more direct power to set railroad rates. After a railroad applied for a rate increase, the ICC would have up to ten months to issue a decision, during which period the old rates would remain in effect. The legislation established a Commerce Court to hear appeals. Shippers were to be a party to the proceedings—a provision that practically guaranteed that every proposed rate increase would at least be contested and delayed. The jurisdiction of the ICC was extended to telephone, telegraph, cable, and wireless communications companies. Among progressives, it was an article of faith that the government should have the power to interfere with market prices. Nobody seems to have given any thought to what the consequences of this meddling might be.

Hugo Richard Meyer was among the very few dissenters. He reported his findings about how the ICC protected regional interests and interfered with the development of a national market in his book *Government Regulation of Railway Rates: A Study of the Experience of the United States, Germany, France, Austria-Hungary, Russia and Australia* (1905), where he also indicated the situation with government-run railroads was even worse in Europe.[104] Perhaps hoping to enlighten progressives who imagined that government ownership of business would solve social problems, Meyer wrote *Municipal Ownership in Great Britain* (1906)[105] and *The British State Telegraphs: A Study of the Problem of a Large Body of Civil Servants in a Democracy* (1907),[106] both chronicles of the disasters of big government.

In May 1910, while the Mann-Elkins bill was being debated, railroad executives decided they could no longer delay action to stop the deteriorating financial condition of the railroads. W. H. Hosmer, chairman of the Western Traffic Association, announced that the twenty-four member railroads planned to introduce a schedule of higher rates for some two hundred commodities.[107] Possibly millions of rates were affected.[108] Eastern railroads individually announced rate increases.[109] According to the Hepburn Act, the new rates would take effect in thirty days, and they could be challenged by the ICC, one rate at a time.[110]

Unfortunately for the railroads, after Roosevelt left office in 1909, the regulatory trend against the railroads actually intensified. President Taft asked Judge David P. Dyer of the U.S. District Court in Hannibal, Missouri, to issue an injunction preventing the railroads from putting their new rates into effect, and he did.[111] Railroad executives made their way to the White House and surrendered. They agreed to suspend their planned rate increases, and the government agreed to withdraw the injunction.[112]

The railroad men had been reduced to a sad and sorry state. Their willingness to take risks was a critical factor enabling markets to function more efficiently so millions of people could prosper as never before, but they were afraid to defend their economic liberty. They had contributed hundreds of thousands of dollars to Theodore Roosevelt's election campaign, only to be denounced and hit with costly new regulations. Roosevelt and others had pressured them to delay rate increases, and they rolled over.[113] After passage of the Hepburn Act, they let four years go by without asserting their right to set rates as they saw fit. The public had become used to a free ride, enjoying railroad improvements the cost of which were not passed on. Railroads negotiated higher-cost labor agreements, and those costs were not passed on, either. The railroad men were expected to continue jeopardizing their businesses while Congress took its time deliberating.

The railroads had few friends in Congress.[114] The progressive movement was in full flower, and progressive intellectuals and politicians indiscriminately denounced railroads. As for railroad leadership, Edward Harriman had died on September 9, 1909, and J. P. Morgan was in the sunset of his career.

Congress passed the Mann-Elkins Act on June 18, 1910, and President Taft signed it into law. Railroad historian Albro Martin noted that the legislation was "the first measure ever adopted by the federal government to establish *de facto* ceilings on a single industry in peacetime and in the midst of a long-term upward trend in prices."[115] Thus did Republicans pioneer price controls in modern America.

The railroads filed an application for higher rates, but after months of deliberations, their application was denied, and except for a few minor adjustments, the railroads did not gain any significant rate increases until 1918.[116] Despite all their lawyers, the railroads continued losing their ability to finance costly improvements.

With price controls, revenue growth deteriorated, while the railroads had to pay higher and higher (unregulated) prices for materials and accommodate costly wage settlements. Woodrow Wilson's Justice Department threatened railroads with criminal prosecution under the antitrust laws, before they were seized during World War I. Government inefficiencies being what they were, during the twenty-six months the railroads were under federal control, the industry lost a reported $900 million.[117]

The U.S. Post Office further undermined the financial condition of the nation's railroads. The volume of mail was growing rapidly, but the Post Office insisted on observing an old law saying that railroads were to be compensated for hauling mail on the basis of the volume of first-class mail they carried, which would be estimated every four years![118] Moreover, the introduction of taxpayer-subsidized parcel post in 1913 further reduced railroad profits. Parcel post rates were lower than the rates charged by private railway express companies such as Adams Express, Southern Express, American Express, and Wells Fargo, which paid the railroads to haul their customers' packages. As those companies lost business to parcel post, the railroads lost revenue, too. To make a bad situation even worse, they were obligated to haul parcel post packages for nothing.[119]

STAGNATION AND COLLAPSE

Writing in 1971, railroad historian Albro Martin estimated that more than $5 billion of investment capital that might have helped upgrade America's railroad system before World War I flowed into other, less regulated and more attractive industries, such as automobiles and communications.[120] He made the following observation: "Developments like the diesel locomotive were delayed twenty years even though the steam locomotive had passed its peak by 1914. Routes that should have been double-tracked, like the western portions of Pennsylvania and the B & O into the important gateway of St. Louis, remained single-track lines. Block signaling expanded with agonizing slowness. Air conditioning of passenger trains lagged behind the introduction of the comfort in practically every other form of public accommodation. The 'first class' surcharge for sleeping and parlor car accommodation, introduced during the war, was retained, and as a result this type of travel went into a decline from which it never recovered. Electrification, a promising development in the prewar decade, languished. The great industries which supplied the railroads withered or diversified into other fields."[121]

In the decades after it was established, the Interstate Commerce Commission did nothing to help expand or improve America's transportation network. The ICC did nothing to help develop the American market or raise living standards. Initially an obstacle to competition, with Theodore Roosevelt's support, the ICC became a threat to the survival of the railroads, a drag on the entire economy, and proof of the bankruptcy of progressive ideas.

CHAPTER FIVE

WHY DID ROOSEVELT'S "PURE FOOD" REGULATORS ATTACK ROAST BEEF, CORN SYRUP, AND COCA-COLA?

Theodore Roosevelt had little apparent concern about the safety of American food until some muckraking journalists began to allege that monstrous things were going on. Then he decided he must rush to the rescue. Once again, Roosevelt assumed the solution would be to increase government power. He urged more "supervision and control by the National Government over corporations engaged in interstate business."[1] He contributed to the myth that wicked capitalists were making fortunes selling unsafe food to Americans and that high-minded government regulators serving the public interest were hard at work to safeguard the American people.

In fact, the biggest advances in food safety owed nothing to government regulation. Many occurred long before Theodore Roosevelt became president and were achieved by private, profit-seeking entrepreneurs. The main effect of food safety laws and regulations was to intensify the political struggles of various interest groups for commercial advantage.

PRIVATE ENTREPRENEURS MADE FOOD
SAFER—BEFORE REGULATION

During the nineteenth century, Americans were living longer than ever before. Statistical evidence suggests that death rates were declining in the United States before Roosevelt became president.[2] A boy born in 1850 had an estimated life expectancy of about thirty-seven years; a girl, about thirty-nine years. By 1900, estimated life expectancy was about forty-six years for newborn boys and forty-eight for newborn girls.[3] People were living longer because, among other reasons, economic liberty led to dramatically increased food production, lower food prices, and technological and scientific advances, which led to better nutrition and consequently better resistance to disease.

During the late nineteenth and early twentieth centuries, there were no epidemics related to commercial food processing.[4] People worried about tuberculosis, diphtheria, typhoid, measles, polio, influenza, and whooping cough.[5] The Spanish-American War and work on the Panama Canal made Americans more aware of yellow fever. Mary Mallon, an Irish household cook who was to become known as "Typhoid Mary," made news after it was discovered that wherever she worked around New York, people became sick. She was believed to have infected forty-seven people with typhoid; three of them died.[6] Evidently, then, the major public health concern was infectious disease, not commercial food processing.

Indeed, early "pure food" laws were aimed more at protecting producers than at protecting the general public. Writing in 1927, historian Gustavus A. Weber traced "pure" food and drug regulations to a June 16, 1848, law empowering the federal government to ban imports. Seemingly high standards were applied to *imported* foods and drugs more than a half century before they were applied to *domestically produced* foods and drugs. The decision about whether to permit an imported food or drug into the United States was apparently made by customhouse clerks rather than by chemists or others with technical knowledge, and the procedures for evaluating a food or drug seemed casual, to say the least. The 1848 law stated that "all drugs, medicines, medicinal preparations including medicinal essential oils, and chemical preparations used wholly or in part as medicine, imported into the United States from abroad, shall, before passing the custom house, be examined and appraised, as well in reference to their quality, purity, and fitness for medical purposes, as to their value and identity specified in the invoice."[7]

Meanwhile, private entrepreneurs were achieving major advances for fresher, more wholesome food. During the early nineteenth century, Nicolas-François Appert, a resourceful French brewer and confectioner whom historian Maguelonne Toussaint-Samat described as "a dynamic and jovial little man despite his bald head and big eyebrows,"[8] developed a new method for preserving food: It was sealed in jars, then boiled. Appert published his findings so that everybody could benefit, and Americans called his process "appetizing."[9] The Dutch developed cans of welded tin plate, used for preserving fish. The English used such cans to preserve fruit in syrup.[10] In 1813, English entrepreneurs Bryan Dorkin and John Hall started the first canning factory. In addition to making food safer, canned goods intensified competition in the food business, because canners could enter distant markets. They gave consumers more variety by making it possible to enjoy wholesome food out of season.

Canned food, noted historian Reay Tannehill, usually was "sold to customers on the American prairies or in the urban slums of Manchester, who had no access to—perhaps had never even eaten—the fresh product. Even if the gastronomic value of the food was minimal, it gave life and variety to an otherwise restricted diet. And because canning combines established themselves where production costs were lowest, customers thousands of miles away were able to buy what were to them exotic foodstuffs at a highly competitive price. Once the canning manufacturers had taken note of Louis Pasteur's discoveries about the part played by micro-organisms in fermentation and putrefaction—discoveries which were gaining general acceptance by the late 1860s and the 1870s—and once the Massachusetts Institute of Technology had charted the most satisfactory processing times and temperatures for different foodstuffs (at the end of the century), it became not only convenient and cheap, but safe and reliable as well."[11]

Gail Borden (1801–1874), a Litchfield, Connecticut, dairy farmer and Texas surveyor, traveled to London hoping to find a market for his invention—a dehydrated meat biscuit that would not spoil. He failed, ran out of money, and had to return to the United States in steerage, where he saw the infants of immigrant mothers dying after having consumed raw milk from infected cows on the ship. Milk was generally a problem because it was shipped in unsanitary oak barrels and spoiled rapidly. Borden developed a process for preserving milk by condensing it in a vacuum container at low heat. He received a U.S. patent for the process in 1856 and the following year established the New York Condensed Milk Company.[12] Borden insisted that the farmers from whom he bought milk observe strict sanitary standards.[13] According to historians Harper Leech and John Charles Carroll, demand for Borden's canned condensed milk "in the Civil War hospitals overcame most of the popular prejudice against the tin food-container."[14] After the war, people bought Borden's condensed milk because of its reputation for dependable quality.

In 1869, Camden, New Jersey, fruit merchant Joseph Campbell and Abraham Anderson, a manufacturer of tin ice boxes, joined forces to produce canned tomatoes, vegetables, jellies, minced meats, and other foods. Seven years later, Campbell dissolved the partnership because he wanted to expand much more rapidly than Anderson. He joined timber and flour merchant Arthur Dorrance to establish Joseph Campbell & Company. In 1897, Dorrance hired his twenty-four-year-old nephew John, an MIT-trained chemist, who developed canned, condensed soup within the year. Because the heaviest ingredient in canned soup was water, reducing by half the amount of water that needed to be added cut shipping costs and lowered the price of a 32-ounce can of soup by two-thirds, from 30 cents to a dime.[15] Consumers added water when cooking the soup. Condensed soup became the core of Campbell's business.[16]

The same year Campbell started his partnership, Henry John Heinz started his business. At the time, most people ate mainly bread, potatoes, root vegetables, and meat that was dried, salted, or smoked. Most fruits and vegetables were unavailable when locally out of season. Heinz's idea was to give people more interesting flavors by bottling condiments, such as pickles and ketchup, in clear glass bottles. Up to that point, the general practice had been to use bottles made with dark-colored glass, which could conceal bits of leaves and turnip filler. Heinz started using clear glass containers, so consumers could see how pure his condiments were.[17] His business prospered on both sides of the Atlantic and eventually around the world.

Artificial refrigeration was a huge advance to reduce food spoilage. In 1842, John Gorrie, a Florida physician, designed a machine to cool air, so that yellow fever patients would be more comfortable. His machine compressed gas that flowed through radiating coils, then rapidly expanded the gas to lower the temperature. In 1851, he was granted a U.S. patent for mechanical refrigeration. Alexander Twinning introduced commercial refrigeration in 1856, and it was adapted for the brewing and meatpacking industries by James Harrison, an Australian.

In 1856, the French engineer Charles Tellier bet that he could transport across the Atlantic Ocean mutton that would be fit to eat about three and a half months later when the ship arrived in Buenos Aires, Argentina. He froze the meat and equipped the ship *Frigorifique* with a freezer. At about the same time, another French inventor, Ferdinand Carré, designed a freezer for the ship *Paraguay,* which delivered some eighty tons of frozen meat to Le Havre, France. The appearance and flavor of the meat reportedly were not great, but it was safe to eat.[18] Over the years, many improvements were made in the freezing process. Perhaps the biggest improvement for flavor was made by the American entrepreneur Clarence Birdseye, who developed the quick-freezing process.[19]

Butter was another health concern at the time. Traditionally, it was churned by farm women, sold to local merchants, and offered or resold without much regard for proper preservation. There were many complaints—from *Uncle Tom's Cabin* author Harriet Beecher Stowe, among others—that rancid butter posed a serious risk to health. In 1873, Hippolyte Mège-Mouriés, a French food chemist, secured a U.S. patent for an inexpensive alternative to butter made with beef fat and flavored with milk and other substances.[20] By 1900, there were almost three dozen patents related to what came to be known as margarine (the name deriving from the ingredient margaric acid). Costing about a third less than butter,[21] margarine was most appreciated by working-class people, who spent an estimated 40 to 50 percent of their incomes on food.[22] When the dairy industry lobbied state legislatures for protection, state governments began passing laws outlawing margarine. More laws may have been passed against margarine than against any other food product in American history.[23]

Like the rest of American business, the food industry was intensely competitive, and the trend was toward more competition—a strong incentive to improve the quality of food and cut cost for consumers. For instance, during the late nineteenth and early twentieth centuries, Royal had the largest share of the cream of tartar baking powder business, but it faced plenty of rivals offering alum baking powder. Altogether, as many as five hundred companies were manufacturing baking powder, which was a cheaper and often safer leavening agent than yeast or eggs.

American food was becoming safer than ever—*before* Theodore Roosevelt signed the Meat Inspection Act and the Pure Food and Drugs Act.

LOCAL BUTCHERS FIGHT
LOW-COST MEATPACKERS

Until the late nineteenth century, butchering was a local business, conducted in places such as farmhouses, old warehouses, and covered docks.[24] A butcher needed a cleaver, a knife, a cauldron for scalding the carcass, and a rope for hanging the carcass so the skin could be scraped and removed and the major pieces of meat cut away.[25]

Traditionally, slaughtering began after the first frost, because cold weather helped to minimize spoilage. Then, in the nineteenth century, slaughterhouses began to acquire and store large quantities of ice cut from midwestern lakes, so their facilities could be turned into icehouses in warm months, enabling business to continue with minimal spoilage year-round.[26] Boston entrepreneur Frederick Tutor—the "Ice King"—developed better methods of storing ice to minimize melting and made money shipping ice from New England to Charleston, New Orleans, and even Bombay.[27] A substantial trade developed in the shipping of live cattle by rail from the West to eastern markets, where they were slaughtered or, increasingly, loaded onto boats bound for Europe. A thousand-pound steer, however, yielded only about 550 pounds of edible meat; everything else was disposed of (this was before resourceful entrepreneurs figured out how to turn waste materials into useful things). Paying the railroads to ship waste materials across the country made no sense. It would be better to do the slaughtering in a central location and then ship the dressed carcasses in refrigerated cars.

In 1857, the first refrigerated shipments of beef went by rail from Chicago to New York. The meat was packed in ice, which caused discoloration and an off-taste. Although it was perfectly safe to eat, consumers balked. What was needed was a way to prevent the meat from touching the ice. George Hammond, a Detroit meatpacker, tried hanging carcasses from racks in cars refrigerated with ice, but the carcasses swayed back and forth and sometimes caused derailments. J. B. Sutherland, also from Detroit, secured the first patent for a refrigerated car in which air circulated past ice bins.[28] T. C. Eastman, a New York meat wholesaler, installed cold-storage units on the Anchor, White Star, and Williams & Gueton steamship lines, which started shipping dressed beef to England. Economic historian Mary Yeager described the dramatic effect of cold storage on the profitability of the business: "The savings as well as profits were enormous. A live steer cost £8 10s. to send from New York City to London in 1878, as opposed to 30s dressed. It cost Eastman about $26 per head for preparation, freight, and cost of transit, including commissions to agents on the other side. The average price realized was about $90, netting him roughly $64 per head!"[29]

More refrigerated car patents were issued, but it was a Chicago meatpacker, Gustavus Franklin Swift, who developed a reliable method of refrigerating the beef during shipment. Swift, working with Boston engineer Andrew Chase, developed a promising design in 1879: The top of each boxcar would be lined with ice, air would be circulated, and the chilled air would naturally fall toward the carcasses, kept stationary in containers to maintain the stability of the cars.[30] This soon proved superior to other designs that had been tried.

Swift tried to persuade railroads to build refrigerator cars according to this design, but they considered refrigerator cars too specialized. So he used his own assets as collateral to borrow money for building ten refrigerator cars. He wanted to enter the big New York market, but William Henry Vanderbilt, president of the New York Central Railroad, refused to let him in. Like other railroads, the New York Central had considerable investments in stock-yards where cattle were watered and fed as they were transported—investments that would be rendered worthless if shipments of dressed meat displaced shipments of live cattle. Moreover, railroads didn't want to pay for refrigerated cars. Their general policy was to handle a maximum amount of freight with a minimum number of cars. In practice, this meant that shippers could not assume that enough railroad cars would be available when they needed them. To ensure timely shipments of perishable meat, the packers themselves had to invest heavily by buying refrigerated cars.

Fortunately, competition among the railroads was intense. Neither the Baltimore & Ohio nor the Grand Trunk lines (which went mainly through Canada, connecting with U.S. railroads in Buffalo) had much cattle business. These railroads were eager to earn money from shipping dressed meat. Swift made a deal with the Grand Trunk Railroad.[31] As a consequence, for the cost of shipping a single steer, Swift could ship three dressed carcasses and offer beef for less. When other railroads began to appreciate the potential volume involved in shipping dressed meat, they began to offer better terms.

How would dressed beef be distributed when the business was set up to handle live cattle? Swift traveled extensively throughout the East, recruiting dealers and forming partnerships with many. Sometimes he cut his prices until dealers understood that the future of the beef business was with Chicago dressed beef, not live cattle slaughtered locally.[32] The next step was to establish cold-storage facilities in major markets and sales networks for small towns. Refrigerator cars made possible dramatically expanded shipments of beef to distant markets, and the big Chicago meatpackers reportedly marketed their products to consumers 1,125 miles away on average.[33] The boom in refrigerator car traffic stimulated the ice-harvesting business. Icehouses began popping up along rail routes, as did facilities for re-icing refrigerated cars. Lakes were purchased for their potential ice yield.[34]

Philip D. Armour and his partner John Plankington moved their meatpacking business to Chicago, where railroad connections were better, and quickly built an efficient new operation there. They learned how to use every part of a hog, thereby reducing waste materials. Armour—who was Swift's biggest rival—explained why: "Even after the packing business had assumed fairly large proportions, the packers were not aware of, or did not appreciate, the value of the offal, and the problem of how to get rid of it at the least expense was ever present. So recently as twenty-five years ago, in Chicago, the blood was allowed to run into the river, and men were paid five dollars a load to cart the heads, feet, tankage, and other waste material out upon the prairie and there bury it in pits and trenches. Instead of being a source of profit, the offal, in this respect, was a distinct source of expense. Gradually there grew up in the vicinity of the packing centers subsidiary enterprises having for their object the utilization of some or all of this waste material. Such concerns turned out glue, oil, tallow, and crude fertilizers. In time, however, the necessities of the business, and the growing competition, forced the progressive packer to include these industries in its own establishment . . . [and] today a large packing plant depends largely for its profit on the intelligent utilization of those so-called waste materials which, in the early days of the packing business, were not only thrown away, but the removal of which was, as I have shown, an actual source of expense."[35]

Local butchers resented the competition spawned by these advances. They claimed that the big Chicago packers sold meat from diseased cattle.[36] Allegations about diseased cattle seem to have originated among midwestern cattlemen and were aimed at competitors in Texas who drove their herds north to markets in Kansas City and increasingly to Chicago. Texas fever and pleuropneumonia were the diseases most often mentioned. Though debilitating for cattle, they appeared not to harm people who cooked meat from affected animals.[37] In 1886, butchers in St. Louis established the Butchers' National Protective Association to organize opposition against Chicago beef.[38] The New York Wholesale Butchers Union claimed that Chicago beef was contaminated with ammonia and warned that continued shipments of Chicago beef would destroy an estimated $100 million of local business. Restaurants were pressured not to serve Chicago beef. Delmonico's, a popular Manhattan eaterie, published a cookbook that belittled the quality of Chicago beef. A number of midwestern states passed laws aimed at limiting the movement of Texas cattle through their territory. The laws were opposed by Texas cattlemen as well as Chicago meat-packers who wanted no restrictions on the supply of cattle.[39] Meanwhile, reports of diseased American hogs led Italy to restrict hog imports in 1879.[40] France followed in 1881. Two years later, Germany restricted imports of hogs from the United States. Belgium, too, restricted American hogs.

Not surprisingly, such claims scared consumers away from American meat. Cattlemen hoped to revive their fortunes by lobbying for state cattle inspection laws.[41] Butchers wanted inspection laws requiring that cattle be inspected in the state where the meat was to be consumed. This regulation would have had the effect of banning meat shipped from out of state. Cattle inspection laws were introduced in Arkansas, Colorado, Kansas, Minnesota, Missouri, Nebraska, New Mexico, Ohio, Pennsylvania, Texas, and Wyoming,[42] and adopted in four of those states.[43] The Chicago packers, already subject to inspection by the Chicago Health Department, the Humane Society, and the State Livestock Association, wanted no more laws.

The inspection laws were tested in Minnesota when a meat-packer named Henry Barber sold a hundred pounds of beef from a cow slaughtered in Illinois, presumably in Chicago. The sale violated a Minnesota law requiring that beef sold in the state come from cattle inspected in the state. Barber was convicted and imprisoned. He appealed, claiming that the U.S. Constitution delegated to Congress the power to regulate interstate commerce. In May 1890, the U.S. Supreme Court agreed and struck down the Minnesota state inspection law. In the majority opinion, Justice John Marshall Harlan wrote: "enactment of a similar statute by each one of the states composing the Union would result in the destruction of commerce among the several states, so far as such commerce is involved in the transportation from one part of the country to another of animal meats designed for human food, and entirely free from disease."[44]

By this time, the big Chicago packers were worried about losing more export business, particularly since Argentina had emerged as a major supplier of meat.[45] The Chicago packers supported proposals for federal inspection of meat entering interstate commerce or export markets. They were also concerned about mounting competition from smaller packers. The number of U.S. meatpackers soared 52 percent from 1899 to 1909.[46] Although Roosevelt characterized the Chicago packers as an all-powerful "trust," they accounted for less than half of the market for meat. Accordingly, they backed what became the Meat Inspection Act of 1891. It authorized the Department of Agriculture to inspect cattle prior to slaughter, but only if they were going to enter interstate commerce. Inspection was not required for meat sold in the same state where the animal was slaughtered. This law was amended three years later to authorize inspection of hogs.

The general public had little or nothing to do with all this political maneuvering. There was no public outcry for meat inspection laws. The allegations against the Chicago packers never made much sense because there were only four big meatpackers—Swift, Armour, Morris, and Hammond—and they spent a lot of effort and money to develop nationally known brand names. If these companies had been so foolish as to sell meat that made customers sick, they would have been exposed immediately, their brands would have been ruined, and they would have incurred big losses as customers avoided the tainted brands.[47]

"EMBALMED BEEF" AND *THE JUNGLE*

After the Spanish-American War, General Nelson Miles, commanding general of the U.S. Army, claimed that American soldiers had been fed what he called "embalmed beef." William Randolph Hearst's *New York Journal* treated this comment as front-page news, running it under the headline "MILES MAKES GRAVE

CHARGES AGAINST THE ADMINISTRATION—POISONS USED IN BEEF MADE THE SOLDIERS ILL—TONS OF BAD MEAT SENT TO TROOPS IN PORTO RICO."[48] General Miles, however, may have been acting on a personal grudge against the McKinley administration. After the outbreak of war with Spain, Miles, who had distinguished himself during the Civil War, hoped for glory in Cuba. He was disappointed when President McKinley assigned him to Puerto Rico, and he complained about the way mobilization for the war had been handled.

Any problems with meat were probably due to the army's logistical problems. Biographer Kathleen Dalton reported, "The tragedy of the war was the army's botched supply and transportation system, which caused inhumane treatment of the soldiers. Mismanagement of the war shocked [Roosevelt]."[49] As for Miles, he was not a believer in refrigerated or canned meat. He urged the army to continue the Civil War practice of shipping live cattle to war and slaughtering them as needed to feed the troops, even though such practices complicated efforts to keep food sanitary in tropical heat.

In February 1899, President McKinley asked General Grenville Dodge to head an investigation of the complaints about bad meat. The Dodge Commission—also dubbed the "Beef Court"—took testimony from witnesses, inspected meatpacking plants, and sampled refrigerated and canned beef. Theodore Roosevelt testified that he would rather eat his old hat than the meat they were served.[50] But when Miles testified, according to historian Ivan Musicant, "he produced none of the promised evidence and actually distanced himself from some of his own earlier comments, even repudiating the press interviews he had given. . . . Actually, Miles disavowed so many of his statements that the court found it difficult to establish just what his charges contained."[51] Altogether, the testimony filled eight volumes.[52] Commission members thought the canned beef was fine, and they dismissed Miles's charges that refrigerated beef had been injected with poisonous preservatives. The commission noted that if there really had been a problem with bad meat, Miles should have reported it at the time to his superiors, including the secretary of war.[53] He had, after all, telegraphed the War Department about American soldiers afflicted with yellow fever.[54]

Overall, then, as economist Gary Libecap summarized, "the record does not indicate that the incidence of diseased cattle or their consumption was very great, and there is no evidence of a major health issue at that time over beef consumption."[55] Carolyn Dimitri, senior economist at the U.S. Department of Agriculture's Economic Research Service, similarly concluded that "During the time period [1880s, 1890s], there are no references to public concern in the U.S. over diseased or unsafe meat. There were, however, frequent references suggesting packers were a trust or combine."[56]

"By 1904," Kolko wrote, "84 per cent of the beef slaughtered by the Big Four packers in Chicago, and 100 per cent of the beef slaughtered in Ft. Worth, was being inspected by the government; 73 per cent of the packers' entire U. S. kill was inspected. It was the smaller packers that the government inspection system failed to reach, and the major packers resented this competitive disadvantage [because inspection raised costs]. The way to solve this liability, most of them reasoned, was to enforce and extend the law, and to exploit it for their own advantage. They were particularly concerned about the shipment of condemned live stock to smaller, non-inspected houses."[57]

In 1905, in a series of articles written for *Everybody's Magazine,* Charles Edward Russell called Chicago packers "The Greatest Trust in the World." They possessed, he claimed, "a greater power than in the history of men has been exercised by king, emperor, or irresponsible oligarchy."[58] Apparently spurred by this publicity, the Justice Department prepared an antitrust case against the packers, but it was dismissed by a U.S. district court.[59] Then the socialist writer Upton Sinclair (1878–1968) joined the attack on the meatpackers. He had written five romantic novels when the socialist newspaper *Appeal to Reason* sent him to Chicago. In 1904, packinghouse workers had gone on strike but failed to win concessions from their employers. Sinclair's assignment was to dramatize the plight of the workers. He spent seven weeks making observations and interviewing stockyard workers.[60] Then he went to a cabin near Princeton, New Jersey, where he wrote *The Jungle*.[61]

Sinclair depicted slaughterhouses as cesspools of filth and disease. His manuscript was rejected by every publisher he approached, because he refused to make asked-for changes. Finally, Doubleday agreed to publish it. The book appeared in 1906. Instead of focusing on the terrible working conditions, as Sinclair had intended, the public was horrified at the prospect of eating bad meat. *The Jungle* became a bestseller and, according to Sinclair, was quickly translated into seventeen languages.[62] Philip Armour replied with a series of articles in the *Saturday Evening Post*, and Sinclair countered with an 8,000-word piece in the April 20, 1906, issue of *Everybody's Magazine*. In the rebuttal, he fervently defended the fundamental accuracy of his story, though he conceded, "I was not able to provide legal proof of men falling into vats and being rendered into pure leaf lard."[63]

Suddenly, it seemed there was a political crisis about food. Roosevelt didn't think much of Sinclair, writing his friend William Allen White: "I have an utter contempt for him. He is hysterical, unbalanced, and untruthful. Three-fourths of the things he said were absolute falsehoods. For some of the remainder there was only a basis of truth."[64] But as a politician, Roosevelt had to do something if he was to remain popular. Biographer H. W. Brands remarked, "Roosevelt didn't eat much canned beef, since he could afford better, but he immediately spotted a winner in a campaign against abuses in the packing industry."[65] So Roosevelt began attacking the Chicago meatpackers. He appointed Commissioner of Labor Charles P. Neill and Civil Service lawyer James Bronson Reynolds to investigate conditions in meatpacking plants. Neither knew much about meatpacking and evidently were horrified as much by slaughtering itself as by anything else.[66] They reported what they considered to be distressing situations.

In congressional testimony that followed the investigation, packinghouse executive Thomas E. Wilson made clear that the big Chicago packers wanted federal regulation to handicap their smaller competitors that could not afford to invest in more modern and sanitary facilities. Federal inspection, as noted, was intended to reassure foreign buyers about the quality of American meat. The big Chicago packers, however, objected to paying the cost of federal inspection. They wanted taxpayers to pick up the $3 million tab.[67]

"Historians have always suggested that Sinclair brought the packers to their knees," observed Gabriel Kolko, "or that The Greatest Trust in the World collapsed before the publication of the Neill-Reynolds report. Given the near unanimity with which the measure passed Congress, and the common agreement on basic principles shared by all at the time, there is an inconsistency in the writing of historians on this problem. If the packers were really all-powerful, or actually opposed the bill, it is difficult to explain the magnitude of the vote for it. The reality of the matter, of course, is that the big packers were warm friends of regulation, especially when it primarily affected their innumerable small competitors."[68]

Like the 1891 Meat Inspection Act, the Meat Inspection Act of 1906, which Roosevelt signed on June 30, applied only to meat shipped out of the state where an animal was slaughtered. Federal inspection was not required when meat was consumed within the state. Upton Sinclair criticized the federal meat inspection as a freebie for the meatpackers. "The Federal inspection of meat," he wrote, "was, historically, established at the packers' request. . . . It is maintained and paid for by the people of the United States for the benefit of the packers. . . . Men wearing the blue uniforms and brass buttons of the United States service are employed for the purpose of certifying to the nations of the civilized world that all the diseased and tainted meat which happens to come into existence in the United States of America is carefully sifted out and consumed by the American people."[69]

JUNK SCIENCE AND "PURE FOOD"

The same day Roosevelt signed the Meat Inspection Act, he signed the Pure Food and Drugs Act. In this case, too, he did not become involved with legislation until the underlying issues became front-page news. The story is more complicated and intriguing than what is commonly conveyed in history books.

Probably the first federal health-related law was the Drug Importation Act (1848), empowering customs officials to board incoming ships, open crates, inspect goods, and decide whether to let them be unloaded. Historian Gustavus Weber pointed out that although "Congress failed to authorize the Department of Agriculture or any other national governmental service to protect the people from domestic food adulteration—the adding of harmful ingredients—it did require the Department of Agriculture and the Treasury Department to give a certain measure of such protection in the case of imported food products . . . [and] the Chemical Division [of the Agriculture Department] devoted much attention to the examination of food products imported into this country."[70] That American consumers were to be protected from foreign producers and not from U.S. producers suggests that the purpose of the legislation was to restrict foreign competition.

In 1879, bills were introduced into Congress proposing to ban food adulterants—specifically oleomargarine and glucose (a sugar made from cornstarch).[71] Although the bills did not yet have enough political support to pass, the targets of the laws were a tip-off that the stated goal of "pure food" was a smoke screen for old-fashioned protectionism—suppressing oleomargarine, which competed with butter (the dairy farmers' lobby), and glucose, which competed with cane sugar (the sugar refiners' lobby). In 1886, Congress passed a law that imposed a tax on oleomargarine and restricted its manufacture and sale. The tax was enforced by the Treasury Department's commissioner of internal revenue.[72] Clearly, public health was not the real issue.

In 1886, Congress had appropriated funds for chemists to analyze adulterants alleged to be in food. Appropriation bills in 1896 and 1902 funded analyses of food adulteration.[73] Then came debate about proposed bills to outlaw the adulteration of foods in interstate commerce—though there was disagreement about what constituted adulteration; large, well-established manufacturers of foods, drugs, and drinks tended to favor regulatory legislation; smaller companies expressed some opposition.[74] Warnings about "adulterated food" soon became a strategy for exploiting consumers, starting with tea drinkers. There were efforts to start growing tea in the United States. The climate was suitable in South Carolina, but the cost of cultivating and harvesting tea there would be perhaps eight times higher than in East Asia. U.S. tea producers could survive only if American consumers were prevented from buying imported teas at lower prices. On March 3, 1883, the Tea Act "to prevent the importation of impure and unwholesome tea" became law.[75] On March 2, 1897, "An Act to prevent the importation of adulterated and spurious teas" became law.[76] The fact that it was to be enforced by the secretary of the treasury suggests that its principal purpose was to protect domestic tea producers, principally in South Carolina, from overseas competition.[77]

By this time, progressives had begun to focus on dietary reform. They recommended consumption of 3,500 calories a day, including 125 grams of protein, 125 grams of fat, and 450 grams of carbohydrates—numbers that would raise more than a few eyebrows today.[78] From a "scientific" standpoint, vegetables were considered a waste of money because they did not have many calories.[79] Ethnic food was condemned as "unscientific."[80]

The most influential crusader against adulterated food was Harvey Washington Wiley, who became chief chemist at the U.S. Department of Agriculture's Bureau of Chemistry in 1882. Roosevelt's biographers have displayed surprisingly little curiosity about Wiley, whose attacks played an important role in Roosevelt's larger campaign against wicked capitalists. Kathleen Dalton just mentioned his name in *Theodore Roosevelt: A Strenuous Life* (2002). Nathan Miller did little more in *Theodore Roosevelt: A Life* (1990). Wiley went unmentioned in Edmund Morris's Pulitzer Prize–winning biography *Theodore Rex* (2001). Historian James Harvey Young, however, described Wiley as having "a knack for eliciting tremendous loyalty, and his personal associations, tending toward the conspiratorial, were as important as his public speaking."[81] Wiley encouraged Americans to consume more sugar, which he considered the hallmark of an advanced civilization. "Childhood without candy," he remarked, "would be Heaven without harps."[82] Wiley lobbied for high sugar tariffs, and he counted on the Louisiana Sugar Producers Association to help protect his job when Democrats were in office.[83]

Wiley fought bureaucratic battles to have his Bureau of Chemistry control all chemistry research conducted by the Department of Agriculture. When the Bureau of Soils published the results of chemistry research done by its own scientists, Wiley asked a friend at the University of California to attack his competitor's findings in the journal *Science*. Within the Department of Agriculture, Wiley dominated work relating to adulterated food. He promoted new government regulations and maneuvered to ensure that he would control how they were administered.

Wiley's "science" was not all that scientific. For example, in 1902, he formed a "Poison Squad." It consisted of a dozen healthy young men who worked at the Bureau of Chemistry and volunteered to consume large amounts of food additives for five years so that Wiley could study their effects. He tested borax, boric acid, salicylic acid, sulfurous acid, benzoic acid, benzoates, formaldehyde, sulphate of copper, and saltpeter.[84] On the basis of the results from those twelve people, Wiley's Bureau of Chemistry issued a report warning that food preservatives were dangerous for health. "Two aspects of the experiments diminished their scientific value," observe economists Coppin and High. "First, there was no control group. Although fluctuations in health, weight, and appetite were recorded, there was no norm with which to compare them. Second, Wiley began his experiments with some firmly entrenched but unusual ideas about digestion and preservatives. Spoilage and digestion, in his view, were the same process, and so preservatives, which interfere with the normal decay of a substance, necessarily interfered with digestion. He also believed that some preservatives, those proven safe by long usage, were less harmful than others. According to him, traditional preservatives—salt, vinegar, spices, wood smoke, sugar, peppers—compensated for their preserving action in the stomach by causing 'the secretion of ferments in the intestinal canal.' As he cited no chemical analysis or laboratory experiment for his beliefs, they were apparently just that—beliefs without scientific foundation even by the scientific standards of the day."[85]

Although the "Poison Squad" report had little scientific value, it helped Wiley generate a lot of publicity. He wrote articles and gave interviews promoting a federal law that would restrict if not ban "adulterated food." At first, he attracted little popular support: People were not dying in the streets because of adulterated food. Consequently, Wiley revised his strategy. He decided to ally with an interest group that would benefit from such a law. What group did this champion of public health choose? The producers of straight whiskey—the expensive stuff served at gentlemen's clubs!

The makers of straight whiskey were eager to crush their competitors who produced rectified whiskey—the cheap stuff sold in saloons.[86] Both types of whiskey involved fermentation, then distillation, but rectified whiskey was distilled again or processed through charcoal. From a nutritional standpoint, the two whiskeys were identical.[87] The main practical difference between them was that the producers of straight whiskey had to pay a "bottled-in-bond" tax. Of course, the revenue stamp on each bottle of straight whiskey implied nothing about the nutritional value or safety of the product, and Wiley conceded as much when he testified before Congress in 1904: "The Government's stamp does not guarantee purity in respect of the origin of the whiskey and its supervision by the government, but of course it does not guarantee . . . that it is pure in the sense of wholesomeness."[88]

After Wiley was asked to defend his claim that rectified whiskey was bad, he launched into a rambling monologue: "If it [rectified whiskey] contained all the elements that nature adds, the chemist would be at sea. But then the connoisseur comes to your help. You get a product that does not taste like the natural product; and if you did have one that tasted like the natural product, then the physiologist comes to your help. It does not have the same physiological effect."[89] He presented no evidence showing that the effects of rectified whiskey on a person's mind and body differed in any way from the effects of straight whiskey.[90] Nevertheless, the Overbolt Company, a straight whiskey producer, sent Wiley a complimentary case of rye whiskey. He acknowledged the gift: "I thank you very much for your courtesy and will take pleasure in bringing the matter of bottling in bond as a guarantee of purity before the Food Standards Committee officially authorized to advise the Secretary of Agriculture in these matters."[91]

Wiley denounced producers of rectified whiskey as the "Whiskey Trust," implying the existence of a monopoly, though in fact the industry was intensely competitive.[92] He branded producers of rectified whiskey as the enemies of wholesome food.[93] He talked ominously about "crooked whiskey coagulating the protoplasm."[94] He persuaded the American Medical Association and women's groups to support new government regulations against rectified whiskey.[95] At the same time, he recommended that physicians prescribe straight whiskey as a medication![96]

Wiley thought a pure food law could be enacted in 1904, and on January 20 the Hepburn-McCumber bill was passed by the House of Representatives.[97] William Peters Hepburn, a Republican congressman from Iowa, drafted this bill (not long afterward he drafted the bill authorizing federal interference with railroad freight rates). Porter James McCumber was a Republican senator from North Dakota. Because of procedural delays and opposition from the producers of rectified whiskey, the bill failed to secure approval in the Senate.[98]

In September 1904, Wiley relaunched his campaign at a meeting of the International Pure Food Congress in St. Louis.[99] His aim was to have regulations authorized by a food law restrict if not ban the estimated 85 to 95 percent of whiskey that was rectified[100]— the poor man's whiskey—thereby appealing to supporters of the growing movement to prohibit alcohol consumption by the unruly masses, many of them recent immigrants to the United States, without upseting the rich and powerful, who enjoyed straight whiskey. But his campaign became confused as he plunged into controversies unrelated to rectified whiskey. In his speech to the International Food Congress, Wiley attacked saccharin, the artificial sweetener produced by the Monsanto Company. Company president John F. Queeney protested that the Hepburn-McCumber bill, which Wiley backed, would have unfairly discriminated against Monsanto. Wiley countered that saccharin, unlike sugar, lacked food value.[101] Many nutritionists today maintain that neither saccharin nor sugar has food value. Sugar consumption has been linked to diabetes and heart disease.

Wiley was deep into the ketchup controversy. He seems to have refrained from making his most critical remarks about food additives because his acquaintance Henry John Heinz had been unable to manufacture a ketchup that would keep more than a few days after a bottle was opened without the additive benzoate of soda.[102] When Heinz announced that he had perfected a process that did not require additives, Wiley resumed his attacks on additives.[103] In effect, Wiley promoted a Heinz ketchup monopoly, for a federal ban on food additives would leave Heinz the only company able to produce ketchup.[104]

While Wiley was crusading for government regulation of food, there were revelations that the Agriculture Department's Bureau of Animal Husbandry had sold inside information about soon-to-be-released crop reports—information of value to speculators who analyzed supply and demand conditions before buying or selling agricultural commodities.[105] The speculators rewarded Agriculture Department statisticians with a share of the trading profits, enabling them to amass big money on a small salary.[106] Why should anybody believe the government could enforce honest dealings if the government itself was so easily corrupted?

Wiley was bailed out by muckrakers who blamed the failure of Congress to enact pure food legislation on special interest lobbying. In his book *Treason of the Senate,* Graham Phillips singled out rectified whiskey producers as corrupting influences.[107] The May 1905 issue of *World's Work* carried an article by Edward Lowry called "The Senate Plot Against Pure Food."[108] Samuel Hopkins Adams wrote "The Great American Fraud," a series of twelve reports on patent medicines that started running in the October 7, 1905, issue of *Collier's, the National Weekly.* In 1906, Adams's reports were gathered together and reprinted as a book by the American Medical Association. Wiley was widely portrayed as a great hero who had defied special interests that poisoned people and corrupted American democracy. Wiley, of course, said nothing about his links to straight whiskey producers, sugar producers, and other special interests.[109] Stirred by all this, the Woman's Christian Temperance Union began lobbying for a pure food law.[110] Theodore Roosevelt finally got on board, backing a food law in his State of the Union address in 1906.

Congress passed the Pure Food and Drugs Act, and it was signed into law on June 30, 1906—but not because there was a food crisis. Despite decades of discussion about "pure food," there still was no evidence that food quality was deteriorating or that commercial food processors posed a threat to public health. On the contrary, food was safer than ever before because railroads brought fresh food to market more quickly than ever before and because canned, refrigerated, and frozen food technologies minimized spoilage. All these advances had been achieved by private entrepreneurs. Wiley had whipped up hysteria about minor, if not entirely spurious, issues.

By the Bureau of Chemistry's own reckoning, there was no food crisis. During the first year the Pure Food and Drugs Act was enforced, this bureau reportedly collected 13,400 food samples, of which 814—6 percent—were considered adulterated enough to warrant prosecution.[111] The regulators seem to have judged 94 percent of the sampled food to be safe.

The Pure Food and Drugs Act was mainly concerned about truthful labeling. In a dispute about the truthfulness of a product's label, the burden of proof was on the government. Wiley's Bureau of Chemistry was given broad discretion to enforce the law. In 1911, in *United States v. Johnson*, the Supreme Court ruled that the labeling requirements applied only to ingredients.[112] The law did not apply to claims made on behalf of patent medicines. Congress responded to this ruling by passing the Sherley Amendment, which outlawed labels making false claims about the effectiveness of patent medicines.

Although truthful labeling is obviously a good thing, statutes as well as common law precedents already covered fraud, and the Pure Food and Drugs Act led to unexpected trouble. Wiley used his power to launch crusades having little to do with health and everything to do with politics. The official guardian of public health and enforcer of one of Theodore Roosevelt's landmark laws went after corn syrup. The demand for it had boomed, in part because it was a low-cost alternative to cane sugar. The price of cane sugar was high because of the tariff on imported cane sugar. Corn syrup was commonly used in table syrups and in inexpensive jams and jellies.[113] Producers of cane sugar called corn syrup an adulterant and insisted that it be legally known as "glucose," a word that newspaper reporters had inexplicably associated with coal tar and other poisons.[114] Wiley agreed that glucose was the proper name,[115] although in his 1907 book, *Foods and Their Adulteration*, he had written that it was all right to call glucose "corn syrup" and said that it was a wholesome food.[116] Producers of corn syrup feared that if they had to sell their product as glucose, consumers would avoid it. They tried countering Wiley by noting that, according to his definition of the word, adding cane sugar to food should also be considered adulteration.[117] Wiley insisted that, according to federal food definitions, corn syrup did not qualify as a syrup. Corn syrup producers replied that the liquid residue remaining after crystallized sugar was extracted from sugar cane also did not qualify as a syrup according to federal food definitions.

At this point, Theodore Roosevelt, who could not restrain himself from interfering with anything, became involved in the controversy. The president of the United States ruled that corn syrup looked like syrup and came from corn so it could be called corn syrup. On February 13, 1908, the secretaries of agriculture, the treasury, and commerce signed Food Inspection Decision 87: "In our opinion it is lawful to label this sirup as Corn Sirup."[118] Wiley, however, got his bureaucratic revenge. Food Inspection Decision 87 required corn syrup to be listed as an ingredient on food labels, but added cane sugar did not have to be listed. This ruling prevailed for three decades.[119]

Wiley then attacked Coca-Cola, America's most popular soft drink. In 1908, he attempted to have the government seize ten barrels and fifteen kegs of Coca-Cola being shipped from Atlanta, Georgia, to Knoxville, Tennessee. He objected to Coke's caramel color and to the presence of caffeine, and he insisted that the beverage was addictive.[120] He compared caffeine to strychnine, commonly used for rat poison, and he claimed that caffeine was as addictive as opium and morphine.[121] Frederick L. Dunlap and George McCabe, members of the Food Inspection Board, disagreed with Wiley's views about caffeine and nixed the seizure.[122] Unfazed, Wiley plotted another seizure but was foiled again. It was pointed out to him that if the Food Inspection Board ruled caffeine was dangerous in Coke, it would have to outlaw coffee and tea.[123] But this time, Dunlap and McCabe ended up siding with Wiley, and forty barrels and twenty kegs of Coke were seized.[124] The trial began on March 13, 1911, in Chattanooga, Tennessee. Apparently Wiley wanted the presiding judge to be Edward T. Sanford, who shared his views.[125]

The two main charges were that Coke was adulterated and that it was mislabeled. It was said to be adulterated because of the small amounts of caffeine added—although caffeine was not on the government's list of poisonous substances.[126] It was said to be mislabeled because it did not make use of the entire coca leaf. Of course, if the entire coca leaf had been used, Coke would have contained cocaine, which would have made it an illegal substance.[127] Wiley may have had something to do with sending seven federal spies to Chattanooga to dig up evidence that the jurors were unable to competently deliberate on the case or had corrupt ties to Coca-Cola.[128] The spies found nothing of consequence.[129]

Notwithstanding Wiley's incessant claims that his methods were "scientific," one of the earliest double-blind experiments that was conducted to test the effects of caffeine was not done under his supervision. Harry and Leta Hollingworth administered caffeine to half of a group of test subjects. The participants didn't know whether they were getting caffeine, some other additive, or no additive of all. They were observed for changes in behavior. Mark Prendergast, author of the "definitive history" of Coca-Cola, reported that "Leta directed the actual experiments, which indicated that caffeine, in moderate amounts, improved motor skills, while leaving sleep patterns relatively unaffected. [Harry] was particularly dismayed by one scientist's conclusion that caffeine caused congestion of the cerebral blood vessels in rabbits, whom [the scientist] had dispatched by a club on the head."[130] Science was not on Wiley's side.

Asa Candler, president of the Coca-Cola Company and formerly an Atlanta pharmacist, denounced Wiley's alleged evidence as "rat, rabbit and frog." Candler suggested that Wiley might be carrying a grudge against Coca-Cola because the company had stopped buying sugar from his friend John Arbuckle, an immigrant Scot who became America's largest coffee importer. Wiley had done work for Arbuckle and accepted many gifts from him. Coke had switched to Henry Havemeyer's American Sugar Refining Company, which sold sugar for less.[131]

Wiley did not seem to be concerned about the caffeine in Arbuckle's coffee, but he had asked Lyman Kebler, head of the Bureau of Chemistry's drug laboratory,[132] to write a report suggesting that the small amount of caffeine in Coke was addictive. "Most addicted," Kebler wrote, "are office people and 'brain workers.' . . . The beverage is in some instances purchased at the fountain by the pitcher, taken home and consumed in the same way that beer is in some families. . . . In many cases soldiers consumed the beverage in undue amounts, particularly those persons who are addicted to the use of alcoholic beverages. The largest quantities are consumed after a prolonged alcoholic debauch." Kebler must have shocked many when he revealed that some soldiers mixed Coke with whiskey to make a " 'coca cola high-ball' . . . which makes the soldiers wild and crazy."[133] Wiley, however, was unable to document any physiological or nutritional differences between the caffeine added to Coke and the caffeine naturally occurring in coffee and tea. He simply denounced the adding of caffeine to Coke as adulteration.[134]

Things became a bit uncomfortable for Wiley when the *St. Louis Post Dispatch* reported that he had given an anticaffeine speech claiming that "coffee drunkenness" was probably more dangerous than whiskey drunkenness. This revelation outraged grocers across America. Wiley replied by writing in *Grocers' Magazine*, "I have never, either by precept or practice, condemned the moderated use of tea or coffee."

Federal agents reportedly tried to influence jurors with offers of alcohol and sex. Coke filed a motion to have the case dismissed, and Judge Edward T. Sanford upheld the motion without resolving the caffeine issue. He ruled that because some caffeine had always been in Coke's formula, it was not an added ingredient. Wiley was furious. He wrote a friend, "It will not be long before a milk dealer will discover that by adding a grain or two of caffeine to his milk it will become more popular which will drive his competitors into similar practices, and soon we will have our bread and our meat treated in the same way. It will open wide the flood gates to drug addiction in our foods through which the muddy waters of wealth and greed will rush."[135] The case was appealed to the U.S. Supreme Court, and on May 22, 1916, Justice Charles Evans Hughes delivered the majority opinion, ruling that all the ingredients of Coke were subject to the Pure Food and Drugs Act and that caffeine was an added ingredient. He referred the case back to the Federal district court.[136] To keep its successful beverage formula secret, Coca-Cola negotiated a settlement with the Justice Department on November 12, 1917.[137] All told, the company spent some $250,000 defending itself. The government returned the barrels of syrup it had seized.[138]

Wiley's power began to fade, but he had built a bureaucratic empire. The annual budget of the Bureau of Chemistry had soared from less than $50,000 with ten employees in 1882 to over $1 million with six hundred employees thirty years later.[139] Although more government money was being spent in the name of "pure" food and drugs, federal officials did not seem to know what they were doing. Writing in 1928, historian Gustavus A. Weber reported, "Early in 1913 it became apparent that the efficiency of the Bureau of Chemistry in administering the Food and Drugs Act was seriously impaired by lack of system. The laboratories, both in and out of Washington, were congested with samples collected by inspectors. The inspectors, who were responsible only to the Chief Inspector in Washington, worked independently of the chemists in the branch laboratories, with resulting loss of efficiency. There was delay in analyzing samples and in detecting adulterations."[140]

Wiley's political support vanished. Producers of straight whiskey and rectified whiskey began working together to counter the efforts of progressive reformers to prohibit the consumption of alcoholic beverages. Heinz Company executives decided that the antipreservatives campaign no longer served their interests, and they apparently became concerned about possible revelations of their ties to Wiley. They began to distance themselves from him. Wiley's longtime backer John Arbuckle was near death. Wiley had alienated Theodore Roosevelt, and in 1912 Wiley backed Democrat Woodrow Wilson for the presidency. Wilson, however, seems not to have liked Wiley, either.[141] On February 29, 1912, Wiley resigned from the Bureau of Chemistry.[142] In May 1912, at age sixty-seven, Wiley became a father—his young son was dubbed the "Pure Food Baby."[143] Despite his energetic crusades against caffeine, he gave a speech titled "The Advantages of Coffee as America's National Beverage."[144] He began writing a column for *Good Housekeeping* magazine, his platform for continued attacks on Coca-Cola.[145]

Years of lobbying for a pure food law, and Wiley's energetic publicity campaigns and bureaucratic maneuvering, did little if anything to improve the health of the nation. How could a campaign to call rectified whiskey one thing rather than another improve people's health? How could a campaign to call corn syrup one thing rather than another improve health? Why did Wiley think he could improve public health by attacking reputable companies and promoting special interests?

Wiley's enforcement of the Pure Food and Drugs Act, according to economists Coppin and High, "did not improve the health of the consumer, the plane of competition among producers, or the honesty and integrity of government officials. If anything, Wiley's enforcement worsened the ability of consumers to make informed judgments about food and drugs. His claims about the healthfulness of various foods and preservatives were not well-founded. He produced no sound evidence that rectified whiskey was more harmful than straight whiskey, that ketchup with benzoate of soda was more harmful than ketchup without it, that 350 milligrams of sulfur dioxide in dried fruit was the proper limit, that syrup made with sucrose was more nutritional than syrup made with glucose. In fact, some of his claims—that rectified whiskey coagulated the protoplasm, that preservatives hindered the digestive process, that added caffeine was more deleterious than naturally occurring caffeine, that sucrose was healthier than glucose—were exaggerated even at the time that he made them, and they certainly have not stood the test of scientific evidence."[146]

Although Roosevelt signed the pure food and drug law Wiley had championed, the two men detested each other. Both had strong, self-righteous personalities. In 1908, they had a contentious meeting. After Wiley condemned saccharine, he recalled: "President Roosevelt turned upon me, purple with anger, and with clenched fists, hissing through his teeth, said: 'You say saccharine is injurious to health? Why, Doctor Rixey gives it to me every day. Anybody who says saccharine is injurious to health is an idiot.' "[147]

Roosevelt wrote, "I tested him personally in reference to corn syrup, the use of saccharine, and the importation of a French vinegar. In each case he had made a ruling which was nonsensical. . . . These instances gave me a great distrust of Wiley's good judgment."[148]

MORE TRUTHFUL LABELING
OF LAWS AND POLITICIANS?

Theodore Roosevelt claimed that there was a food safety crisis and that America needed new laws to mandate meat inspection and require truthful labeling. Politicians like Roosevelt could have used some truthful labeling themselves.

There was no food safety crisis. Thanks to a succession of privately developed food preservation technologies and the increasing efficiency of the railroads that brought food to markets, nobody was dying in the streets because of unsafe food. The 1906 Meat Inspection Act had its main impact on small, undercapitalized slaughterhouses that were going out of business anyway, as the big Chicago meatpackers increased their share of the American market. In any case, federal meat inspectors had already been assigned to slaughterhouses as a result of the 1891 Meat Inspection Act. The 1906 Pure Food and Drugs Act empowered the Agriculture Department's notorious quack, Harvey Washington Wiley, to conduct crazy crusades against foods competing with the interest groups he served. Yet, incredibly, generations of historians have praised Theodore Roosevelt's Meat Inspection Act and Pure Food and Drugs Act for providing a sound basis for more government regulation.

CHAPTER SIX

WHY WERE ROOSEVELT'S "CONSERVATION" POLICIES WASTEFUL AND DESTRUCTIVE?

T HE NATIONAL PARK SERVICE today calls Theodore Roosevelt the "Father of Conservation." Roosevelt crusaded to preserve America's resources from being exploited by greedy corporations. He declared that America was running out of natural resources, and consequently the president needed more power to save the environment. But what did Roosevelt actually do to protect America's land and natural resources?

The conservation movement began as a huge scramble for federal pork barrel subsidies, as some interest groups used their political clout to exploit other interest groups. Organizations in the West lobbied for government funds extracted from eastern taxpayers, and there were bitter conflicts among people maneuvering for advantages in the West. The most active lobbying organizations were the Lakes-to-the-Gulf Deep Waterway Association, American Forestry Association, National Rivers and Harbors Congress, American Cattle Growers Association, National Irrigation Congress, National Irrigation Association, National Drainage Association, Interstate Mississippi River Levee Improvement Association, National Water Users Association, American National Livestock Association, Public Domain League, Mississippi Valley Levee Association, Louisiana Development League, and National Reclamation Association.[1] Members of these lobbying groups hoped to enrich themselves with "conservation"—free dams, free waterway improvements, cheap water, cheap timber, cheap access to grazing lands, and other goodies, at somebody else's expense.[2] And many groups were successful, thanks in a large part to the efforts of Theodore Roosevelt.

Roosevelt expanded the power of the executive branch at the expense of Congress. Without congressional approval he established "conservation" commissions and spent federal money on "conservation" projects. In effect, he forced his conservation program on people, for there was not much general support for it. Despite the lobbying of many groups representing various special interests, people in western states did not want Washington telling them what must be done with their land.[3] Nor did people in the East want their money going to subsidize far-off projects. But Theodore Roosevelt got his way, and we are still feeling the negative effects.

THE PROGRESSIVE BATTLE CRY
FOR FEUDALISM

Roosevelt's conservation policies represented a radical break from American tradition. By the time Roosevelt became president, the government still controlled some 557 million acres of land in America, and his goal was to maintain federal control of it and keep it off the market.[4] Since the colonial era, however, the trend had been toward privatizing government land. Converting government land to private property was, in fact, hugely important for the spirit of Americans and the wealth of the country.

The earliest American settlements, in Jamestown, Virginia, and Plymouth, Massachusetts, began with common property. They failed because it was in each settler's interest to take as much as possible from common property and contribute as little as possible to it. As a result, the property did not yield enough to support the community. The situation in Jamestown began to turn around only after one of the Virginia Company's backers, Edwin Sandys, offered a "headright"—fifty acres of land—to each new immigrant.[5]

William Bradford, governor of Plymouth, saved his colony by privatizing the land. "At length, after much debate of things," he recalled, "the Governor (with the advice of the chiefest amongst them) gave way that they should set corn every man for his own particular, and in that regard trust to themselves. . . . And so [he] assigned to every family a parcel of land."[6]

The prospect of acquiring land proved a powerful inducement for immigration to Britain's North American colonies. Although technically the colonies belonged to the king of England, squatters could not be stopped from appropriating and developing government land. The British tradition of individual landholding was upheld in America by common law judges who had some independence from the king. The American system stood in remarkable contrast to the feudal landholding systems enforced in both Spanish America and New France. According to historian Albro Linklater, "Individual landholdings were so rare that during the half-century when Spain ruled California, from 1769 to 1821, fewer than thirty families were permitted to acquire their own rancheros, or estates. . . . In French America . . . the Crown owned the land and chose who could settle there; Protestants, for example, were banned. It created monopolies to exploit the fur and timber. The habitant who actually worked the soil never had clear rights to it."[7] Consequently, the population of the British colonies dwarfed that of Spanish America and French America.

The demand for private property surged after the American Revolution, and the best bet for paying off Revolutionary War debts was selling land acquired from the British. In 1787, Congress encouraged settlement of the Northwest Territory, as the lands west of the Appalachian Mountains were called, by passing the Northwest Ordinance. This law provided that land north of the Ohio River and east of the Mississippi River would be divided into three to five states (eventually Ohio, Indiana, Michigan, and Wisconsin), able to join the Union on equal terms with the original thirteen. The Northwest Ordinance established that the United

States would expand by creating new states rather than by expanding old states.

Thomas Jefferson and his political foe Alexander Hamilton agreed on the importance of privatizing land. Hamilton's primary interest was in selling the land as quickly as possible to the highest bidders, generating revenue for the new federal government. Jefferson believed that enabling people to become independent property owners was a key to securing American democracy. He helped develop a plan to sell property as efficiently as possible by dividing the land into square plots that could be easily surveyed and valued.

In 1796, Congress passed a law specifying that land must be divided into six-mile-square townships, then subdivided into one-mile-square (640-acre) sections. The government had a hard time selling these units. A mile-square section was too big and expensive for most people, and even those interested in purchasing land had difficulty getting information about specific parcels—for example, whether the land was well suited for crops. By the time President Jefferson approved the Louisiana Purchase (1803)—more than 800,000 square miles of land from France—Congress recognized that land had to be made available in much smaller units if it was to sell. It was offered in quarter sections (160 acres). In 1820, still less expensive half-quarter sections (80 acres) were offered. Finally in 1832 quarter-quarter sections (40 acres), considered the minimum acreage needed to support a typical farm family, were offered. "When Congress made it possible to sell public land by the quarter-quarter section," explained Linklater, "the squatter had only to step out 250 double paces, or 440 yards, toward the sun at noon, stick in a marker, then march 250 double paces toward the point where the sun set. . . . That was it: 440 yards by 440 yards made a 40-acre lot."[8]

States were eager to raise cash, boost their population, and develop their land, so as soon as surveyors had done their work, land was offered for sale.[9] Much of it was purchased by speculators who provided funds for the emerging American real estate market and assumed the risks of holding land, which were considerable. How much were particular parcels worth? Who would buy them? Who would be able to use the land successfully? Government officials didn't know. No one could tell for sure where railroad lines might be extended, where canals might be built, where towns might develop. Many speculators guessed right about what would happen but guessed wrong about how long it would take, and they went broke carrying the cost of the land.

There were widespread fears that big speculators might establish an aristocratic landholding system such as prevailed in Europe, but that did not occur. Why didn't it? One reason was that the speculators assumed big risks. "By claiming 320 acres instead of 160," historian Paul W. Gates explained, "[a speculator] had to bear a heavier portion of the cost of road construction and maintenance; his [government] school costs were increased or the establishment of schools was delayed and his children were denied educational opportunities; the expense of county and state government, in a period when the land tax was the principal source of government revenue, was burdensome. Other social institutions like churches, granges, and libraries came more slowly because the population was so dispersed. Furthermore, railroads, which all settlers wanted in their vicinity, could not be pushed into sparsely settled areas without large subsidies. State and county subsidies required special assessments upon the already overburdened taxpaying farmers."[10]

Meanwhile, the sheer numbers of squatters determined to acquire and improve government land forced officials to begin streamlining the process for securing recognition of property rights. According to Gates, legislators supported "the two great principles of equity in [U.S.] statutory law: The right of occupants . . . to their improvements and the right of settlers on privately owned land, unchallenged for seven years and paying taxes thereon, to a firm and clear title to their land no matter what adverse titles might be outstanding."[11] In 1812, Kentucky passed a law requiring that squatters expelled from their land must be compensated for the value of improvements they made. The U.S. Supreme Court struck down the law in the 1821 case of *Green v. Biddle*, but the outraged response of squatters highlighted the importance of landholding issues to western politicians.[12]

In 1832, Congress enacted a law saying that a squatter who occupied and cultivated government land would qualify for 160 acres. Congress renewed the law three times, extending the rights of squatters.[13] Between 1834 and 1856, states enacted pro-squatter laws similar to the Kentucky law struck down by the Supreme Court.[14]

These measures extended property rights to millions of people who had previously been outside the legal system. They now had incentives to continue improving their property—after all, they could profit by selling the land, passing the title to the buyer. Without a title, they might be able to continue working their land, but they could not sell it. Plus, there was the risk that somebody might come along and order them off the land, and they would lose the value of improvements they had worked hard to build. With a title to their property, they could borrow money, using their land as collateral. They could raise investment capital for a project on their property, and they could insure it.

By contrast, in most other countries back then, as now, comparatively few people had a title to the land they worked. They could continue growing the crops they and their predecessors had grown for generations, but they had little incentive to improve their land, because they could not profit from improvements. They could acquire no additional land, because their neighbors lacked titles. Without a title and insurance, people in most countries bore the entire risk of casualties such as fire, floods, and high winds.

Even in the United States, however, the government was slow to provide an efficient system for assigning titles to land. Complex property laws, imprecise titles, and rival claims made it difficult for anybody to secure clear titles. There was a tremendous amount of costly litigation. Seeking remedy in court was beyond the means of many people. "Between 1785 and 1890," economist Hernando de

Soto reported, "the United States Congress passed more than five hundred different laws to reform the property system, ostensibly based on the Jeffersonian ideal of putting property into the hands of private citizens. The complicated procedures associated with these laws, however, often hampered this goal. To confuse matters further, individual states developed their own rules of property and land distribution that largely benefited and protected only their own propertied elite. As a result, attempts to reform the property system only served to heighten the nation's land difficulties while making migrants extremely wary about losing what semblance of title they may have possessed."[15]

The most famous of the land laws was the Homestead Act (1862), which ended the Hamiltonian policy of maximizing revenue from land sales. The aim of the Homestead Act was to encourage farming. If an individual was at least twenty-one years old and a head of household, he could claim 160 acres. He could go to a federal Land Office, identify a 160-acre parcel he was interested in on a map, and pay a $10 filing fee to temporarily claim the parcel. He had to live on the property, build a home, and make improvements for five years, then find two neighbors to verify what he did before he received the title to his land.

Because the Homestead Act attracted poor people into farming, many farmers were undercapitalized—particularly for the harsh conditions west of the hundredth meridian (running through the western part of the Dakotas, Nebraska, Kansas, Oklahoma, and Texas), where settlers faced drought, locusts, and other hazards. Altogether in the United States, less than half of homesteaders persisted and secured titles to their property.[16] In Kansas and Nebraska alone, some ninety-three thousand homestead claims were abandoned.[17]

Moreover, large numbers of settlers applied for titles and transferred them to timber companies, mining companies, or cattlemen. Historians have characterized these transactions as corrupt, but the practice reflected the reality that a lot of land had a higher value as a source of timber, minerals, or grazing land. As Paul W. Gates recounted, "Land office reports, accounts of the cattle and lumber industry, and other government documents are replete with stories of the use of dummy entrymen by individuals and companies eager to get control of large areas of the public lands. . . . As competition for land intensified, compensation to dummy entrymen reached as high as $1,000 for a quarter section."[18]

Officials were wrong to insist that land with widely varying characteristics was best suited for farming. It would have been better to acknowledge that the land was being valued through trial and error in the marketplace. Even where land really was suited for farming, claims were often combined to form larger farms than had been originally intended, suggesting that bureaucrats might have underestimated the optimum size of farms.

Ironically, to the extent that the federal government's homesteading policies increased the total number of farmers and farm production, they contributed to declining farm prices and farm incomes—complaints about which sparked the populist movement. The amount of U.S. land devoted to farming soared from 407.2 million acres in 1860 to 841.2 million acres in 1900 and 958.6 million in 1920, by which time homesteading laws had had their effect.[19]

Unfortunately, Theodore Roosevelt did not recognize this reality. By 1900, an estimated 250 million acres of government land had been privatized, unleashing stupendous human energies for industry and trade as well as agriculture.[20] But Roosevelt insisted on keeping millions of acres under federal control and unavailable for sale. "I acted on the theory," he wrote, "that the President could at any time in his discretion withdraw from entry any of the public lands of the United States and reserve the same for forestry, for water-power sites, for irrigation, and other public purposes. Without such action it would have been impossible to stop the activity of the land thieves."[21]

ROOSEVELT'S "RECLAMATION" SQUANDERS
RESOURCES IN THE DESERT

Even before Theodore Roosevelt became president, some politicians began looking to Washington to assert its control over federal lands and, beyond that, to use taxpayer money to fund development out west. By the late nineteenth century it was clear that the effort to encourage settlement of America was generally failing west of the hundredth meridian. There, annual rainfall was less than twenty inches, and many places, such as Arizona and Nevada, received only about four inches of rain per year. Winters were as brutal as the droughts. Large numbers of pioneers perished as bitter-cold Arctic air and blizzards swept down from Canada. "No one knows how many lost their lives," Marc Reisner wrote of western pioneers, "but when the spring thaw finally came, whole families were discovered clutching their last potatoes or each other, ice encrusted on their staring, vacant eyes."[22]

Little wonder, then, that during the 1880s Kansas and Nebraska lost between 25 and 50 percent of their populations and that only about 400,000 families lasted on their homesteads out of more than a million who had initially tried. Reisner asked, "How could you settle a region where you nearly froze to death one year and expired from the heat and lack of water during the next eight or nine?"[23]

The only hope for farming such regions was irrigation, though of course that offered no help in dealing with the harsh winters. Hundreds of entrepreneurs established companies to develop irrigation systems. These entrepreneurs figured that if land could be acquired cheaply enough, and if it could be irrigated, then it could be farmed profitably. But recouping the substantial infrastructure costs involved proved difficult. Almost all the companies went bankrupt. Reisner cited a Colorado legislator who lamented the "crushed and mangled skeletons of defunct [irrigation] corporations . . . [that] suddenly disappeared at the end of their brief careers, leaving only a few defaulted obligations."[24]

States tried to step in where private businesses failed, but they lost money, too. The states issued bonds and defaulted. There were huge political fights about where dams and reservoirs would be located. There were even bigger fights about who would benefit from the water that taxpayers were forced to subsidize. State-run irrigation systems were noted for their corruption and waste. In California, state-run irrigation systems had been a disaster. Despite all these failures, progressives, with their inordinate faith in federal politicians and bureaucrats, believed that the federal government could successfully manage irrigation.

Western congressmen and senators became interested in building dams after it became clear that dams might attract more people to their states, which would in turn increase the politicians' influence. It didn't matter that building dams would lose money; western politicians would be increasing the population of their states at somebody else's expense. One strategy was to have the federal government force eastern taxpayers to subsidize western irrigation projects so that farmers could make a living on arid land. In 1888, Congress authorized that studies be done, and in the late 1890s the powerful lobbying group the National Irrigation Congress demanded federal subsidies for irrigation. Other groups joined the effort, including the National Board of Trade, the National Association of Manufacturers, and the National Business Men's League. Irrigation projects could not be justified as financially sound investments, so lobbyists like California lawyer George H. Maxwell stressed other benefits that would come from federal irrigation subsidies: not just increased population out west, but also expanded markets for eastern businesses and even a solution to social problems. (Maxwell claimed that social problems were caused by people living close together, and that irrigation would enable people to spread out and farm arid land.)[25]

Easterners opposed paying for irrigation subsidies. Eastern farmers objected because subsidies would mean giving western farmers unfair advantages at their expense.[26] Theodore Roosevelt's

own Republican Party represented the principal voice for easterners; in fact, President William McKinley, under whom Roosevelt
served as vice president, withheld his support from the proposed irrigation subsidies. When Roosevelt assumed the presidency, however, he was determined to encourage settlement with irrigation
subsidies, apparently fearing that if large regions of the West were
unpopulated, a foreign power might be tempted to seize territory.
He joined forces with pro-subsidy western politicians, most notably
Francis G. Newlands of Nevada, who was concerned about the ex-
odus of people from his desert state.

Newlands wanted to divert water from the Truckee and Carson
rivers to allow farming on the arid land.[27] He imagined that revenues from land sales might provide the funding.[28] If the government irrigation projects lost money, the deficit would be covered by
the U.S. Treasury—in other words, everybody who had not received
any irrigation subsidies. Since Newlands's aim was to encourage
western population growth, he favored limiting subsidies to 80
acres per family. Perhaps because of campaign contributions from
interest groups that wanted bigger irrigation subsidies, the cap was
raised to 160 acres.

President Roosevelt joined Newlands and other western politicians in promoting "reclamation," which meant taxing people in
the East to subsidize the construction of dams and irrigation systems, enabling settlers to farm arid western land. This was something that the National Irrigation Association had long been
lobbying for.[29]

A Senate bill was introduced in 1902 to provide subsidies for the
construction of dams and irrigation systems in sixteen states west
of the hundredth meridian where agriculture did not make much
sense. Newlands's stated aim was to "nationalize the works of irrigation."[30] Congress passed and Roosevelt signed the Reclamation
Act (also known as the Newlands Act) in March.[31]

To administer the Newlands Act, President Roosevelt ordered
the creation of the U.S. Reclamation Service (later renamed the

Bureau of Reclamation). It was curious that Roosevelt, who crusaded against private monopolies, approved of the Reclamation
Service as a dam-building monopoly. The Reclamation Service became what historian Reisner called "an unparalleled experiment in
federal intervention in the economy."[32] "Public power"—a euphemism for government monopoly—became a progressive battle cry.

Although progressives like Roosevelt spoke of making land suitable for settlement, western interest groups quickly seized on the
Newlands Act as a way to get generous federal subsidies. For
example, the railroad industry provided significant funding for the
National Irrigation Congress, which actively lobbied for government-subsidized irrigation projects that would increase the value of
arid western lands owned by railroads.

The Reclamation Service's first project was for Francis Newlands's home state of Nevada—the Truckee-Carson ditch. It linked
the Truckee River, which drained Lake Tahoe, to the Carson River
basin, where irrigation would be available. By 1908, Roosevelt's last
year in office, only three hundred plots had been sold, and further
settlement was soon ended because there wasn't enough water. The
project had to be significantly expanded before settlement could re-
sume. Roosevelt acknowledged that the population in reclamation
areas was "small when compared with that in the most closely in-
habited East."[33]

There was a speculative scramble for sites that might benefit
from contemplated dams. Historian E. Louise Peffer reported, "Activity in initiating claims or in acquiring public land under any of
the applicable laws was so great in the year following the passage of
the Reclamation Act that the receipts from the entry and disposi-
tion of public lands flowed into the reclamation fund." A common
tactic was to have individuals claim to be homesteaders filing for
land, then sell their titles to investors. Roosevelt ordered federal
agents to harass homesteaders who viewed federal subsidies as another gold rush. Peffer explains: "Roosevelt instituted the practice

of having every final entry scrutinized by special agents in an attempt to prove nonfulfillment of the terms of the land laws. . . . These special agents had made their presence felt and resented that they became the subject of numerous attacks in Congress. . . . It became increasingly difficult for a homesteader to get his patent. . . . The West did not approve this way of doing things. . . . It hindered the flow of lands into private ownership."[34]

Midwestern farmers objected that their taxes were going to subsidize western farmers—competitors—who were getting unfair advantages: the government dams and irrigation systems. But western lobbyists prevailed in the scramble for goodies, as politicians became eager to secure projects for their home states. According to Reisner, Congress "was soon writing 'omnibus' authorization bills, in which bad projects were thrown in, willy nilly, with good ones."[35] For example, by 1907, nine irrigation projects were under construction in the upper Missouri River basin, but they were there, Reisner noted, "mainly for political reasons: the Missouri Basin states contributed a lot of money to the Reclamation Fund." The Reclamation Act required projects to pay for themselves within forty years, but none of these nine projects would ever produce enough revenue to pay back the Treasury. Together they were short by nearly $40 million.[36]

Farmers were supposed to pay the government for the cost of irrigating their land, providing what Roosevelt called a "revolving fund" for future irrigation projects.[37] Interest on the government's capital investment was waived for ten years, and Congress could (and did) extend the interest-free period.[38] Despite such generous terms, the government had a hard time collecting, as Roosevelt acknowledged. There was "an organized effort to repudiate the obligation of settlers to repay the Government for what it has expended to reclaim the land."[39]

This became a serious problem because, as Roosevelt reported, "Although the gross expenditure under the Reclamation Act is not yet as large as that for the Panama Canal, the engineering obstacles to be overcome have been almost as great, and the political impediments many times greater. The Reclamation work had to be carried out in widely separated points, remote from railroads, under the most difficult pioneer conditions. The twenty-eight projects begun in the years 1902 to 1906 contemplated the irrigation of more than three million acres and the watering of more than thirty thousand farms. Many of the dams required for this huge task are higher than any previously built anywhere in the world. They feed main-line canals over seven thousand miles in total length, and involve minor constructions, such as culverts and bridges, tens of thousands in number."[40]

Despite the less than overwhelming response from prospective users of subsidized irrigation, it did increase the value of arid land. How much? Apparently the government experts didn't know, because there was quite a bit of speculation, and no matter how hard they tried to stamp it out, it flourished. Land in irrigation regions was to remain under government control except for homesteads, but those homesteads became a notorious loophole. People bought land supposedly as a homestead, held it for a while, and when its value increased enough, they sold it. Government officials—including President Roosevelt himself—continued to complain about speculation. What else could they possibly expect when they transferred resources from the productive East to the arid West?

Subsidized irrigation put irrigation-dependent farmers and city dwellers concerned about water supply in conflict with timber companies serving the demand for wood houses, paper, and many other things. Those focused on water supply believed that forests retained more water than open land did, so they opposed cutting down trees. Timber companies wanted to retain as much flexibility as possible for their operations.

Moreover, Samuel P. Hays wrote in his history of the conservation movement, "The Bureau [of Reclamation] thought in terms of maximum development of all Western rivers, while the people of each local area considered their own welfare first. Plans formulated by the Bureau frequently called for reservoirs in the tributaries to store excess runoff until it could be used during the dry season on lands further down the river. Upper river residents, however, resented the use of 'their' water elsewhere, frequently in another state. For example, the Bureau planned a series of reservoirs in the upper Rio Grande in Colorado to provide water for lands in Texas and New Mexico. Residents in southern Colorado, however, hoped to use the same sites to store water for their own use. The Bureau of Reclamation turned down their applications for rights-of-way on the grounds that their plans would interfere with the larger Rio Grande project. The conflict actually involved disagreements between upper and lower Rio Grande water users. . . . Colorado groups demanded that it leave them alone to develop their own state."[41]

Subsidized irrigation encouraged waste on a colossal scale. Farmers paid less than they otherwise would have, so they had fewer incentives to conserve water. They undoubtedly used water on less valuable crops, such as alfalfa, than would have been the case if they had had to pay the full cost of irrigation. Many farmers didn't know how to maintain their irrigation systems, so the systems gradually fell apart.[42] Large numbers of farmers poured their life savings into irrigation farming, only to find that it made no sense. They went bankrupt. After World War I, the nations of western Europe resumed agricultural production, and this, together with excess capacity in the United States and other countries that had filled the gap during the war, led to chronic farm surpluses. It was ludicrous to subsidize costly irrigation farming when crop surpluses were driving down prices of agricultural commodities.

ROOSEVELT APPROVES CALIFORNIA'S SECRET WATER GRAB

In his great "conservation" crusade, Theodore Roosevelt championed a remarkable double standard. While he continually hectored private businessmen for their alleged moral shortcomings, he defended the government's corrupt practices. The government's heavy-handed tactics were perhaps most visible in its suppression of water markets and creation of government water monopolies—an endeavor in which Roosevelt himself played an important role.

In 1905, the city of Los Angeles bribed Bureau of Reclamation engineer Joseph B. Lippincott to promote city interests in the Owens River, which was the most promising source of municipal water despite being some 250 miles away. The river flowed through the 100-mile-long Owens Valley, between the Sierra Nevada and Death Valley. Lippincott had a clear conflict of interest, since the Bureau of Reclamation planned diverting the Owens River for local irrigation. Lippincott escorted Los Angeles officials around Owens Valley, determining where they would need to acquire water rights. He hired Fred Eaton, former mayor of Los Angeles, to tell landowners that he wanted to become a rancher and buy water rights. As Reisner observed, Lippincott's deal with Los Angeles "was, if not exactly illegal, an apparent violation of the most basic ethical standards for government officials."[43] Theodore Roosevelt, however, ignored the government's conflicts of interest and deception. He declared, "It is a hundred or a thousand-fold more important to state that this water is more valuable to the people of Los Angeles than to the Owens Valley."[44]

The Reclamation Service subsequently canceled its project to divert the Owens River for local irrigation, but it did not reopen the land for sale to homesteaders. Roosevelt's conservationist adviser, Gifford Pinchot, declared most of Owens Valley to be a national forest, even though it had no trees. According to the law, Pinchot could not arbitrarily rule that any piece of land was a "national forest"; the highest value of the land was supposed to be as a forest. But as Reisner pointed out, "The valley's irrigated orchards were infinitely more valuable than the barren flats and scattered sagebrush that characterized the new national forest, so Pinchot's action was incontrovertibly a violation of the legislation that put him in business." Pinchot maintained that he was trying to ensure that Los Angeles had quality water, but much of what he labeled "national forest" fell below the L.A. aqueduct's intake.[45]

The progressive idea of subsidized living in the desert was extraordinarily wasteful. Reisner described what the city of Los Angeles had to build to complete the aqueduct from the Owens River: 120 miles of railroad, 500 miles of roads, 240 miles of telephone line, 170 miles of power lines, a huge concrete plant to support all this construction, two hydroelectric plants to run the machinery. It took several thousand workers six full years to complete the project.[46]

Roosevelt played an important role suppressing water markets. Fred Eaton, who had spent his own money acquiring Owens River water rights on behalf of Los Angeles, for which he was later compensated, wanted to operate the Owens Valley end of the aqueduct as a private business. This probably would have meant market prices for water. But Roosevelt backed the view that the municipal government of Los Angeles should monopolize the entire aqueduct system, thereby ensuring that the price of water would be politically driven below costs, providing incentives for more people to move to Los Angeles and make the water situation worse.

Roosevelt-style progressivism spawned rebellion, too. The people in Owens Valley bitterly resented the unethical way Los Angeles officials had appropriated their water, and rebels repeatedly dynamited the aqueduct. William Mulholland, head of the Los Angeles Department of Water and Power, derided everybody who lived in Owens Valley as "dynamiters."[47] More acts of sabotage followed the department's report that recommended destroying irrigation. Local citizens descended on the Alabama Gates and switched the weirs so that the Owens River flowed into what had been Owens Lake instead of to Los Angeles. Mulholland dispatched Los Angeles police to regain control of the Alabama Gates. Rebels countered by dynamiting the No Name Siphon, a big pipe that brought water over a Mojave hill toward Los Angeles.

As with other reclamation efforts, land sales never came close to paying for all these dams and irrigation systems. Even with lavish subsidies from eastern taxpayers, western desert farmers couldn't make a living and defaulted on their payments. Congress extended payment terms to fifty years.

The much-reviled speculators in desert land, reported Reisner, "were often better at paying their water bills than the stone-broke small farmers."[48] Blinded by antibusiness bias, Theodore Roosevelt and other progressives failed to see that untrained, undercapitalized settlers had little chance to make a decent living in the brutal American desert. It was a cruel hoax to promote desert farming as the American dream.

BAILING OUT WATERWAY NAVIGATION

As America's railroad networks expanded during the late nineteenth century, waterways handled a declining share of the freight business. "In 1851–52," explained economic historian Robert Fogel, "boats carried six times as much freight as railroads; in 1889–90 railroads carried five times as much freight as boats."[49] People preferred railroads because they delivered goods much faster, and railroad rates had been going down. Thus towns and companies that depended on waterways faced declining fortunes, and they lobbied for the federal government to spend large sums improving waterways. This Roosevelt was only too happy to do.

In 1907 Roosevelt and Gifford Pinchot enjoyed a free ride down the Mississippi River courtesy of the Lakes-to-the-Gulf Deep Waterway Association, a lobbying group. Roosevelt spoke at the association's convention in Memphis.[50] Soon thereafter he announced an ambitious scheme to bail out the waterway shipping business. He decided that the federal government should spend more and more money on waterways used by comparatively fewer and fewer people. The president was undoubtedly mindful that such a scheme might mollify midwesterners about their tax dollars going west to irrigate deserts.

In his State of the Union address of December 1907, Roosevelt declared, "Our great river systems should be developed as national water highways, the Mississippi, with its tributaries, standing first in importance, and the Columbia second, although there are many others of importance on the Pacific, the Atlantic, and the Gulf slopes. The National Government should undertake this work, and I hope a beginning will be made in the present Congress; and the greatest of all our rivers, the Mississippi, should receive special attention. From the Great Lakes to the mouth of the Mississippi there should be a deep waterway with deep waterways leading from it to the East and the West. Such a waterway would practically mean the extension of our coastline into the heart of our country. It would be of incalculable benefit to our people."

Lobbyists with the Lakes-to-the-Gulf Deep Waterway Association were overjoyed. They dreamed of having the U.S. Army Corps of Engineers, at taxpayers' expense, digging a deep channel from Chicago to New Orleans. Chicago businessmen hoped to affirm their commercial leadership of the Midwest. St. Louis businessmen hoped to regain advantages lost when railroads found it more efficient to route grain shipments to Memphis. Manufacturers throughout the Midwest hoped to more easily reach a wider market—including Latin America. The St. Louis Latin American Club touted the wonders of the Lakes-to-the-Gulf project.

But the Army Corps of Engineers estimated that the cost would be high. In political wrangling over the Rivers and Harbors Act (1907), Congressman Theodore Burton of Ohio used his influence to defeat funding for the Lakes-to-the-Gulf project.

That did not stop Roosevelt, however. He was interested in more grandiose projects than navigation anyway. Gifford Pinchot, the one-armed explorer John Wesley Powell, and Powell's assistant W. J. McGee recommended multiple-use water projects—electric power, flood control, navigation, and irrigation. They believed that such projects required scientific experts and presidential power to enforce a plan over the objections of local interest groups. Historian Hays, sympathetic to this view, explained: "Congress, far more responsive to the demands of local constituents than to the requirements of scientific planning, could not select projects rationally."[51]

So in 1907, Roosevelt established the Inland Waterways Commission as an executive agency to assert control over water projects, an attempted end run around the House Rivers and Harbors Committee. "The time has come for merging local projects and uses of the inland waters in a comprehensive plan designed for the benefit of the entire country," he insisted. "Such a plan should consider and include all the uses to which streams may be put, and should bring together and coordinate the points of view of all users of water."[52]

After spending most of its time trying to decide what might be done for the declining business of shipping via waterways, the commission offered platitudes promising something for everybody: "Plans for the improvement of navigation in inland waterways . . . should take account of the purification of the waters, the development of power, the control of floods, the reclamation of lands by irrigation and drainage, and all other uses of the waters or benefits to be derived from their control."[53]

But some of those aims conflicted with others. If the primary purpose of a dam was to produce hydroelectric power, there had to be a reasonably full reservoir behind it. If the primary purpose was flood control, however, a reservoir had to be empty so there would be capacity for floodwater. If a reservoir was empty, or if water was substantially drawn down for irrigation or for industrial or household use, navigation would be impossible.

In December 1907, Senator Newlands introduced a bill to establish a government agency that would somehow resolve such conflicts. He affirmed the progressive faith: "Large powers and a comparatively free hand should be given to an administrative body of experts."[54] Roosevelt pressured his secretary of war, William

Howard Taft, to support the bill, but the Army Corps of Engineers asserted its view that dams could not offer something for everybody and that navigation had to take precedence. Congressman Theodore Burton, now chairman of the Inland Waterways Commission, declared that he was against establishing a government agency independent of Congress.

There was considerable public debate about the claims made by Roosevelt and Newlands. How much would various waterway improvements cost? Could they really be paid for by having the government sell hydroelectric power? What about the Army Corps of Engineers' claim that dams and reservoirs could not provide complete protection against floods?[55] As the debate went on, it became increasingly clear that government did not have the answers. Nonetheless, Roosevelt and other conservationists were determined that government should have the power.

WHAT TIMBER FAMINE?

During the late nineteenth century, more and more trees were being cut down to accommodate the needs of a growing economy, and there were fears that America was running out of wood. Having cut down old-growth forests they owned in the East, timber companies bought and cleared forests in the Great Lakes region, then began working in the Pacific Northwest and the South.

Some observers warned darkly of a "timber famine." They weren't concerned about the aesthetic or spiritual values of a wilderness experience. Nor were they concerned about endangered habitat. They wanted to make sure there would be enough wood for homes, furniture, paper, and numerous other things.

Gifford Pinchot was among the doomsayers. Roosevelt hailed him as "the foremost leader in the great struggle to coordinate all our social and governmental forces in the effort to secure the adoption of a rational and farseeing policy for securing the conservation of all our national resources."[56] Not surprisingly, he bought Pinchot's gloomy view. "If the present rate of forest destruction is allowed to continue," Roosevelt told the American Forest Congress in January 1905, "a timber famine in the future is inevitable."[57]

Pinchot seems to have inherited his wealthy father's fear of a "timber famine." James Pinchot encouraged him to engage in socially worthwhile pursuits, among them forestry—the business of managing forests. So after graduating from Yale in 1889, Pinchot went to Europe, where the comparative scarcity of trees, after centuries of cutting, spurred a study of forest management. A German forester, Dietrich Brandis, became Pinchot's mentor, explaining how trees could be grown as a crop. Pinchot returned to the United States and accepted an offer to manage about 5,000 acres of forests at George W. Vanderbilt's Biltmore estate in Asheville, North Carolina. But he became convinced that expanding government control over forestland was the only solution to the coming timber famine.

Fear of a timber famine provided the rationale for what came to be known as the conservation movement. It didn't seem to matter that timber prices, like other commodity prices, had begun a long decline after the Civil War and continued declining amid the hysteria about a timber famine. The fear that America was running out of wood created urgency, brought people together with something like religious fervor, and focused their energies on new laws intended to conserve trees. Without the fear of a timber famine, there wouldn't have been a conservation movement as it developed.

In 1891, Congress passed "An Act to Repeal Timber Culture Laws and for Other Purposes," empowering the president to set aside government land as forest reserves. The idea was to save some forests for the future, because conservationists like Pinchot presumed that free markets were incapable of allocating commodities between present and future needs. President Benjamin Harrison established six forest reserves—some 3 million acres—but this meant only that the government retained title so that the land wouldn't be transferred to private owners.[58] The government did nothing to manage or protect the land.

As president from September 14, 1901, to March 4, 1909, Roosevelt reportedly set aside 141.2 million acres of national forests, 79.6 million acres of coal lands, and 213,886 acres of national parks.[59] The claim here, as with previous land retained by the federal government, was that bureaucrats and politicians were better than private property owners at predicting future needs and balancing present needs against future needs. Yet nobody ever presented any evidence of superior forecasting by bureaucrats and politicians.

There were scandals, of course. As historian Peffer explains, the government created forest reserves even in places where many acres of the land had already passed into private ownership. In 1897, Congress passed a law saying that when the government seized private land, the government would provide the owner with equivalent acreage somewhere else. But, Peffer pointed out, the law did not say that the government had to provide land of equivalent value.[60] Sure enough, some California and Oregon speculators bribed officials to gain title to worthless land, then lobbied General Land Office officials to have their land included in forest reserves so they could exchange the acreage for more valuable property.[61] The schemes, exposed in September 1902, made clear how government control of land bred corruption. This wasn't the kind of corruption Roosevelt liked to talk about in his business-bashing speeches.

"By the early 1900s," reported Gerald W. Williams, a U.S. Forest Service historian, "the nation was becoming aware of the massive land frauds in the West. Inspired by a series of exposés in the *Portland Oregonian* newspaper in 1901–04, federal prosecutors were urged to investigate and prosecute those indicted for fraud, especially related to the establishment of new forest reserves. The bulk of the prosecutions took place in Oregon. In 1905, U.S. Senator John Mitchell and a U.S. Representative, both from Oregon, were found guilty of fraud and taking bribes. Several county clerks, as well as a number of people who were willing co-conspirators, were convicted of land fraud. Another Oregonian, Binger Hermann, commissioner of the U.S. Department of the Interior General Land Office in Washington, D.C., came to trial for aiding the 'land fraud ring,' but he was never convicted. Several years later, Stephen A. Douglas Puter, as the self-described 'King of the Oregon land fraud ring,' published a book with the title *Looters of the Public Domain* (1907) . . . [written] in the Multnomah County jail in Portland, Oregon, where he was serving time for a land fraud conviction."[62]

Moreover, from the very beginning, national forestlands were extensively damaged by overgrazing. Homesteaders and ranches with property bordering public land treated the public land as common property, which meant it was in every herder's interest to consume as much grass as possible and to do nothing to maintain the value of the public grazing lands because somebody else would benefit. In 1905 the Public Lands Commission reported, "The general lack of control in the use of public grazing lands has resulted, naturally and inevitably, in overgrazing and the ruin of millions of acres of otherwise valuable grazing territory."[63]

Bills were introduced in Congress to limit grazing on national forestlands, but they reached a deadlock. Homesteaders protested that such bills would drive them out. Many ranchers denounced homesteaders as speculators. Small ranchers claimed that they would be devastated if they couldn't graze their herds on national forestlands. Congressmen from eastern states generally didn't care what happened out west.[64]

Although Roosevelt, Pinchot, and other progressives denounced large landowners, such landowners had strong incentives to maintain—conserve—the value of their private property. Among the most successful forestland speculators was Cornell University. Established as a land grant educational institution in 1865, it was entitled to a million acres of land. Cornell claimed a half-million acres of forests in Wisconsin. The land was well managed and gradually sold off at steadily rising prices. By the time the last of the properties was sold in 1925, net proceeds were around $5 million.[65]

Timber entrepreneurs like Frederick Weyerhaeuser also bought millions of acres of land. In 1900, for instance, Weyerhaeuser made one of the largest land purchases in U.S. history, buying some 900,000 acres of Washington State timberlands from James J. Hill, the railroad entrepreneur. The Northern Pacific Railroad had been awarded the acreage for its role in building the transcontinental railroad.[66]

Big timber companies were accused of wasteful forestry practices, although they had the resources to introduce technologies that helped conserve wood. Historians Ralph W. Hidy, Frank Ernest Hill, and Allan Nevins explained, for instance, how the "indiscriminating advance of innumerable oscillating saws in the gangs had worked against quality, and promoted waste." The companies wanted to be able to produce higher-grade lumber, especially without rot or other defects that made wood harder to sell. The introduction of the band saw, a more precise tool, allowed timber companies to "get the most high-grade lumber out of the log. In every respect the band [saw] conserved raw material."[67] By contrast, small owners lacked the resources to harvest timber efficiently. "When conservation became an issue," Hidy, Hill, and Nevins wrote, "they did not have the means or the inclination to adopt sound forestry practices."[68] One would never learn these things by reading Theodore Roosevelt's speeches.

Gifford Pinchot knew a lot about trees but apparently had a limited understanding of how markets worked. As economist Sherry Olson explained, foresters like Pinchot viewed "demand as a quantity consumed *regardless of price*."[69] Pinchot assumed that people would consume as much wood next year or in five years as they consumed last year, even if the price went up, because they needed wood. In fact, of course, higher prices provided incentives for consumers to consume less and to explore substitutes, while producers had incentives to produce more. Lower prices provided incentives for consumers to consume more and incentives for producers to produce less. Prices were powerful signals that affected human behavior.

In addition, Pinchot seemed unaware that markets were the most efficient discovery process, reflecting the knowledge not just of a few experts like himself but of all market participants, particularly those who stood to make money or lose money depending on how well they understood market trends. As economists Terry L. Anderson and Donald R. Leal explained, "Prudent investors would only forgo cutting if they expected [the] value [of forestland] as standing timber to increase faster than the return on alternative investments. Typically, forestland was inspected, appraised, purchased, and sold to lumber mills, activities that depended on current and future prices. The decision for an owner was whether and for how long to hold timber and at what rate to harvest it. If he expected to earn a higher rate of return by placing his assets in some alternative form of investment, then holding onto timber was a losing proposition. In this case, the economic decision would have been to sell the timber (presumably to be cut and processed) and put the proceeds into stocks, bonds, or other investments. A timber owner would have been foolish to sell trees that he expected to increase in value at a rate higher than the prevailing return on other investments."[70]

In 1908, in an effort to generate political support for the conservation movement, Roosevelt established the National Conservation Commission. He did this without congressional authorization.[71] The commission compiled a three-volume inventory of America's natural resources and estimated when they would be exhausted. Pinchot served the group dealing with forestry, which warned that annual timber cutting exceeded annual forest growth by 250 percent and that soon there would be no more trees—a timber famine.

Timber prices, however, were rising slowly along with inflation, suggesting that few people were worried about a timber famine. Pinchot complained, "We have got to make the public see that cheap timber is not good for forest conservation."[72] In March 1909, Pinchot urged the House Ways and Means Committee to promote higher timber prices by raising tariffs on imported lumber.[73]

By this time, there were some signs that a timber famine was never going to happen. During the railroad boom following the Civil War, railroads consumed between one-fifth and one-quarter of annual U.S. timber production.[74] But in the first decades of the twentieth century, the railroads were taking steps to reduce their wood consumption. Eastern railroads switched from wood-burning to coal-burning engines. As freight trains carried heavier loads, wooden trestles, bridges, and other structures were rebuilt with steel. For a while, railroads took federal foresters' advice to grow trees. They planted millions of trees and lost money. By 1905, railroad managers were coming to the conclusion that they could cut their crosstie replacement budgets by using wood preservation techniques—especially creosote—which would significantly extend the life of crossties and make possible the use of less expensive wood previously avoided because of its vulnerability to boring insects. Wood preservation techniques were to cut railroad crosstie replacement budgets by one-third.[75] Moreover, wood was used less and less as an industrial fuel, and the increased efficiency of farming enabled fewer farmers to produce more food.[76] The clearing of forests for agriculture would pretty much be over by 1920.[77]

The rationale of the conservation movement—the idea that politicians and bureaucrats needed more power to conserve disappearing resources because they were uniquely qualified to predict the future and balance future needs against current needs—was collapsing. As it happened, politicians and bureaucrats did a poor job anticipating the future, perhaps because they made political decisions rather than independent judgments based on market conditions.

In 1915, Ernest A. Sterling, a director of the American Forestry Association, observed: "The phantom of timber famine has never been very real, and its use as a bugaboo or club has been a boomerang."[78]

CONSERVATION PROMOTES MONOPOLY, CORRUPTION, AND WASTE

There was probably more hypocrisy in Theodore Roosevelt's conservation policies than in anything else he did. He denounced private monopolies while promoting a government dam-building monopoly and a government land monopoly involving millions of acres. He posed as a champion of honest government, yet he supported corrupt practices when California secretly schemed for water rights in Owens Valley. Roosevelt's restrictions on the distribution of public domain land invited corruption, and he knew it. Supposedly for "conservation," Roosevelt engaged in pork barrel politicking, urging that the taxpayers' hard-earned money be spent in a hopeless effort to stem the long-term decline of river-borne freight traffic. Roosevelt made a mockery of "conservation" by squandering resources on a vast scale. He transferred resources from the East and Midwest, where natural precipitation made possible efficient farming, to arid western regions where farming was impossible without dams, aqueducts, and other costly infrastructure for irrigation that required continuing subsidies. And eventually irrigation resulted in rising salinity in the soil, leading to the abandonment of farmland. Where is the enlightened thinking in any of this?

CHAPTER SEVEN

WHY DID ROOSEVELT PUSH TO IMPOSE AN INCOME TAX ON AMERICANS?

T HEODORE ROOSEVELT revived the idea of a federal income tax after it had been given up for dead. In December 1906, he declared that "there is every reason why, when next our system of taxation is revised, the National Government should impose a graduated inheritance tax, and, if possible, a graduated income tax."[1]

Progressive politicians who wanted big government at the expense of "the rich" began promoting an income tax amendment to the Constitution. Several years later, President Woodrow Wilson signed the income tax into law. Like so many laws, it took on a life of its own. It turned out to be a people's tax, inflicting a serious burden on tens of millions of ordinary people who certainly were not rich. And like so many of Theodore Roosevelt's pet causes, the income tax had pernicious effects that Roosevelt never considered, or at least never mentioned.

THE EARLY PUSH FOR AN INCOME TAX

Agitation for an income tax began during the late nineteenth century, when many entrepreneurs were becoming wealthy by providing necessities for millions of ordinary consumers—rather than luxuries for the rich—simply because ordinary folks were a bigger market. They voted with their dollars for their preferred brands of meat, soup, clothing, farm tools, transportation, and other goods and services. They were tough taskmasters because they switched from old providers to new providers that offered better quality at lower prices and greater convenience.

Many Americans, however, resented the very existence of great fortunes, apparently never stopping to think that they came to be in large part because entrepreneurs were providing newer, better, and cheaper goods and services that consumers desired. Lists of the wealthiest Americans were compiled, and claims were made about their share of the total wealth in the United States, as if anybody knew the total value of all the land, homes, factories, tools, and other assets in the country. Progressive social critics implied that it was unfair for some people to be rich while others were poor. The enormous size of some personal fortunes—such as that of John D. Rockefeller, who reportedly earned some $40 million a year—was itself considered immoral.

This debate was not about criminal behavior. There were plenty of laws dealing with force, the threat of force, or fraud. True enough, a few wealthy people did participate in nefarious schemes. But all were defamed, regardless of whether they were guilty. Later, in the early 1930s, they were as a group called "robber barons," and the name stuck.[2]

The income tax enacted during the Civil War to raise revenue was repealed in 1872, but Farmers in the West and South hoped to revive it so they could push the cost of government onto somebody else. Many of these farmers were having a hard time getting by because of intensifying competition as more and more people became farmers. Between 1850 and 1900, the number of farms nearly quadrupled, and farm acreage nearly tripled. In 1900, farmers accounted for over 40 percent of the U.S. population.[3] The federal government's homesteading policies had encouraged poor people to become farmers in regions with little rainfall, notably west of the hundredth meridian. With limited capital or expertise, most of these people were doomed to failure. Large numbers of homesteads were abandoned.[4]

It should be noted, however, that large numbers of farmers made good decisions about where to locate and what to grow. Improved farm tools, such as Cyrus McCormick's reaper for harvesting grain, made possible enormous gains in efficiency. The estimated value of farmland and buildings soared fivefold between 1850 and 1900.[5]

Frustrated farmers generated so much political pressure that in 1874 two income tax bills were introduced in Congress. For the next two decades, in almost every session of Congress, representatives from the West and South introduced an income tax bill. "Most of the agitation for this tax during this period was by those active in the 'share-the-wealth' and 'soak-the-rich' campaigns," reported historians Roy G. Blakey and Gladys C. Blakey.[6] Each income tax bill died in the House Ways and Means Committee.

Newspaper magnate Joseph Pulitzer, who loved to go on crusades for reform, embraced the income tax. In 1883, he urged: "Tax luxuries. Tax inheritances. Tax large incomes. Tax monopolies. Tax the privileged corporation."[7]

Columbia University economist Edwin Robert Anderson Seligman, another prominent income tax advocate, envisioned "a system of taxation which no one could escape."[8] He conceded that political support for an income tax was based on envy of businesspeople and others who anticipated market trends and prospered. Undoubtedly, too, government officials wanted an income tax because of its potential to generate more government revenue.

Seligman acknowledged that enforcing an income tax would be a problem. "It is notorious that the ascertainment of individual income is exceedingly difficult," he wrote. "If the attempt to reach the income of the individual rests upon the declaration of the taxpayer himself, we are putting upon him a strain which, in the present state of the relations of the individual to the government, may be characterized as exceedingly severe. . . . If the declaration of the individual is sought to be controlled by official action, officials inevitably find considerable difficulty in reaching a conclusion as to the exact amount of income." Seligman also anticipated how an income tax could subvert individual liberty: "If [tax officials] are lenient, the results are apt to be a farce; if they are stringent, the danger is that it will lead to a system of bureaucratic inquisition, which may end by becoming intolerable to the taxpayer."[9] To avoid such a problem, he recommended that taxes be withheld at the source,[10] but not out of benevolent concern for taxpayers. After all, the avowed aim of the system that he proposed was to extract as much revenue from them as possible.

An income tax inevitably meant being rough with people—snooping into their private business, inflicting fines and prison terms on those who objected. It is a supreme irony that the advocates of more government interference with private life styled themselves "progressives" and that an income tax with graduated (discriminatory) rates become known as "progressive."

Agitation for an income tax intensified during the administration of Republican president Benjamin Harrison, who signed the unpopular McKinley Tariff (1890) and went along with the "Billion Dollar Congress," which wiped out a big federal budget surplus by doling out money for Civil War veterans and business subsidies. Calls for an income tax grew even louder under Harrison's successor, Democrat Grover Cleveland, when the panic of 1893 caused bank failures, railroad bankruptcies, a business contraction, and plunging federal tariff revenues. An income tax looked like the only way to resolve a budget crisis. The philosophical issues of an income tax were widely debated at this time—not two decades later, when the Sixteenth Amendment ushered in a permanent income tax.

William Jennings Bryan first made his mark as a Nebraska congressman by denouncing tariffs, which, he declared in 1894, were "conceived in greed and fashioned in inequity." He charged that tariffs plundered customers and enriched politically connected businessmen without being an efficient source of federal revenue. As an alternative to tariffs, he advocated an income tax: "There is no more just tax than the income tax, nor can any tax be proposed which is more equable; and the principle is sustained by the most distinguished writers on political economy."[11] Displaying what biographer Paolo E. Coletta characterized as his tendency to "argue vehemently against whatever he thought wrong,"[12] Bryan claimed Adam Smith, the author of *Wealth of Nations* (1776) and a champion of laissez-faire, as a backer of the income tax. Bryan quoted Smith as saying, "The subjects of every State ought to contribute to the support of the Government, as nearly as possible, in proportion to their respective abilities."[13]

That gross misrepresentation of Smith's ideas reveals the desperation of those who promoted an income tax. In *Wealth of Nations*, Adam Smith provided an insightful commentary on the problems with various taxes: "Capitation taxes, if it is attempted to proportion them to the fortune or revenue of each contributor, become altogether arbitrary. The state of a man's fortune varies from day to day, and without an inquisition more intolerable than any tax, and renewed at least once every year, can only be guessed at. His assessment, therefore, must in most cases depend upon the good or bad humour of his assessors, and must, therefore, be altogether arbitrary and uncertain."[14] Smith also anticipated some of the reasons why the income tax is widely hated: "An inquisition into every man's private circumstances, and an inquisition which, in order to accommodate the tax to them, watched over all the fluctuations of his fortune, would be a source of such continual and endless vexation as no people could support."[15]

Among the best-known opponents of an income tax was Senator Nelson Aldrich, Rhode Island Republican. Aldrich warned that advocates of an income tax wanted a "redistribution of wealth."[16] An income tax was, as he maintained, a form of robbery. Unfortunately, Aldrich undermined the credibility of his position by promoting tariffs, which were another form of robbery.

A more persuasive opponent of an income tax was Yale University sociology professor William Graham Sumner, who had long denounced tariffs as robbery. "In the recent debates on the income tax," he wrote in 1894, "the assumption that great accumulations of wealth are socially harmful and ought to be broken down by taxation was treated as an axiom."[17] Earlier, in 1883, he had denied "the notion that 'the State' owes anything to anybody except peace, order, and the guarantees of rights." He also had pointed out how power corrupts: "It is the extreme of political error to say that if political power is only taken away from generals, nobles, priests, millionaires, and scholars, and given to artisans and peasants, these latter may be trusted to do only right and justice, and never to abuse the power. . . . They will commit abuse, if they can and dare, just as others have done. The reason for the excesses of the old governing classes lies in the vices and passions of human nature—cupidity, lust, vindictiveness, ambition, and vanity. These vices are confined to no nation, class, or age. . . . What history shows is, that rights are safe only when guaranteed against all arbitrary power."[18]

In January 1894, West Virginia Democrat Benton McMillin, chairman of the House Ways and Means Committee, introduced an income tax bill. It proposed taxing annual income above $4,000. Treasury Department officials estimated that average income was about $1,000 and that 85,000 Americans would be taxpayers—that is, one-tenth of 1 percent of the 65 million people in the United States.[19] Congressmen were paid $5,000, which meant they could not be accused of escaping taxes they imposed on others, although they would be taxed at the lowest rate.[20] The income tax bill was added to the Revenue Act of 1894, which was mainly about tariffs because tariffs provided the lion's share of federal revenue. Many congressmen were likely to go along because they wanted the other provisions in the legislation.[21]

In an effort to win votes for the income tax, politicians made fantastic claims. Congressman David A. De Armond of Missouri topped even the rhetorical excesses of William Jennings Bryan, proclaiming: "The passage of the bill will mark the dawn of a brighter day, with more of sunshine, more of songs of birds, more of the sweetest music, the laughter of children well fed, well clothed, well housed. Can we doubt that in the brighter, happier days to come, good, even-handed, wholesome Democracy shall be triumphant?"[22]

After the House passed the income tax bill by a large majority, William Jennings Bryan and Congressman Henry St. George Tucker of Virginia carried Ways and Means chairman McMillin out of the House chamber on their shoulders as members cheered. The *New York Tribune* exulted that the House had "hatched a Populist chicken."[23]

The Senate subsequently passed the income tax bill by a big enough margin to overcome a veto by President Grover Cleveland. The income tax became law on August 20, 1894, without the president's signature.

The tax was quickly challenged. On behalf of Charles Pollock, a Massachusetts businessman who owned shares in Farmers Loan & Trust Company, New York lawyer William D. Guthrie filed a lawsuit seeking an injunction to prevent the bank from paying what he claimed was an unconstitutional tax.[24] Guthrie filed a similar lawsuit on behalf of Lewis H. Hyde, who owned shares in Continental Trust Company. Guthrie assailed the income tax as discriminatory, citing Article I, Section 8, of the Constitution (taxes "shall be uniform throughout the United States"). He declared that "Congress cannot sacrifice one—the lowliest or the richest—for the benefit of others."[25]

Guthrie retained fellow New York attorney Joseph H. Choate (Harvard College 1852, Harvard Law School 1854) as senior counsel. Guthrie and Choate believed that America's Founders had aimed to prevent any individual or faction from amassing the kind of tyrannical power that had plagued people for centuries. They noted that the Constitution limited the central government to powers that were specifically delegated, and that powers not delegated to the central government were reserved for the states or the people. The Constitution further limited the government with an ingenious system of checks and balances that made it difficult for one faction to control everything.

More specific to the income tax question, the Constitution placed limitations on taxes. Beyond what Guthrie originally cited—Article I, Section 8 ("all duties, imposts and excises shall be uniform throughout the United States")—the Constitution dealt with taxes in two other clauses. Article I, Section 2, declared: "Representatives and direct taxes shall be apportioned among the several States which may be included within this Union, according to their respective Numbers." Article I, Section 9, stated: "No capitation, or other direct, tax shall be laid, unless in proportion to the census or enumeration herein before directed to be taken."

In advising government lawyers on how to defend the income tax, Edwin Seligman claimed that because the clauses pertaining to direct taxes had taken shape in the context of debates about slavery, they were never intended by the drafters of the Constitution to limit the government's taxing power.[26]

Choate countered that America's Founders, having dealt with tyrannical kings and tyrannical majorities, were definitely concerned that some people might try to exploit others. He pointed out that the Civil War income tax generated 80 percent of its revenue from four states—Massachusetts, New Jersey, New York, and Pennsylvania—that had only 20 percent of the representation in the House. Thus, he insisted, the Civil War income tax was a direct tax not in proportion to population and therefore contrary to the Constitution.

The Pollock and Hyde cases were consolidated as *Pollock v. Farmers' Loan & Trust Co.*, and Choate took his arguments to the U.S. Supreme Court. He thundered against the thievery that resulted when some people enacted taxes to be paid by other people: "If it goes out as the edict of this judicial tribunal [the Supreme Court] that a combination of States, however numerous, can unite against the safeguards provided by the Constitution in imposing a tax which is to be paid by the people in four States or in three States or in two States, but of which the combination is to pay almost no part, while in the spending of it they are to have the whole control, it will be impossible to take any backward step. You cannot hereafter exercise any check if you say now that Congress is untrammeled and uncontrollable."[27] Choate also warned that an income tax would open the door to attacks on private property and to increases in federal spending. He declared, "I do not believe that any member of the Court ever has sat or ever will sit to hear and decide a case the consequences of which will be so far-reaching as this."[28]

In a moment of candor, Seligman remarked that "it is undoubtedly a fact that the enthusiasm for the tax came chiefly from those who were thus assured freedom from its burdens."[29] U.S. Attorney General Richard Olney, who took the lead defending the income tax, acknowledged that "an income tax is preeminently a tax upon the rich."[30]

One of the Supreme Court justices could not participate in the proceedings, and on April 8, 1895, the litigants learned that the eight remaining justices were evenly split. Four of them agreed that a tax on land was a direct tax, but they did not agree about whether it invalidated the entire law. Because of that and other unresolved issues, the tie vote settled nothing. There was another hearing, with all nine justices. The result was a 5–4 decision against the income tax, issued on May 20. Chief Justice Melville Weston Fuller wrote the majority opinion. Just four months earlier, he had written the majority opinion limiting the application of the Sherman Anti-Trust Act, but *Pollock v. Farmers Loan & Trust Co.* was probably the most important case he handled as chief justice.

First Fuller had to acknowledge that in 1880, in *Springer v. United States*, the Supreme Court had upheld the Civil War income tax by ruling that it was an excise and not a direct tax.[31] That case involved an Illinois lawyer, William M. Springer, who had refused to pay his 1865 income tax. The government proceeded to collect the tax by seizing and selling Springer's homestead.[32] Fuller wrote that in the *Springer* case, the government was trying to collect a tax on a man's income from professional services and from U.S. bonds. In contrast, he maintained, the 1894 income tax applied to all income, including income from real estate, and a real estate tax was clearly a direct tax. Fuller thus denied that the *Springer* decision was a precedent that could support the 1894 income tax.[33]

Writing for the majority, Chief Justice Fuller vigorously attacked the income tax law: "First, we adhere to the opinion already announced [in the first decision], that, taxes on real estate being indisputably direct taxes, taxes on the rents or income of real estate are equally direct taxes. Second. We are of opinion that taxes on personal property, or on the income of personal property, are likewise direct taxes. Third. The tax imposed by sections 27 to 37, inclusive, of the act of 1894, so far as it falls on the income of real estate, and of personal property, being a direct tax, within the meaning of the constitution, and therefore unconstitutional and void, because not apportioned according to representation, all those sections, constituting one entire scheme of taxation, are necessarily invalid."

Promoters of the income tax must have found this decision deeply troubling. It was written not by a rich man but by a man from Maine who practiced law for many years before earning more than $2,000. Republicans generally supported high tariffs and opposed the income tax, but Fuller was a Democrat, and Democrats were supposed to support the income tax. Promoters of the income tax could not easily smear Fuller as a lapdog of the rich.

Supporters of the income tax nevertheless denounced the Supreme Court's decision. Appealing to envy and resentment, the *New York Journal* published a list of rich people who would save money without an income tax.[34]

In spirited dissents, three different justices argued in defense of the income tax, using the overheated rhetoric that Theodore Roosevelt and other progressives would later use to push for an income tax. Justice Henry Billings Brown denied that the Constitution imposed limitations on the federal government's taxing power and complained that the government might face an emergency and need revenue from an income tax—even though there was no emergency when the Revenue Act of 1894 became law. "My fear," he wrote, "is that in some moment of national peril this decision will rise up to frustrate its will and paralyze its arm. . . . I cannot escape the conviction that the decision of the court in this great case is fraught with immeasurable danger to the future of the country, and that it approaches the proportions of a national calamity."[35] He did not indicate what kind of "national calamity" he was referring to.

Justice John Marshall Harlan similarly warned that the decision to strike down the income tax "cannot be regarded otherwise than as a disaster to the country."[36] He expressed the desperation of politicians who wanted to get their hands on more money, even when there was no urgent need to spend it. He was furious that, as a result of the Supreme Court's ruling, "Congress cannot subject to taxation—however great the needs or pressing the necessities of the government—either the invested personal property of the country, bonds, stocks, and investments of all kinds, or the income arising from the renting of real estate or from the yield of personal property."[37] What Congress might do with more money, Harlan didn't say.

Justice Edward Douglass White said that by striking down the income tax, the Court was acknowledging that large sums had been wrongfully collected from the American people by previous income taxes, and he worried that there could be huge claims for refunds. "This consequence shows how necessary it is that the court should not overthrow its past decisions," White wrote.[38] He seemed to be saying that when the government is wrong, it must never admit it.

THEODORE ROOSEVELT REVIVES
THE INCOME TAX

Chief Justice Fuller would be the last Supreme Court justice to strike down a federal income tax in the United States. But at least for a time his ruling seemed decisive. Fuller's decision was viewed as such an effective blow that for a number of years progressives gave up on the idea of an income tax. Even William Jennings Bryan stopped talking about it.

Then Theodore Roosevelt's favorite war escalated the government's demand for cash. Washington politicians did not immediately embrace the idea of an income tax. Rather, they began to look longingly at an inheritance tax. Many people, such as the economist Richard T. Ely, had been promoting socialism and an inheritance tax.[39] Seligman, having failed in his effort to save the 1894 income tax, urged a graduated inheritance tax. The idea had been popularized by Edward Bellamy's novel *Looking Backward* (1888), about a Boston man who falls into a hypnotic sleep for more than a hundred years and wakes up to find himself in a socialist paradise. The book featured an inheritance tax that seized everything beyond what the government considered "an ample income." *Looking Backward* reportedly sold more than a million copies.[40]

An inheritance tax was part of the 1898 revenue act financing the Spanish-American War. It was upheld by the Supreme Court in *Knowlton v. Moore*. Justice Edward Douglass White wrote the majority decision. White, who had previously supported an income tax, wrote that an inheritance tax was an excise tax on the transmission of an estate and was therefore subject to the requirement in Article I, Section 8, of the Constitution that excises be "uniform throughout the United States." The likelihood was great that inheritance tax revenue, like income tax revenue, would be paid primarily by people in a few states, but White ruled that the tax would pass constitutional muster as long as it was administered uniformly. Even so, by 1902, with the Spanish-American War long over, all war taxes had been repealed, including the inheritance tax.

Several years later, President Theodore Roosevelt suddenly reinvigorated the tax debate. In April 1906, in a speech at the laying of the cornerstone of the House Office Building, Roosevelt seemingly out of the blue urged "the adoption of some such scheme as that of a progressive tax on all fortunes beyond a certain amount either given in life or devised or bequeathed upon death to any individual—a tax so framed as to put it out of the power of the owner of one of these enormous fortunes to hand on more than a certain amount to any one individual; the tax, of course, to be imposed by the National and not the State government."[41] Democrats were thrilled. Many Republicans were horrified. The *Philadelphia Record* editorialized that Roosevelt provided "more encouragement to state socialism and centralization of government than all the frothy demagogues have accomplished in a quarter-century."[42]

On December 3, 1906, in his State of the Union address, Roosevelt plugged "a graduated inheritance tax by which a steadily increasing rate of duty should be put upon all moneys or other valuables." He went on to say that an income tax "is most certainly desirable." He acknowledged that the Supreme Court's *Pollock* decision was an obstacle and that the most likely solution was an income tax amendment to the Constitution. "The difficulty of amending the Constitution is so great," he said. "Every effort should be made in dealing with this subject."[43] In June 1907, he remarked that "most great civilized countries have an income tax and an inheritance tax."[44]

Roosevelt's words seemed to energize Democrats such as Congressman Cordell Hull of Tennessee, who promoted an income tax as an alternative to tariff revenue.[45] Hull later acknowledged in his memoirs that he was motivated by envy: "I was keenly impressed with the income-tax doctrine in the light of our lopsided tax condition in 1907, in which wealth was shirking its share of the tax burdens. Revenue for the expenses of the national Government was then obtained largely from customs duties on imports and excise taxes on such items as whisky and tobacco. Obviously this system was unfair to the poorer classes because they, with their small incomes, were paying the same taxes on such products as the rich, with their large incomes."[46]

Why should some people pay more for government services than others? That would amount to discriminatory pricing, for which progressive politicians had denounced the railroads. If it was wrong for a private company to practice discriminatory pricing, then it was wrong for the government to practice discriminatory pricing. In fact, there was a reasonable case for railroad rebates, for they occurred as a consequence of excess railroad capacity and competition for rail traffic. There always tended to be discounting when supply exceeded demand. Moreover, some shippers got rebates because they provided railcars that were less costly to load and unload. But there was no moral case for overcharging certain classes of taxpayers. That amounted to charging some people for government services used by other people. Although people with big houses and big companies might use more local services, those people paid more local property taxes, too. Rich people did not use more federal services—such as national defense—than poor people. "Graduated" taxation was a polite way of referring to discriminatory taxation by the biggest bully on the block.

Hull believed it was unfair to finance federal expenditures with consumption taxes such as tariffs and excise taxes, because poor people spent a higher percentage of their incomes on consumption items than rich people did. Neither Hull nor any of his progressive colleagues seemed to consider how poor people would suffer if graduated rates taxed away investment capital, making it harder to create jobs. And so on December 19, 1907, Hull introduced an income tax bill.[47] He talked to as many of his colleagues as possible but could not line up much political support.

THE REPUBLICAN ANTI–INCOME TAX STRATEGY BACKFIRES

As the 1908 election approached, Theodore Roosevelt prepared to leave office, but his campaign for an income tax was only beginning. That year, the Democratic Party adopted a platform with this plank: "We favor an income tax as part of our revenue system, and we urge the submission of a constitutional amendment specifically authorizing Congress to levy and collect a tax upon individual and corporate incomes, to the end that wealth may bear its proportional share of the burdens of the federal government."[48]

The Republican Party platform said nothing about an income tax, despite Roosevelt's enthusiasm for it. The Republican nominee that year, William Howard Taft—Roosevelt's vice president—did say: "In my judgment, an amendment to the Constitution for an income tax is not necessary. I believe that an income tax, when the protective system of customs and the internal revenue tax shall not furnish income enough for government needs, can and should be devised which, under the decisions of the Supreme Court, will conform to the Constitution."[49] Taft, who won the election, made no mention of an income tax in his March 3, 1909, inaugural address. He did say, "I recommend a graduated inheritance tax as correct in principle and as certain and easy of collection."

Soon, however, Taft faced a fiscal crunch because of the depression that followed the panic of 1907. Federal revenues fell from $665.8 million in 1907 to $601.8 million in 1908 and recovered only a little in 1909, to $604.3 million. Federal spending jumped from $579.1 million in 1907 to $659.1 million in 1908 and $693.7 million in 1909. Taft faced the biggest federal budget deficits since the Civil War.[50]

Congressman Sereno Payne of New York, chairman of the House Ways and Means Committee, proposed a bill to raise tariffs on imported food and clothing. Even Taft was wary of that, but it was not clear what other revenue sources there might be. Nobody seemed to seriously consider the possibility that the government might cut spending enough to live within its means. There was talk about a 2 percent tax on corporate dividends, which Taft had reportedly suggested. The Ways and Means Committee declined to pursue that idea and instead included an inheritance tax with the tariffs.

Then, in March 1909, Democratic congressman Ollie M. James

of Kentucky, with support from progressive Republicans, introduced a resolution asking President Taft to advise Congress about "the need for an income tax."[51] Congressman Frederick Clement Stevens, Minnesota Republican, subsequently introduced an income tax bill, the purpose of which was—in true progressive fashion—to make possible more government spending. He favored "internal improvements," a category that typically included enormous boondoggles.

Cordell Hull reintroduced his income tax bill, saying that some people ("the rich") should not "shirk" from paying more for government service than others.[52] He denounced tariffs for "exempting the Carnegies, the Vanderbilts, the Morgans, and the Rockefellers, with their aggregated billions of hoarded wealth."[53] Thus did Hull corrupt a proper attack on tariffs with envious sniping at entrepreneurs who had done much to increase output, create millions of jobs, and lower prices for millions of American consumers.

In the Senate, Republicans and Democrats joined the income tax crusade that Theodore Roosevelt had started. Senator Joseph W. Bailey, Texas Democrat, introduced an income tax bill of his own, stressing the alleged justice of the tax and the government's appetite for more money.[54] Senator Albert B. Cummins, Iowa Republican, introduced a bill for graduated taxation of individual incomes. His fellow Republican William E. Borah of Idaho expressed his support for an income tax.

Other Republicans stepped up to oppose the income tax. Senator Nelson Aldrich, who had led the opposition to the 1894 law, again emerged as the most outspoken opponent of an income tax. His points were well taken, but he continued to defend tariffs that involved as much robbery as an income tax. Apparently one reason why Aldrich opposed an income tax was that by generating government revenue, it would reduce the need for tariff revenue and thus increase political pressure for lower tariffs. On April 20, 1909, a *New York Times* editorial observed, "Anyone can see that if an income tax is imposed and death duties collected, the tariff would have to come down. It is not the present intention of the Republican party to lower the tariff."[55]

Senator George Sutherland, Utah Republican, also expressed opposition. He attacked the income tax bills for creating multiple levels of taxation, and he affirmed the view that they were unconstitutional. (Sutherland was later appointed to the Supreme Court, where he courageously helped strike down some of the excesses of Franklin D. Roosevelt's New Deal.)

Rather than pushing for an income tax, President Taft in his June 16, 1909, message to Congress said that corporations should pay an excise tax for "the privilege of doing business as an artificial entity."[56] He had Attorney General George W. Wickersham draft a bill for a 2 percent tax on corporate earnings above some amount such as $100,000.[57] Taft claimed that the tax would reduce alleged corporate abuses, apparently because all the information in corporate tax returns would be open for public inspection (no pretense of confidentiality).[58] Of course, Taft had more than a passing interest in the estimated $25 million of revenue that the federal government would collect from the proposed corporate tax. Business executives were opposed because it would mean upward pressure on consumer prices, which could affect their competitive position, and they did not like the idea of federal officials snooping through their financial records.

Senator Aldrich was willing to accept a corporate income tax because such a bill would divert attention away from an income tax on individuals.[59] Supporters of an income tax decided to take what they could get, and they lined up to support Taft's corporate income tax.

When the politicians started to draft a bill for Taft's corporate excise tax, however, they realized it would cause problems. The higher the tax was, the greater would be the incentive for corporations to generate capital by issuing bonds (debt), rather than by offering stock (equity), which would increase their taxable earnings. There was a debate about whether to prevent corporations from deducting the interest paid to bondholders. The politicians were playing with fire and could easily have disrupted companies that had created millions of jobs. They retreated a bit, granting exemptions to a wide range of businesses, reducing the likely harm but increasing the complexity of the tax code. Republicans did not want to raise so much money that the case for maintaining high tariffs would be undermined.[60]

Still, Senator Aldrich was intent on preventing an income tax from becoming law. So on June 29, 1909, when Senator Joseph Bailey of Texas was away from the Senate, Aldrich announced consideration of Bailey's income tax amendment to the tariff bill. He proposed substituting the corporate excise tax amendment. He vowed, "I shall vote for a corporate tax as a means to defeat the income tax."[61]

Senator Albert Cummins of Iowa argued that a personal income tax would be better than the proposed corporate income tax, because a personal income tax would penalize the rich and generate a lot of money for the government. Cummins urged that an income tax be adopted in addition to, not as a substitution for, tariffs.

The Senate passed the Aldrich tariff bill, 45–34, with the corporate excise tax amendment. Ultimately both the House and the Senate approved compromise legislation developed in a special conference attended by representatives from each house of Congress. This version kept the corporate income tax—which required every corporation doing business in the United States to pay 1 percent of its net income above $5,000 derived from all sources, except for dividends from corporations paying the tax—and supposedly reduced average tariff rates (though Democrats who analyzed the morass of tariff schedules concluded that average rates actually rose almost 2 percent).

Although progressives considered themselves champions of democracy and had been urging that U.S. senators be elected by the people rather than by state legislatures, they went to great pains to minimize public discussion of the new taxes they were pushing through Congress. As Roy G. Blakey and Gladys C. Blakey point out, the bill originated not in the House of Representatives but in the Senate, even though Article I, Section 7, of the Constitution specifies that "All bills for raising revenue shall originate in the House of Representatives." Also, because the final bill was developed in conference, the full House had only a short time to review it, and in any case, the bill made it through with support from Republicans largely because President Taft had pushed the measure.[62]

Moreover, just a few years after passing the Pure Food and Drugs Act to outlaw mislabeling of commercial products, Congress itself mislabeled this corporate "excise" tax amendment. The tax was not an excise tax imposed on products where they were manufactured. It was a tax on corporate incomes—an income tax. If the amendment had been truthfully labeled, it might have been more vulnerable to being struck down by the U.S. Supreme Court. So much for progressives' claims that politicians were morally superior to private individuals and should have more power to enforce truth and justice.

The new corporate "excise" tax survived a challenge in the Supreme Court. Chief Justice Melville W. Fuller, who had written the opinion striking down the 1894 income tax law, had suffered a fatal heart attack on July 4, 1910, and there had been other changes to the Court as well. A new justice, William R. Day, appointed by Theodore Roosevelt on January 29, 1903, delivered the majority opinion in *Flint v. Stone Tracy Co.* (1911), upholding the corporate "excise" tax.[63] Although the tax was levied directly on corporations, it was not, Day asserted, a direct tax and therefore was not at odds with the Constitution. Day accepted Taft's claim that the tax was for the privilege of doing business as a corporation.

Small businesses protested against having their tax returns made public. To those complaints, Taft responded, "To me the publicity feature of the law is the only thing which makes the law of any special value." Why? Because, the president remarked, the new tax "is not going to be a great revenue producer."[64]

ROOSEVELT'S SUCCESSOR LAUNCHES
THE CAMPAIGN FOR A FEDERAL
INCOME TAX AMENDMENT

If Senator Aldrich had hoped that a corporate income tax would fend off a personal income tax, he was disappointed. President Taft's June 16, 1909, message to Congress had supported not only a corporate excise tax but also a constitutional amendment permitting an income tax.[65]

Like sharks smelling blood, numerous congressmen rose to propose income tax amendments. They were not clear about what the government would do with all the money, but they wanted it. Aldrich worried about rushing through a new tax that could generate large amounts of money that the government did not need, but he (like many others at the time) reasoned that a constitutional amendment for an income tax would never be ratified by three-quarters of the states, as the Constitution required.

In July 1909, the Senate and House overwhelmingly approved an income tax amendment, which read: "The Congress shall have the power to lay and collect taxes on incomes from whatever source derived, without apportionment among the several States, and without regard to any census or enumeration."[66]

In arguing for ratification of the amendment, Cordell Hull used the same sort of national security appeal that Theodore Roosevelt used to justify all sorts of extensions of federal power. In a January 1910 speech before Congress, Hull declared, "The wonderful flexibility and certain productiveness of this tax enables it to meet every requirement of peace or war emergencies. . . . During the great strain of national emergencies an income tax is absolutely without a rival as a relief measure. Many governments in time of war have invoked its prompt and certain aid. It enabled England to conquer Napoleon. It came to the relief of our depleted Treasury during the Civil War, when the customs revenues were at a low ebb, and saved the rapidly sinking credit of the nation. We cannot expect always to be at peace. If this nation were tomorrow plunged into a war with a great commercial country from which we now received a large portion of our imports, our customs revenues would inevitably decline and we would be helpless to prosecute that war or any other war of great magnitude without taxing the wealth of the country in the form of incomes."[67]

Roosevelt, who longed to be back in the political arena, began speaking out on the income tax amendment. On August 31, 1910, he delivered a speech at Osawatomie, Kansas, spelling out a more radical creed than he had embraced before. He declared, "I am for men, not for property." He made a spurious distinction between "human rights and property rights"—property rights are human rights in property, starting with property in one's own body. Other property rights include the right to keep one's earnings and to be secure in one's home as well as in other assets acquired through honest labor and trade. The purpose of Roosevelt's devious language was to make his attacks on private property more politically acceptable.

Roosevelt introduced his slogan "the New Nationalism," by which he meant "executive power as the steward of the public welfare." He called for "far more active government interference with the social and economic conditions of this country . . . an increase in government control is now necessary." Then Roosevelt said, "I believe in a graduated income tax on big fortunes, and in another tax which is far more easily collected and far more effective—a graduated inheritance tax on big fortunes."

MAKING SOMEBODY ELSE PAY

Alabama was the first state to ratify the income tax amendment, in 1909. By February 1913, the Sixteenth Amendment was part of the Constitution. Only Connecticut and Florida rejected it.[68] Nelson Aldrich and many others had been wrong about ratification.

The process of debating and drafting actual income tax laws quickly revealed the emptiness of the lofty rhetoric Theodore Roosevelt and other progressives had used to impose an income tax on Americans. Cordell Hull, who had proposed so many income tax bills over the years, did most of the initial drafting. So began decades of wasteful wrangling for advantages as lobbyists promoted one bureaucratic definition of "taxable income" over another, argued for exempting some businesses from particularly onerous terms, demanded seemingly technical changes to push liabilities onto somebody else, and on and on. Politicians on the tax-writing congressional committees soon began accepting campaign contributions from interest groups whose lobbyists hoped to negotiate better breaks in the next tax bill. Most outrageous, federal, state, and local officials were exempted from having to pay an income tax.[69] Why this corrupt logrolling, arm-twisting, and political deal-making, set in motion by the progressive income tax, was considered reform beggars the imagination.

The following exchange in the Senate suggests the quagmire that the reformers got themselves into:

MR. CUMMINS: If I understand this aright, if I had a farm and sell it for a thousand dollars, the money I would receive as the purchase price of the farm would be accounted as income; but if anyone were to give me a thousand dollars during the year, or if I were to receive it by bequest . . . that would not be accounted as income. . . . If the one is income, why is not the other?

MR. SHIVELY: Mr. President, if I understand the Senator correctly, he is inquiring, for the purpose of illustrating what he has in mind, whether the price of a piece of land sold during the year would be regarded as income. My answer is that it would not be. The price of that land would be principal . . .

MR. CUMMINS: But suppose 10 years ago I had bought a horse for $900, and this year I had sold him for $1,000, what would I do in the way of making a return?

MR. WILLIAMS: That thousand dollars is a part of the Senator's receipts for this year, and being part of his receipts, that much will go in as part of his receipts, and from it would be deducted his disbursements and his exemptions and various other things.

MR. CUMMINS: Would the price I paid for the horse originally be deducted?

MR. WILLIAMS: No, because it was not part of the transactions in that year; but if the Senator turned around and bought another horse, that year, it would be deducted.

MR. BRISTOW: As I understand the question of the Senator from Iowa, it was, if he bought a horse 10 years ago for $100.

MR. CUMMINS: Nine hundred dollars.

MR. BRISTOW: And sold it this year for a thousand dollars, whether or not that thousand dollars would be counted as part of his income for this year, regardless of what he paid for the horse 10 years ago. Is that correct?

MR. WILLIAMS: No, I did not say that. It would be part of his gross receipts for the year, of course, but it may not necessarily be part of his net proceeds, and therefore not a part of his income that is taxable.

MR. CUMMINS: But I asked the Senator from Mississippi specifically whether, in the case I put, the price that was originally paid for the horse could be deducted from the price received.

MR. WILLIAMS: The price paid 10 years ago? No, of course not.[70]

The Senate debate focused on exemptions and graduated tax rates. Initially, the income tax rates seemed small enough—1 percent on incomes from $3,000 to $50,000 (incomes below $3,000 annually were exempt); 2 percent on incomes from $50,000 to $75,000; 3 percent on incomes from $75,000 to $100,000; 4 percent on incomes from $100,000 to $250,000; 5 percent on incomes from $250,000 to $500,000; and 6 percent on incomes above $500,000.[71]

But the problem was the very principle of graduated tax rates. If private businesses charged consumers of bread, clothing, cars, and other things according to their income, they surely would have been prosecuted for immoral price gouging, price discrimination, or monopolistic pricing. When the government did the same thing, it was called social justice.

Without the accountability of a roll call, the House approved the income tax bill on May 8, 1913. Although progressives fancied themselves to be democratic reformers, they prevented senators from voting on the income tax law by itself. Senators were presented with a tariff bill including an income tax. They could take or leave the whole thing.[72] Presumably the reason for this approach was to make opposition more difficult. A large number of senators wanted to vote for tariffs favored by their campaign contributors, and the only way they could do so was to swallow an income tax. President Woodrow Wilson signed the bill on October 3, and Americans have been burdened with an income tax ever since.

The constitutionality of the 1913 income tax was challenged when a stockholder of Union Pacific Railroad filed a lawsuit in an effort to prevent the company from paying income taxes. Writing for the majority, Chief Justice Edward Douglass White, who had been elevated to that post following the death of Melville Fuller, upheld the tax in a decision issued on January 24, 1916.[73]

If peace had prevailed, federal income tax rates might have remained low for a long time. But there was a war in Europe. Theodore Roosevelt, who was eager for America to plunge into it, hectored President Wilson about the need to increase military expenditures in the name of preparedness.

In 1916, President Wilson and his treasury secretary, William G. McAdoo, made what historian W. Elliott Brownlee called "the single most important financial decision of the war." As Brownlee explained, "They chose to cooperate with a group of insurgent Democrats in arranging wartime financing on the basis of highly progressive taxation. Led by Congressman Claude Kitchin of

North Carolina, who chaired the House Ways and Means Committee, the insurgent Democrats attacked concentrations of wealth, special privilege, and public corruption."[74] Despite their moralistic rhetoric about soaking the rich, they were looking for money to pursue their war.

Wilson's regime introduced the doctrine of "excess" profits, which simply meant big profits, without taking into account big risks. "Alone among all the World War I belligerents," Brownlee pointed out, "the United States placed excess-profits taxation—a graduated tax on all business profits above a 'normal' rate of return—at the center of wartime finance. Excess-profits taxation turned out to be responsible for most of the tax revenues raised by the federal government during the war. Taxes accounted for a larger share of total revenues in the United States than in any of the other belligerent nations."[75]

Businessmen vehemently opposed "excess" profits taxes, but they had lost the debate years earlier when they failed to present a persuasive case against income taxation. They had sought pragmatic solutions, while progressives prevailed with their moralistic case for making somebody else pay. Thus are we left dealing with the consequences of yet another of Theodore Roosevelt's "reforms."

WHAT WAS THEODORE ROOSEVELT'S REAL LEGACY?

W ITH HIS BIG TOOTHY SMILE, twinkling eyes, and colossal energy, Theodore Roosevelt remains an unforgettable personality. His vision of a strong executive branch inspired later presidents—with unfortunate consequences for the American people.

Democrat Woodrow Wilson, who introduced major restrictions on the private sector and pursued a catastrophic war policy, seems not to have had many kind words for his Republican rival, although biographer August Heckscher reported that Wilson "was an admirer of [Roosevelt's] combative, newsmaking style of action."[1]

Roosevelt influenced Franklin Delano Roosevelt, who probably had a greater impact on twentieth-century American history than any other president. According to biographer Frank Freidel, FDR first "fell under the spell of his remote cousin" while in prep school, and Theodore Roosevelt was for him an even "greater ideological influence than Harvard." It is no coincidence that when FDR became president, he ushered in the modern era of big government. As Freidel noted, FDR found appealing Theodore Roosevelt's belief "in using to the utmost the constitutional power of the president." To cope with the Great Depression, he immediately launched the New Deal, accurately described by Freidel as "a program emphasizing national planning in the tradition of Theodore Roosevelt." Freidel noted that "in words reminiscent of Theodore Roosevelt, FDR declared 'the duty rests upon the Government to restrict [high] incomes by very high taxes.'"[2]

Lyndon Baines Johnson, who simultaneously launched huge domestic entitlement programs and escalated the undeclared Vietnam

War, also looked to Theodore Roosevelt as a model of an active president. Johnson admired "the hyperactive White House of Theodore Roosevelt," according to historian Eric F. Goldman.[3] Johnson reportedly remarked, "Whenever I pictured Teddy Roosevelt, I saw him running or riding, always moving, his fists clenched, his eyes glaring, speaking out."[4]

Richard M. Nixon, who dramatically expanded federal regulation of the economy, liked Theodore Roosevelt "because of his great dynamic drive and ability to mobilize a young country."[5]

Why do so many people view Theodore Roosevelt as an American hero? Surely his dynamic personality plays a role, but there is a more substantive reason for his lasting influence. Roosevelt successfully promoted the interests of politicians and bureaucrats, which led to a vast expansion of federal power, particularly presidential power. The consequences, as they played out over the decades, have been disastrous for ordinary people. The principal consequences include:

1. The United States has entered other people's wars and tried to build other people's nations, and tragically hundreds of thousands of American soldiers have died without enhancing U.S. national security.

America's Founders lived during an era of constant warfare. They well understood how destructive wars were, how they burdened people with heavy taxes, how they promoted the concentration of government power and the suppression of civil liberties. Conscription, confiscation, and censorship were consequences of war. America's Founders had no illusions about the glory of warfare. In an effort to reduce the likelihood that a president would drag the country into war, the Constitution requires a congressional declaration of war. This process is supposed to create opportunities for discussion, debate, and rational thinking.

America's Founders realized, too, how extraordinarily difficult it would be to develop a free society. It required people who were determined to live independent lives, who respected the equal rights of others, and who embraced a rule of law. Certainly one nation could not establish a free society elsewhere by sending in soldiers and money. If people were to be free, they had to make their own choices.

Theodore Roosevelt believed war was glorious, even healthy for a nation. He thought that reasons for participating in a war should not be limited to national defense. He insisted that the United States should intervene in the affairs of other nations and enter other people's wars to do good.

He has become famous for his exaggerated role in a war that never should have happened. In 1976, decades after the Spanish-American War, Admiral Hyman Rickover headed an investigation of the sinking of the *Maine*. His conclusion: The ship sank not because of Spanish treachery but because of the spontaneous combustion of explosive coal gases in the ship's coal bins. Such explosions had occurred before.[6] Debate has continued about what caused the sinking of the *Maine*. The only thing that is clear is the overwhelming desire for war at that time.

Roosevelt poisoned relations with the United States' neighbors. As historian Samuel Flagg Bemis put it in 1943, "Theodore Roosevelt confused the Latin American policy of the United States by identifying intervention in the Dominican Republic with the Monroe Doctrine, thus making that Doctrine, which had said 'hands off' to Europe, seem to say 'hands on' for the United States."[7]

Theodore Roosevelt's arrogant interventionism generated so much ill will toward the United States that Franklin D. Roosevelt found it necessary to announce a "Good Neighbor" policy for Central and South America. At the Montevideo Conference in December 1933, Cordell Hull, FDR's secretary of state, supported a resolution saying that "no state has the right to intervene in the internal or external affairs of another."[8] John F. Kennedy, too, was probably mindful of a need to make amends for Theodore Roosevelt's arrogance when, in 1961, he proposed an "Alliance for Progress" in Central and South America.

Perhaps Theodore Roosevelt's proudest achievement was the Panama Canal, but it isn't clear how the canal improved U.S. national security. The canal certainly made it easier for the U.S. navy to move ships from the Pacific Ocean to the Atlantic Ocean and back, but a response to an attack against the United States is far more likely to come from aircraft or missiles. A case might be made that the Panama Canal undermined national security by making it easier for the United States to enter wars that it should have stayed out of.

In order to push his interventionist agenda—and extend executive power at the expense of Congress—Roosevelt significantly expanded the use of "executive agreements," which were agreements made on the president's authority, without the approval of the U.S. Senate. For example, when the Senate would not ratify a treaty giving the United States authority to administer the Dominican Republic's customs revenues, Roosevelt simply issued an executive agreement. He later remarked, "I put the agreement into effect, and I continued its execution for two years before the Senate acted; and I would have continued it until the end of my term, if necessary, without any action by Congress."[9] He also made a secret executive agreement with Japan that, in the words of historian Arthur Schlesinger Jr., "bestow[ed] American approval on the Japanese military protectorate in Korea—an agreement that remained unknown until the historian Tyler Dennett unearthed it nearly twenty years later in the Roosevelt papers."[10] Then, ignoring Congress's constitutional power to declare war, Roosevelt told Germany and France that if they allied with the Soviet Union in a war against Japan, the United States would back Japan.[11]

Roosevelt's use of executive agreements set a dangerous precedent. His successor, William Howard Taft, intervened in Latin America, insisting on "the right to knock their heads together until they should maintain peace between them."[12] Sure enough, in 1911 Taft dispatched the U.S. marines to Honduras to protect U.S. investments in the banana business, and the following year he sent twenty-six hundred soldiers to Nicaragua, where the United States maintained a military presence for two decades.[13] Ever since, American presidents have launched military actions without benefit of a declaration of war from Congress, in Korea, Vietnam, and elsewhere.

As for Roosevelt's interventionist agenda, it has had a huge impact on U.S. foreign policy. In 1914 Woodrow Wilson intervened in Mexico, aiming to install a good government and to catch a bandit (Pancho Villa).[14] He failed on both counts. But it seems not to have occurred to him that the interventionist doctrine was flawed, because in 1917 he pushed the United States into the far more complicated European war—as Theodore Roosevelt had been urging him to do. Though Wilson portrayed the First World War as a noble cause to make the world "safe for democracy," American entry into the war enabled the French and British to win a decisive victory and impose vindictive surrender terms on the Germans, triggering the bitter nationalist response that generated political support for Hitler. The unintended consequence of Wilson's intervention was that the United States helped make the world safe for dictators, as I document in my book *Wilson's War*. Just as troubling, Wilson pressured and bribed Russia's Provisional Government to stay in the war. Russia was already deteriorating as a result of incompetent generals, ammunition shortages, inflation, and corruption, among other things. The government stayed in the war, unintentionally accelerating the collapse of the Russian army, which made it possible for Lenin to seize power on his fourth try. The Communists established concentration camps and launched a reign of terror that lasted for decades.[15]

In short, the first great test of Theodore Roosevelt's interventionist agenda backfired catastrophically.

Since Theodore Roosevelt's time, U.S. interventions abroad have become more common and less connected to U.S. national security. In the undeclared war that the United States entered in Korea in 1950, some thirty-eight thousand Americans lost their lives. This occurred despite the fact that the invasion of South Korea by North Korea's Soviet-backed dictator, Kim Il Sung, began a civil war that posed no threat, direct or indirect, to the United States. Only six months before President Harry Truman sent American troops into the conflict, his own secretary of state, Dean Acheson, had excluded Korea from Asian territories that the United States would protect from Communist aggression. Truman's decision to march forces north to destroy Kim Il Sung's regime provoked the Chinese government to intervene and led to further American bloodshed.

The United States then got sucked deeper and deeper into a conflict involving Communist guerrillas in Vietnam. Americans first became involved there after World War II, as they helped France try to maintain its colonial empire in Southeast Asia. When the Communists defeated the French in the Battle of Dien Bien Phu in 1954, the United States took on a more active role as the Communists infiltrated South Vietnam and continued to clash with pro-French forces. President John F. Kennedy and his successor, Lyndon B. Johnson, escalated U.S. involvement in the war, sending almost 400,000 soldiers to Vietnam before it became apparent that the conflict was a pointless tragedy. President Richard M. Nixon negotiated the U.S. withdrawal. Some 58,000 Americans died, and some 303,000 were wounded. The Communists took over, but U.S. national security wasn't affected.

Since then, inspired to a significant degree by Theodore Roosevelt, U.S. presidents have entered wars in Africa, the Balkans, the Middle East, and elsewhere. It often turns out that alleged U. S. national security interests were exaggerated, and the principal outcomes have been to make enemies and squander American lives in dubious missions.

2. Escalating government regulations have disrupted employers, destroyed jobs, and forced consumers to pay more for practically everything.

Theodore Roosevelt claimed that politicians and bureaucrats could achieve fairness by interfering with the economy. This was a remarkable claim, because government subsidies figured in the biggest financial scandals of his era. Roosevelt had personally witnessed corruption in the New York State legislature. He backed Republican presidential candidate James Blaine, who had packed payrolls with cronies. Roosevelt encountered plenty of fraud in the federal Civil Service system. He had to deal with New York City policemen who, when they weren't sleeping on the job, extorted bribes from shopkeepers. Roosevelt ought to have recognized that neither politicians nor bureaucrats had the moral authority to tell private individuals how they should live their lives. His experience affirmed Lord Acton's view that "power tends to corrupt, and absolute power corrupts absolutely."

Yet Roosevelt worked to gain more power over the economy. He targeted America's biggest industry, the railroads. In 1887, the railroads had helped establish the Interstate Commerce Commission, because limiting the railroads' ability to set prices for their services would end competitors' discounts that eroded their bottom line. Discounting reduced railroad rates for everybody, but the discounting railroads had achieved enough efficiencies to cut their costs so they could still make money. The higher-cost railroads, which lobbied most aggressively against discounting, were the principal losers.

Roosevelt helped antirailroad interests gain control of the regulatory apparatus, and they used it to prevent railroads from recouping costs and competing for capital—even though the railroad industry needed huge infusions of capital to handle growing traffic volumes and to consolidate rail networks. The decline of the railroad industry began with the Hepburn Act, which Roosevelt signed into law on June 29, 1906.

Following Roosevelt's lead, the federal government escalated its interference in the economy as the years went by. During World War I, the War Industries Board was set up to assert government control over American industries that figured in the war effort. Historians

Samuel Eliot Morison, Henry Steele Commager, and William E. Leuchtenburg report, "Baby carriages were standardized, traveling salesmen were limited to two trunks, and the length of uppers was cut down. It was such a regimentation of the economy as had never before been known, and it later served as a model for the New Deal mobilization of 1932."[16] Congress established the Emergency Fleet Corporation, a subsidiary of the Shipping Board, which seized control of private shipping and shipyards. Congress authorized the federal takeover of American railroads and accelerated the consolidation of a national rail network; when private individuals such as J. Pierpont Morgan and Edward Harriman had tried to do this, Theodore Roosevelt had hit them with antitrust lawsuits. The Food Administration fixed food prices, monopolized the grain trade, controlled the meat business, and bought the entire U.S. sugar crop.[17] The War Labor Board compelled companies to accept union contracts, going so far as to seize plants that rejected proposed union contracts.[18]

When Franklin Delano Roosevelt came to power during the Great Depression, he embraced his cousin Theodore's conception of a strong executive and a federal government that took control of the economy. With the New Deal, FDR established dozens of government agencies and issued thousands of regulations. His most audacious scheme was the National Recovery Administration, which enforced cartels in some seven hundred industries. The cartels limited output, enforced above-market prices that discouraged consumers from buying, and enforced above-market wages that discouraged employers from hiring. Furthermore, just as Theodore Roosevelt had promoted higher taxes, FDR *tripled* taxes in the New Deal era (1933–1940), reducing the amount of money consumers had for spending and the amount of money employers had for hiring. FDR harassed large employers with antitrust lawsuits as Theodore Roosevelt had done, except FDR did it on a much larger scale. Theodore Roosevelt, back in 1915, had urged federal spending for so-called public works projects, and FDR did, too. His biggest was the vast Tennessee Valley Authority power-generating monopoly.[19]

The next big burst of regulations came during the 1960s and early 1970s. President Lyndon Johnson signed a bill that attacked freedom of association, subjecting employers to costly antidiscrimination lawsuits if the racial and sexual mix of employees varied from statistical standards. The Equal Employment Opportunity Commission has issued orders about what it considers the proper number of varsity positions on men's and women's athletic teams and pay levels for men's and women's sports (regardless of revenue generated by the sports).[20] President Richard Nixon's Endangered Species Act (1973) has had the unintended effect of accelerating the destruction of species, because it imposes on private landowners the cost of maintaining a species. If an endangered species is believed to be in an area, the law gives landowners incentives to destroy the trees or whatever a species might need, rather than have regulations immobilize land and impose losses on the owner.

Theodore Roosevelt was a major inspiration for all this regulation, and the costs have been staggering. According to estimates by economists W. Marl Crain and Thomas D. Hopkins, the cost of federal regulations was $843 billion in 2000. Confirming the magnitude of the regulations' economic impact, economist Clyde Wayne Crews Jr. estimated a total regulatory cost of $860 billion for 2002.[21] There are three principal categories of cost: (1) the costs of compliance, which include hiring accountants, lawyers, and other advisers; (2) losses incurred as a result of regulations—for instance, reduced output or reduced efficiency; (3) transfer costs such as are incurred when import restrictions raise the cost of materials that manufacturers need. Beyond that, as Steven J. Entin of the Institute for Research on the Economics of Taxation observed, are the additional costs that come as a "result of the reactions of workers and savers to the lower returns and higher prices forced on them by the regulatory burden, which reduces economic output per unit of capital and per hour worked, and so reduces the real rate of return. . . .

As suppliers of labor and capital respond to these disincentives by withdrawing their services from the market, the resulting reduction in gross domestic product and income constitutes a further cost of regulation . . . on the order of 2 percent to 3 percent of GDP."[22] This is real money, for the 2004 gross domestic product was estimated to exceed $11 trillion.[23]

These regulations are a serious drag on the U.S. economy—a legacy of Theodore Roosevelt.

Roosevelt's championing of centralized federal power has had still more troubling economic consequences. In January 1912, while positioning himself for another run at the White House, Theodore Roosevelt met with Paul Moritz Warburg and twenty other bankers and economists who sought his support for the central bank scheme that was to become the Federal Reserve System. After an economist wondered whether they could find an individual capable of running it, Roosevelt remarked, "Why not give Mr. Warburg the job? He would be the financial boss, and I would be the political boss, and we could run the country together."[24]

Agitation to establish a central bank in the United States had begun during Roosevelt's presidency. During the panic of 1907, New York banks didn't have enough cash to pay depositors, because the bulk of deposits were loaned to businesses and couldn't be called back on short notice. J. P. Morgan and his associates arranged loans for the banks they thought were most likely to survive. Subsequently, there was much talk about developing a banking system that could ensure the availability of plenty of cash for such emergencies.

Roosevelt, as it turned out, backed away from supporting the Fed, in part because his fellow progressives attacked it as a banker's cabal—they wanted a government-controlled central bank. When Woodrow Wilson signed the Federal Reserve Act into law in December 1913, it helped fulfill Roosevelt's vision of centralized federal power. The act established an association of regional Federal Reserve banks supervised by a seven-member Federal Reserve Board.

Any of the Federal Reserve banks could engage in open market operations that involved buying or selling gold or government securities.

Theodore Roosevelt never recognized the fatal flaw of giving a few people enormous power over the entire economy. He assumed that only the best people would be in power and that they would always be right. But of course the government, like private employers, makes hiring mistakes, and some people with great résumés turn out to be poor performers. People might not be able to agree about what needs to be done. It's notoriously difficult to interpret conflicting economic data and predict the future. Since the consequences of a Fed decision often take more than a year to play out through the economy, much harm can be done before a mistake is recognized. Because of the Fed's vast power, its mistakes are likely to harm the entire country, not just a local community, a state, or a region.

Historian Allan H. Meltzer maintained that human failings undermined the Fed: "Many of the principals responsible for policy in the 1920s, and during 1929 to 1933, were weak men with little knowledge of central banking and not much interest in developing their knowledge. There were a few strong-minded individuals, but they were often at loggerheads."[25]

The Fed presided over the 1920–1921 depression, which economists Milton Friedman and Anna Jacobson Schwartz describe as "extremely severe in its later stages, when it was characterized by an unprecedented collapse in prices."[26] What's more, as Friedman and Schwartz made clear, bungled Fed policies were primarily responsible for the one-third monetary contraction that brought on the Great Depression of the 1930s. Their massive documentation appears in *A Monetary History of the United States* (1963), *Monetary Statistics of the United States* (1970), and *Monetary Trends in the United States and the United Kingdom* (1982).

The Banking Act of 1935 further concentrated power in the hands of a few Fed officials, magnifying the consequences of human errors. The Fed misjudged the economic situation and dramatically increased bank reserve requirements, causing banks to cut back lending, the bond market to decline, business to suffer, and unemployment to surge—hence, the depression of 1938–1939. Subsequently, Fed expansion of the money supply contributed to rising inflation during the 1950s and 1960s, then to the stagflation of the 1970s, which combined double-digit inflation with chronic high unemployment. Fed chairman Paul Volcker hit the monetary brakes, stopped inflation, and brought on the severe recession of the early 1980s.

Today, the Federal Reserve remains as vulnerable as ever, belying Theodore Roosevelt's belief that the government can always get the best people who will correctly interpret conflicting information, predict the future, and agree about what needs to be done.

3. Antitrust laws have punished companies that saved consumers money.

Antitrust laws were based on the assumption that the American economy was riddled with monopolies during the late nineteenth century, when in fact it was intensely competitive. More and more companies were being formed, even in such supposedly monopolized sectors as petroleum refining. The number of new patents increased significantly every year, and companies developing new technologies displaced companies relying on old technologies. Output expanded and prices declined—the opposite of what would have happened if monopoly had been the norm.

Since then, a number of studies have failed to find evidence of a trend toward monopoly in the United States.[27] Freer trade—considered by many economists to be the most effective antitrust policy—has undermined the market share of the formerly dominant "big three" Detroit automakers and the Pittsburgh steel producers. U.S. textile producers have complained that American consumers are buying too much from foreign competitors. Rapidly changing technology has led to the decline of computer companies that lag trends. Cable TV as well as the Internet have ended the dominance of the big television broadcasters. Federal antitrust lawsuits had nothing to do with any of these developments.

Antitrust was premised on the assumption that a market would be competitive only if there were a large number of companies. But very few companies are needed to ensure a dynamic market. With free trade, there's always the prospect of a foreign company entering a market. When capital markets are free, firms outside an industry can enter it. The entry of financially strong, sophisticated companies usually intensifies competition. In addition, companies in one industry may find themselves competing with companies in another industry—for instance, metals competing not only with metals but also with fiberglass and plastics.

A startling number of antitrust cases have punished low-cost competitors. Theodore Roosevelt's most famous antitrust target, Standard Oil, was an efficient competitor cutting prices. It cut the price of its principal product, kerosene, from 30 cents per gallon in 1869 to 3 cents by 1885.[28] When electric light began to replace kerosene lamps, prices of other petroleum products were cut, too.

Theodore Roosevelt's successors have continued the trust-busting crusade he started. One of the most bizarre antitrust cases involved Alcoa (Aluminum Company of America). Alcoa achieved dominance in the aluminum industry by managing its operations efficiently and pursuing new technologies that enabled it to extract alumina from low-grade ores. In 1941, four years after the Justice Department filed a complaint against the company, Judge Learned Hand of the U.S. Court of Appeals for the Second Circuit (New York, Connecticut, and Vermont) ordered that Alcoa be broken up. Judge Hand conceded that Alcoa had pioneered the aluminum business, expanded output, and cut prices (aluminum declined from $2 per pound during the 1890s to about 22 cents when the case went to trial).[29] He also conceded that Alcoa had conducted its business fairly. The company should be broken up, he said, because it was so successful. He deliberately overstated Alcoa's market share by counting only the market for primary ingot aluminum and disregarding the market for scrap aluminum.

Judge Hand faulted Alcoa for taking the initiative to expand and keep introducing new technologies: "Nothing compelled it to keep doubling and redoubling its capacity before others entered the field," he wrote. "It insists that it never excluded competitors; but we can think of no more effective exclusion than progressively to embrace each new opportunity as it opened and to face every newcomer with new capacity already geared into a greater organization, having the advantage of experience, trade connections, and elite personnel."[30]

Similarly, the Microsoft case involved a company known for cutting prices. National Economic Research Associates estimated that the Windows 98 operating system—the latest system when the Justice Department filed its lawsuit in 1998—cost one-fifth as much as the operating system Microsoft offered in 1989, and Windows 98 included features such as modem support, fax utilities, and CD-ROM drives that a decade earlier had cost more than Windows 98. But was Microsoft a monopoly, as the Justice Department and trial judge Thomas Penfield Jackson claimed? Writing in 1999, Cato Institute analyst Robert Levy emphatically said no and offered three reasons for his opinion: "First, roughly 1 customer in 8 doesn't use Microsoft. Alternatives are available—MacOS, Unix, OS/2 and Linux to name a few. Apple alone, with 13 million users, has reported substantial recent gains in market share. Second, it's not just existing but potential competition that matters. Network computing, digital TVs and other consumer electronics devices may radically alter the scope, nature and function of the operating system. . . . Third, Microsoft must compete against itself. Even if the company were to get out of the business this afternoon, all of its installed systems would continue to function indefinitely. So in order to sell a new product like Windows 98, Microsoft must convince its customers to pay more money, learn a new system and run the risk that other software applications will be incompatible. That imposes powerful discipline on Microsoft's behavior."[31]

Why would antitrust officials act against the interests of consumers? It used to be thought that individuals in government pursue the public interest and those in the private sector pursue their self-interest, but clearly individuals in and out of government look out for themselves. Theodore Roosevelt and other politicians promoted trust-busting because they believed it would advance their careers. Justice Department lawyers pursue antitrust cases, hoping to boost their careers.

Economists William F. Long, Richard Schramm, and Robert D. Tollison analyzed all the antitrust cases from 1890 to 1969 to see how many involved monopoly pricing. The answer was very few. Converting monopoly pricing to market-rate pricing, they reported, "appeared to play a minor role in explaining antitrust activity." Companies were most likely to become targets of an antitrust lawsuit if they reported large sales and had comparatively high profits and a high market share.[32] But sales, profits, and market share do not say anything about the degree of competition in an industry. In competitive markets, companies that offer consumers the best value and do the best job of marketing their products tend to achieve the highest market shares.

According to William F. Shughart II, Jon D. Silverman, and Robert D. Tollison, funding for the Justice Department's Antitrust Division and for the Federal Trade Commission tended to increase when foreign producers increased their share of the U.S. market. Their study suggests that "antitrust enforcement operates in part to protect small domestic firms against their foreign rivals at the expense of larger domestic firms and consumers."[33]

Paul H. Rubin surveyed economics journals for articles assessing twenty-three of the biggest antitrust cases, involving Standard Oil, American Tobacco, Alcoa, Du Pont, ReaLemon, Schwinn, Xerox, AT&T, IBM, and other companies. Fourteen of them were viewed as justified from the standpoint that the defendant pursued anticompetitive behavior. Nine cases were considered unjustified. Of the fourteen justified cases, the government won nine, the defendants six. Of the nine unjustified cases, the government won seven, the defendants two. "Based on this sample," Rubin explained, "it appears that if antitrust performs a deterrent function, it is as likely to deter efficient as inefficient behavior."[34]

These conclusions are particularly troubling because the number of private antitrust cases has soared in the past six decades. Under the terms of the Sherman Anti-Trust Act, private companies may sue their competitors, hoping that judges will award the advantages—especially triple damages—that eluded them in the marketplace. The "explosion of private cases," explained Richard A. Posner, may "reflect a recent rash of procedural rulings highly favorable to antitrust plaintiffs."[35] Now, typically more than a thousand private cases are filed annually, compared with fewer than one hundred government cases.[36] Private antitrust cases are perhaps the clearest indication that Theodore Roosevelt's trust-busting has become a battle cry to throttle competition.

4. Probably more people have been killed than saved by federal food and drug regulations.

Theodore Roosevelt believed that public health depends on high-minded government officials, but he was wrong. The biggest advances for food safety were achieved by private, profit-seeking entrepreneurs, not government regulators. The development of new food preservation methods—canning, freezing, refrigeration—the building of efficient railroad networks, and the introduction of reliable brand-name products substantially eliminated bad food as a major source of death long before Roosevelt's Meat Inspection Act and Pure Food and Drugs Act became law in 1906. Americans enjoyed a wider variety of food than ever before, and they were living longer.

Although the Pure Food and Drugs Act was presented as a solution to a crisis that did not exist, it is hard to object to the idea that labels should be truthful. The trouble is that government programs tend to take on a life of their own and have consequences very different from what was intended, as bureaucrats pursue their interests—bigger staff, bigger budgets, more power.

This became immediately clear as Dr. Harvey Washington Wiley, the first enforcer of the Pure Food and Drugs Act, launched crusades against corn syrup, margarine, and rectified whiskey, serving the interests of his friends who produced rival products—cane sugar, butter, and straight whiskey. In 1929, long after he had been forced out following his crusade against Coca-Cola, Wiley wrote *History of a Crime Against the Food Law,* which affirmed the view that supposedly high-minded food and drug regulators were in cahoots with special interests.

All this occurred when the government's mission was simply to seek truthful labeling and identify adulterated food. The government began to do more harm after it assumed more responsibility for public safety.

In 1927, the Food, Drug, and Insecticide Administration (which became the Food and Drug Administration) was established as a regulatory agency. Eleven years later, following revelations that the liquid form of the drug sulfanilamide contained a lethal solvent, Congress passed the Food, Drug, and Cosmetic Act, which provided that a drug could not be marketed until the FDA had determined it was safe. A new drug would be automatically approved if the FDA did not rule against it within 180 days—which period could be extended if the FDA needed more information.[37]

In 1959, Tennessee Democrat Estes Kefauver, chairman of the Senate Subcommittee on Antitrust and Monopoly, was fishing for a political issue and began hearings on the pharmaceutical industry. He thought the industry was spending too much money on inconsequential innovations, as if a politician such as he would know more than prescribing physicians or researchers, investors, and others with a stake in a pharmaceutical company's fortunes. Kefauver considered a lot of drug research wasteful. He introduced amendments to the Food, Drug, and Cosmetic Act (1) providing that a drug could not be introduced until the FDA had determined that it did what it was supposed to do and (2) eliminating any limit on the time the FDA might take to announce a decision about a new drug.[38] The amendments passed in 1962 on the strength of political support resulting from the thalidomide tragedy. (It turned out that the sedative thalidomide, which the FDA had been moving toward approving, severely harmed fetuses if it was taken by women during pregnancy.[39])

In truth, the Kefauver amendments had little to do with safety. The FDA already had the power to ban unsafe drugs. The principal purpose of the amendments was to secure the FDA's position as a monopoly source of information on drugs. The FDA now determines how new drugs must be tested and how the tests must be reviewed. As Robert M. Goldberg, director of the Manhattan Institute's Center for Medical Progress, reported, when the FDA approves a drug, "it prohibits drug companies from providing doctors and patients with verbal or written information about medical research demonstrating how a drug approved for one medical problem might help solve another." Even if doctors test other uses and publish their findings in prestigious, peer-reviewed medical journals such as the *Journal of the American Medical Association* or the *New England Journal of Medicine,* "drug companies are prohibited from even handing out reprints of such articles." It's the American public who suffers. "An analysis of unapproved drug use suggests that the vast majority of such applications are not only safe and effective but essential to patient health," Goldberg concluded. "Furthermore, it appears that in cases where the FDA has aggressively sought to limit the spread of information about 'off-label,' i.e. unapproved, uses, it has undermined the public health in the process."[40]

According to economist Sam Peltzman, in the decade following the Kefauver amendments the number of new drugs introduced annually declined about 60 percent. By 1974, Peltzman reports, the

Kefauver amendments had delayed the introduction of new drugs by about two years. FDA officials became more risk-averse: Politically they had everything to lose if they approved what turned out to be a bad drug, because of all the bad publicity that would follow. But they seemed to have little to lose if they rejected what turned out to be a good drug. Who would ever know? Peltzman estimated that the costs of FDA delays exceeded the benefits by 3 or 4 to 1.[41]

Although some of Peltzman's findings have been disputed, evidence has been mounting that FDA delays have resulted in hundreds of thousands of needless deaths. For examples, Alexander T. Tabarrok of the Independent Institute reported that "practolol, a drug in the beta-blocker family, could save ten thousand lives a year if approved in the United States. Although the FDA first approved a beta blocker, propranolol, in 1968, three years after that drug had become available in Europe, it waited until 1978 to approve propranolol for the treatment of hypertension and angina pectoris, its most important indications. Despite clinical evidence available as early as 1974, only in 1981 did the FDA approve a second beta blocker, timolol, for prevention of second heart attack. The agency's dilatory action with regard to beta blockers alone was thus responsible for probably tens of thousands of deaths."[42]

During the three and a half years the FDA spent evaluating Interleukin-2—which had proved itself as an effective treatment for kidney cancer in nine countries—several thousand Americans died from kidney cancer. Eugene Schoenfeld, president of the National Kidney Cancer Association, remarked that "Il-2 is one of the worst examples of FDA regulation."[43]

Since then, the FDA introduced a "fast-track" process for evaluating new drugs, but it has reflected political pressures. When Democrats controlled the White House, AIDS drugs were given "fast-track" priority. When Republicans came to power, they gave priority to cancer drugs. "The sudden shift in cancer policy reveals the moral bankruptcy of the FDA's approach to drug development," Robert M. Goldberg observed in 1996. "It used to claim that accelerated approval was limited to drugs that held out a last-ditch hope of postponing or averting death. Under the new cancer policy, drugs that in some way will improve the quality of life will also get fast-tracked. If accelerated approval is no longer limited to potentially life-saving drugs, why leave drugs that might help patients with other serious diseases and conditions on the slow track? Where is the public health benefit of giving faster access to one group of Americans while denying access to others?"[44]

The time required to develop a new drug soared to as long as fifteen years during the 1990s. Goldberg explained why: "The number of people used in clinical trials has increased. The number of clinical procedures per patient has doubled, and the amount of information the FDA demands before accepting a new drug application has skyrocketed. In particular, the number of clinical procedures required in testing new cancer drugs increased 153 percent [during the 1990s]."[45] All this has been in pursuit of an impossible standard—"safe and efficacious." But whether a drug is "safe and efficacious" depends on the age, sex, and overall health situation of particular patients, among other factors. An interesting but substantially undocumented new cancer treatment would be viewed very differently by a patient who was helped by conventional treatments and a patient for whom conventional treatments did no good.

Because of FDA regulatory requirements, the cost of developing a new drug has soared to more than $800 million.[46] This situation has particularly harsh implications for patients with rare diseases. Facing higher and higher drug-development costs, pharmaceutical companies naturally focus on big markets offering reasonable prospects of recovering costs—diseases such as hypertension, stroke, diabetes, and major forms of cancer that afflict millions of people. The companies find it financially impossible to take on the FDA-mandated costs that arise when small numbers of patients are involved. So patients with rare diseases continue to have few, if any, good options.[47]

FDA delays might be justified if they actually improved safety, but apparently they do not. For example, Tabarrok estimated in 2000 that 3 percent of FDA-approved drugs were subsequently withdrawn from the market because of safety issues. The comparable percentages in, respectively, Spain and Great Britain—countries with *less stringent* drug approval procedures—were 3 percent and 4 percent.[48]

The FDA is wedded to decades-old procedures whose limitations are increasingly clear. "Their system just cannot test enough people to identify all possible side effects before a drug is approved," charged Goldberg in 2004. "But the added cost and delay will deny people with serious illness access to new drugs, denying them the chance of living fuller and longer lives." With new technologies making possible a more targeted approach, such as by tailoring drugs "to treat patients who are at risk for a certain disease or condition based on their genetic makeup," some have argued that decades of FDA regulations should be set aside and all drugs should be readily available with full disclosure of the risks.[49] With knowledge of the risks, doctors and patients could make informed choices, deciding whether, in their specific circumstances, the risks would be worth taking.

That approach would challenge everything that Theodore Roosevelt's heirs have assured us about the alleged benefits of federal regulation. But those benefits were overhyped from the very beginning. After the Pure Food and Drugs Act was passed in 1906, the *New York Times* gushed that "the purity and honesty of the food and medicines of the people are guaranteed."[50] Nearly a century later, the *Times* acknowledged a more realistic view in a story headlined "A Reminder That No Drug Is Risk-Free."[51]

5. "Conservation" policies have degraded our environment.

Supposedly a champion of "conservation," Theodore Roosevelt may be responsible for more environmental destruction than any other U.S. president. The worst corporate polluters were pikers compared to Theodore Roosevelt.

The fatal flaw of Roosevelt's conservation policies was the assumption that there was only one right way to do things and it should be enforced everywhere. When bad decisions were made, they harmed not only a locality or a region but the entire country. Because bureaucracies have aggressively pursued their interests, always seeking bigger staffs, bigger budgets, and more power, it has been almost impossible to alter bad decisions or repeal bad programs.

Conservation bureaucrats since Roosevelt's time have claimed to practice "scientific management," but they have been as prone to human error as anyone else. As economists Roger A. Sedjo and Marion Clawson explained, "The capacity of American forests to regenerate naturally, and to grow wood, has been repeatedly and seriously underestimated by foresters generally and by the Forest Service in particular." The Forest Service has consistently displayed "little or no regard for the effect of economic factors on the willingness of forest owners to grow more timber in response to favorable economic conditions."[52]

In 1902, when Roosevelt established the Bureau of Reclamation, he said that the federal government's taxing power would be used to transfer vast resources from more productive uses in the East to less productive uses in the West. He specifically channeled funds into the highest-cost type of farming—farming in deserts—when more efficient types of farming were producing food in ever greater abundance. Over the years, the government has continued this inefficient policy. The Bureau of Reclamation has built more than six hundred dams around the United States, destroying beautiful valleys, building up salinity in irrigated soil, and drying up rivers. In August 2002, Barry Nelson of the Natural Resources Defense Council wrote, "Nothing demonstrates [the Bureau of Reclamation's] antiquated policies more dramatically than the fact that the Colorado River . . . often no longer flows to the sea."[53] The bureau also wastes stupendous amounts of water by building reservoirs in hot, arid regions, where water standing out in the sun simply evaporates. In 1997 in testimony before a House subcommittee, Sierra Club president Adam Werbach reported the Lake Powell reservoir in Arizona loses nearly 1 million acre-feet of water per year—"enough for a city the size of Los Angeles."[54]

Why does Theodore Roosevelt's disastrous dam-building program continue? It continues because western farmers who benefit from the subsidies aggressively defend it. According to the Western Water Alliance, in Seattle, "the subsidies go well beyond the interest subsidy originally built into the Reclamation program." Congress has given irrigators as much as forty extra years to repay the capital cost of projects. "Moreover, if the repayment price for water exceeds an irrigator's 'ability to pay,' the Bureau transfers the balance to project power users. . . . The Bureau also charges the lowest possible 'power project' rates for the energy required to pump water to its customers—a tiny fraction of market rates for that electrical power."[55] With these and many other cushy regulations and loopholes in place, it is little wonder that recipients of the government's largesse lobby vigorously to preserve the federal program.

Government-subsidized water made it possible to grow palm trees in the desert and spurred a great migration to California. The pressure on scarce water supplies intensified, all because of subsidies that shielded people from the full cost of living in the desert. Far fewer people would have made the move if they had known they would have to pay steep prices for water. Incredibly, despite California's dramatic population growth, agriculture—subsidized irrigation—continues to consume about 80 percent of the state's water.[56]

By establishing the federal government's monopoly control of millions of acres of national forests, Theodore Roosevelt ensured the vast degradation of America's natural environment. The national forests, another of Roosevelt's supposed achievements, have suffered the fate of all common property: It's in all users' interest to take as much as they can and in nobody's interest to spend money to maintain the value of common property, because someone else would gain the benefit of any investment. From the very beginning, overgrazing has plagued national forests. In 1918, Supreme Court justice Louis Brandeis identified the problem when he wrote the majority opinion in *Omaechevarria v. State of Idaho*. Cattle and sheep graze "on the public domain of the United States," Brandeis wrote. "This is done with the government's acquiescence, without the payment of compensation, and without federal regulation."[57] Some forty years later, historian Wesley Calef complained that the politically weak Bureau of Land Management "does not exert sufficient control over range grazing use to insure conservation of the federal lands."[58]

That's not all. There have been unintended consequences of federal bureaucrats' decision to suppress forest fires. Before this, frequent, low-intensity fires typically thinned out forests and replenished the soil. Fire suppression has resulted in much denser growth and ever-decreasing amounts of sunlight reaching the forest floor. Large numbers of trees have died, creating a dangerous buildup of tinder. When fires do occur, they tend to be large and hard to control; they destroy essential microorganisms, sterilizing the soil and making it more vulnerable to erosion; and they destroy species that would have survived low-intensity fires.[59] Excessive density also has contributed to widespread insect infestation in national forests. According to economist Robert H. Nelson, "On the Lincoln National Forest in New Mexico, 57 percent of the ponderosa pine acreage is infected with round-headed beetles."[60]

By contrast, privately owned forests tend to be intensively managed, because it's in the self-interest of owners—whether a paper company or a timber company—to maintain the value of their assets. One can tell from an airplane window whether one is flying over a national forest or a privately managed forest. For instance, Nelson explained: "Idaho national forests have 33 percent greater wood volume per acre than state and private forests. The state and private forests have in general been more intensively managed, involving higher timber harvest levels per acre and greater application of labor and capital for thinning, disease control, reforestation, and other purposes."[61] Also: "There is wide agreement that the national forests are a greater fire hazard than industry forests, mostly because intensive private forest management prevented the fuel buildup that has occurred on the federal lands."[62]

Despite accumulating evidence that bad policies need to be changed, the Forest Service appears to be paralyzed. This condition is due, in part, to the Endangered Species Act (1973), the Federal Land Policy and Management Act (1976), and other laws that established byzantine procedural requirements and provided many opportunities for opponents to block proposed action.[63]

What of the "timber famine" that was the rationale for Theodore Roosevelt's conservation movement? According to the U.S. Forest Service, "In the 1920s, timber growth nationally was about half the rate of harvest. By the 1940s, improving forest growth rates and modestly declining harvest rates resulted in timber growth and harvest coming into approximate balance. . . . Since the 1950s, timber growth has consistently exceeded harvest."[64] Today, there is more forested acreage than there was in 1900.[65] In some cases, this increase is due to the decline of industries dependent on extensive tree-cutting—for example, leather tanning, which used tannic acid derived from bark. More important has been the increased efficiency of farming, which makes it possible for fewer people, cultivating less land, to produce more food. Consequently, millions of acres of farmland have reverted to forestland. Today, many a stone wall runs through suburban woodlands, reminding us of farms that used to dominate the countryside. Dramatic reforestation has occurred on millions of acres of private lands that are not subject to U.S. Forest Service policies.

The decades have not been kind to Theodore Roosevelt for having expanded the National Park system. The parks have deteriorated under government control. The government has been unable to protect them from damage by visitors. For example, there are a reported 55,000 snowmobiles in Yellowstone National Park during winter months. Besides making a lot of noise and spewing carbon monoxide into the air, snowmobiles are estimated to dump between 50,000 and 60,000 gallons of unburned fuel into the snow, and much of it ends up in springs and streams. Snowmobiles are in Yellowstone because of political pressure from towns that border the park. They claim they would lose business if snowmobiles were banned. West Yellowstone prides itself as the "snowmobile capital of the world."

The National Park Service budget is a serious problem. A major reason why is that revenues generated by the parks are not retained by the parks. Ever since the Progressive era—in 1918, to be exact—park revenues have gone to Washington, D.C., and the National Park Service has had to lobby congressional committees for appropriations. It competes with many government programs, such as Medicare and the Defense Department, that are far larger and more effective at securing appropriations. Consequently, the number of park rangers has declined, and some $6 billion worth of park maintenance has been postponed. Roads, trails, buildings, sewage systems, and other infrastructure are in disrepair.

Some three hundred parks compete for a share of the National Park Service budget. Generally the best way to get money is to talk about overcrowding. So the need for government funding creates incentives to encourage overcrowding. Perhaps that is one reason why the National Park Service charges fees below the market value of park recreation. The most popular parks charge the same admission fees as less popular parks. Some parks charge nothing at all. Visitors are not charged according to the length of their stay. Seniors and young children often pay nothing. Although there are fees for entering and camping in parks, there typically are no fees for other activities such as fishing.

Because the National Park Service does not control its revenues, it lacks incentives to control its costs.[66] Reportedly one-third of National Park Service construction costs go for overhead and overruns. National Park Service projects cost perhaps three times more per square foot than standard office construction. *USA Today* reported in 1997 that the National Park Service spent $1 million to build a four-hole outhouse in Glacier National Park; the project was a priority of Montana's three-member congressional delegation.[67]

Such congressional politicking has become common. When Senator Robert Byrd of West Virginia chaired the Senate Appropriations Committee, he pushed through a $10 million appropriation for Wheeling National Heritage Area, then made sure it became a national park. Congressman Joseph McDade of Pennsylvania, on the House Appropriations Committee, played a key role establishing Steamtown as a National Historic Site in Scranton. The National Park Service budget also has had to cover a multimillion-dollar project at Boston Public Library, a $2 million walkway near Tacoma, Washington, and a $2.1 million renovation of the Thomas Stone National Historic Site in Port Tobacco, Maryland (which attracts about ten visitors per day).

Just as the Forest Service has mismanaged forests, the National Park Service has mismanaged wildlife. Environmentalists have encouraged a do-nothing policy with the idea of conjuring up the kind of primeval wilderness that existed eons ago. But most national parks are small enough that factors beyond their borders affect the balance of wildlife. Forest rangers did nothing when the elk population surged in Yellowstone and ate just about all the willows and aspens. Beaver, ptarmigan, and bighorn sheep subsequently disappeared. Without beavers, many wetlands dried up, and other animal populations declined.[68] Early America wasn't like that. Chronic overgrazing by elk or deer is a problem at other national parks, including Rocky Mountain, Mount Rainier, Olympic, Glacier, and Acadia.

Contrary to what Theodore Roosevelt expected, politicians and bureaucrats have not been good stewards of our parks. Our natural wonders probably would have been better protected as deed-restricted private property whose owners were free from political pressures.

6. "Soak the rich" income taxes soak everybody.

Theodore Roosevelt and other progressives embraced an income tax with ever steeper rates because they imagined that somebody else—"the rich"—would pay for government. From the very beginning, that was an illusion.

In 1914, following the outbreak of World War I, President Woodrow Wilson asked for, and Congress approved, higher taxes to generate some $105 million of additional revenue. The bill hiked excise taxes on beer, wine, gasoline, and other things that ordinary people purchased. Income tax rates were left as they were.[69] As military spending increased—even when the United States was supposed to be a neutral power—the Revenue Act of 1916 raised the normal income tax to 2 percent for individuals and corporations and added a surtax ranging from 6 percent (on incomes over $20,000) to 13 percent (on incomes over $2 million).[70] A new federal estate tax—on top of estate taxes levied by thirty-three states—ranged from 1 percent (on estates worth $50,000 to $100,000) to 10 percent (on estates worth more than $5.5 million).[71] Munitions manufacturers were assessed a 12.5 percent tax on their next profits, on top of the corporate income tax.

War spending drove tax rates up, but ordinary people, not the rich, bore roughly half the tax burden. In 1917, the federal government collected $180.1 million of personal income taxes and $207.2 million of corporate income taxes, compared with $284 million of excise taxes on alcohol and $103.2 million of excise taxes on tobacco.[72]

The income tax truly became a war tax after Wilson persuaded Congress to declare war in 1917 and the government's demand for money exploded. The War Revenue Act of October 3, 1917, displayed the raw power of the income tax perhaps for the first time, and progressives like Republican senators Robert M. LaFollette of Wisconin and William Borah of Idaho were thrilled. The normal income tax rate doubled, to 4 percent on individuals and

6 percent on corporations. The war excess profits tax ranged from 20 percent to 60 percent. Corporations were hit with a 10 percent penalty on profits not distributed to shareholders (where they would be subject to income taxes and surtaxes). Among other things, the government increasingly "double-dipped," taxing profits when earned by corporations and again when distributed to shareholders.[73]

Before 1915, the income tax had produced negligible revenue. The following year, it accounted for 16 percent of federal revenues. By 1920, it provided almost 60 percent of federal revenues. The tariff ceased to be a major revenue source.[74] The income tax had proved itself as a revenue generator. So even though federal tax rates began to decline after the war ended, it was only a matter of time before the government again turned to the income tax as a quick way to drum up money.

Franklin Delano Roosevelt became well known for his "soak the rich" taxes, but until 1937, federal excise taxes on beer, wine, cigarettes, soft drinks, chewing gum, radios, and other things that ordinary people purchased generated more revenue than the federal personal income tax and the federal corporate income tax combined. In 1936, the federal government reported $674.4 million from the personal income tax, $753 million from the corporate income tax, and $1.5 billion from excise taxes.[75] Despite big income tax hikes, the federal excise tax continued to be the single largest source of federal revenue until World War II. So FDR's New Deal was financed on the backs of the middle class and poor people who bought things subject to the federal excise tax. To hear one of FDR's "fireside chats," Americans had to pay one federal excise tax on a radio and another on the electricity needed to run it.

By 1942, the income tax became the federal government's biggest source of revenue. It was no longer paid only by a few rich people as in Theodore Roosevelt's day. The income tax was a people's tax. During World War II, everybody had to pay a federal income tax. Everybody was subject to the exasperating complexity of tax regulations. Everybody had to suffer the indignities of tax audits and other Internal Revenue Service intrusions into personal life, thanks to Theodore Roosevelt and his fellow progressives.

In 2002, 11.3 million business returns and 130.3 million personal income tax returns were filed. Most of those taxpayers weren't rich.[76] Economist James L. Payne has identified more than thirty costs incurred by taxpayers to comply with tax regulations. Among them are costs for tax planning, record keeping, data processing, filling out forms, audit preparation, and appeals preparation. According to Payne's estimate, in 1993 the cost of compliance—borne by taxpayers—was approximately equal to 65 percent of the proceeds from the personal income tax.[77]

LIBERTY AND PEACE

What can we learn from Theodore Roosevelt's experience?

First of all, it should be noted that his policies were not inevitable. If ideas had been different, there probably would have been different choices and different outcomes.

Instead of intervening in the affairs of other nations and promoting American entry into World War I, it would have been better if Theodore Roosevelt had used his personal charisma to help keep America at peace. He could have used his "bully pulpit" to promote American neutrality while wars raged in the Old World. He could have defended American exceptionalism, the view that the United States was established as a special place, a sanctuary for liberty and peace—a republic, not an empire. If Roosevelt had taken that position, his successors might have been more inclined to stay out of other people's wars, and Americans would have avoided many of the horrors that developed during the twentieth century.

Government programs take on lives of their own and often have unexpected consequences as bureaucrats pursue their self-interest by lobbying for bigger staffs, bigger budgets, and more power. The more power bureaucrats wield, the greater is the harm they do with their imperfect information and poor judgment. It would have been better not to establish regulatory agencies, such as the FDA for the safety of food and drugs, and instead to rely on competition (good brand names driving out bad products), on the enforcement of existing laws against fraud, and on tort remedies for damages.

People take care of their own property better than they take care of other people's property, because they stand to profit by improving property values. If Theodore Roosevelt had accelerated rather than slowed the transfer of government land to private ownership, the environment would be in much better shape today. There would have been countless experiments to find the best ways to manage resources. People who wished to preserve natural wonders could have done so with private deed restrictions. There would have been no Bureau of Reclamation building hundreds of dams that blocked and drained rivers for subsidized irrigation in arid regions where farming made no sense. Without national forests, Washington bureaucrats would not have had the power to enforce policies that contributed to catastrophic fires affecting millions of acres.

Politicians and bureaucrats are incapable of running an economy. The political decisions they make tend to be bad business decisions. They lack incentives to be careful with taxpayers' money. Rather than denouncing successful entrepreneurs, interfering with their ability to price their services and compete for capital, and threatening them with antitrust lawsuits and discriminatory taxes, Theodore Roosevelt could have promoted competition. He could have championed unilateral free trade—the most effective antitrust policy—by seeking the repeal of tariffs that protected monopolies and robbed consumers. He could have worked to abolish government subsidies and government-enforced barriers to entry in various businesses. If Roosevelt had opposed an income tax and government regulations, he might have thwarted the expansion of government power that was making it harder for entrepreneurs to create growth and jobs. Greater prosperity is the best bet for lifting people out of poverty.

Contrary to what Theodore Roosevelt claimed, the weak are best protected from the strong by strict limits on government power. The strong tend to do well in any society. When government expands, the strong, with their lawyers and lobbyists, gain more power than they would otherwise have. They get laws and regulations serving their interests at the expense of everyone else. We would all be better off with fewer burdens on our backs and strangers in our pockets.

What we need, most of all, is liberty and peace.

NOTES

INTRODUCTION

1. William Roscoe Thayer, *Theodore Roosevelt: An Intimate Biography* (New York: Grosset & Dunlap, 1919), p. 445.
2. Edmund Morris, *The Rise of Theodore Roosevelt* (New York: Coward, McCann & Geoghegan, 1979), pp. 17, 24.
3. David McCullough, *The Path Between the Seas: The Creation of the Panama Canal, 1870–1914* (New York: Simon & Schuster, 1977), p. 249.
4. Kathleen Dalton, *Theodore Roosevelt: A Strenuous Life* (New York: Knopf, 2002), p. 12.
5. State of the Union message, December 2, 1902.
6. "Tax Freedom Day® Arrives April 11 in 2004," Tax Foundation, www.taxfoundation.org/.
7. Theodore Roosevelt, *An Autobiography* (New York: Macmillan, 1913), p. 389.
8. Henry F. Pringle, *Theodore Roosevelt* (New York: Barnes & Noble, 1956), p. 181.
9. Roosevelt, *An Autobiography*, p. 389.
10. William J. Olson and Alan Woll, *Executive Orders and National Emergencies: How Presidents Have Come to "Run the Country" by Usurping Legislative Power* (Washington, DC: Cato Institute, 1999), p. 15.
11. Senate Special Committee on National Emergencies and Delegated Emergency Powers, *Executive Orders in Times of War and National Emergency*, 93rd Cong., 2nd sess. (1974), pp. 40–46.
12. Dalton, *Theodore Roosevelt: A Strenuous Life*, p. 210.
13. H. W. Brands, *T.R.: The Last Romantic* (New York: Basic Books, 1997), p. 419.
14. Theodore Roosevelt, *The Foes of Our Own Household* (New York: George H. Doran Company, 1917), p. x.
15. Quoted in Henry F. Pringle, *Theodore Roosevelt* (New York: Barnes & Noble, 1956), p. 207.
16. Howard K. Beale, *Theodore Roosevelt and the Rise of America to World Power* (Baltimore: Johns Hopkins University Press, 1956), p. 38.
17. Theodore Roosevelt to Henry Cabot Lodge, January 28, 1909, *Correspondence of Theodore Roosevelt,* vol. 6; selected and edited by Elting E. Morison (Cambridge: Harvard University Press, 1951–1954), pp. 1497, 1498.
18. Arthur M. Schlesinger Jr., *The Imperial Presidency* (Boston: Houghton Mifflin, 1973), p. 88.
19. McCullough, *The Path Between the Seas*, p. 385.
20. Theodore Roosevelt, speech delivered at Provincetown, Massachusetts, August 20, 1907. The phrase "malefactors of great wealth" was cited by FDR in a speech he

delivered in Chicago on October 14, 1936. See www.presidency.ucsb.edu/site/docs/pppus.php?admin=032&year=1936&id=180.

21. State of the Union message, December 2, 1905.

22. *Historical Statistics of the United States, Colonial Times to 1970* (Washington, DC: Bureau of the Census, 1975), part 2, p. 728; Douglass C. North, *Growth and Welfare in the American Past* (Englewood Cliffs, NJ: Prentice-Hall, 1966), p. 111; *Historical Statistics of the United States, Colonial Times to 1970*, part 2, p. 912.

23. Gabriel Kolko, *The Triumph of Conservatism: A Reinterpretation of American History, 1900–1916* (Chicago: Quadrangle, 1963), p. 5.

24. See, for instance, William F. Shughart II, "Private Antitrust Enforcement—Compensation, Deterrence, or Extortion?" *Regulation,* Fall 1990, pp. 53–61.

25. Albro Martin, *Enterprise Denied: Origins of the Decline of American Railroads, 1897–1917* (New York: Columbia University Press, 1971), p. 361.

26. See the National Park Service website, www.cr.nps.gov/logcabin/html/tr5.html.

27. President's Commission on Privatization, *Privatization: Toward More Effective Government* (Washington, DC, March 1988), p. 242.

28. James Ridenour, *The National Parks Compromised: Pork Barrel Politics and America's Treasures* (Merrillville, IN: ICS Books, 1994), p. 108.

29. Marc Reisner, *Cadillac Desert: The American West and Its Disappearing Water* (New York: Penguin Books, 1986), p. 115.

30. Ibid., pp. 514, 515.

31. Robert H. Nelson, *A Burning Issue: A Case for Abolishing the U.S. Forest Service* (Lanham, MD: Rowman & Littlefield, 2000), p. 8.

32. See, for example, Gary D. Libecap, "The Rise of the Chicago Packers, and the Origins of Meat Inspection and Antitrust," *Economic Inquiry,* April 1992, pp. 242–62.

33. Edmund Morris, *Theodore Rex* (New York: Knopf, 2001), p. 438.

34. Clayton A. Coppin and Jack High, *The Politics of Purity: Harvey Washington Wiley and the Origins of Federal Food Policy* (Ann Arbor: University of Michigan Press, 2002), p. 31.

35. John F. Witte, *The Politics and Development of the Federal Income Tax* (Madison: University of Wisconsin Press, 1985), p. 72.

36. Willard L. King, *Melville Weston Fuller* (New York: Macmillan, 1950), p. 195.

37. "Tax Stats at a Glance," Internal Revenue Service, www.irs.gov/taxstats/article/0,,id=102886,00.html.

38. "Individual Income Tax Returns with Positive Adjusted Gross Income (AGI): Number of Returns, Shares of AGI and Total Income Tax, AGI Floor on Percentiles in Current and Constant Dollars, and Dollar Average Tax Rates, by Selected Descending Cumulative Percentiles of Returns Based on Income Size Using the Definition of AGI for Each Year, Tax Years 1986–2000," www.irs.gov/pub/irs-soi/02in01ts.xls.

39. See R. J. Rummel, *Death by Government* (New Brunswick, NJ: Transaction, 1994).

40. Theodore Roosevelt, *Oliver Cromwell* (New York: Scribner, 1900), p. 216.

CHAPTER ONE

1. Theodore Roosevelt, "The New Nationalism," speech in Osawatomie, Kansas, August 31, 1910.

2. Quoted in Page Smith, *America Enters the World* (New York: McGraw-Hill, 1985), p. 185.

3. Quoted in Forrest McDonald, *A Constitutional History of the United States* (Malabar, FL: Robert E. Krieger, 1986), p. 166.

4. James Russell Lowell, "Scotch the Snake, or Kill It?" *North American Review*, July 1865, p. 192, reprinted in *The Complete Writings of James Russell Lowell*, vol. 6 (New York: AMS Press, 1966), p. 299.

5. *Historical Statistics of the United States, Colonial Times to 1970* (Washington, DC: Bureau of the Census, 1975), part 2, p. 1104. Federal budget expenditures increased from $63.1 million in 1860 to $1.2 billion in 1865.

6. Jeffrey Rogers Hummel, *Emancipating Slaves, Enslaving Free Man: A History of the American Civil War* (Chicago: Open Court, 1996), p. 329.

7. *Historical Statistics of the United States, Colonial Times to 1970*, part 2, p. 1104.

8. Hummel, *Emancipating Slaves, Enslaving Free Man*, p. 331.

9. Quoted ibid., pp. 331, 332.

10. Henry Adams, letter to Henry Cabot Lodge, June 7, 1876, cited in William C. Widenor, *Henry Cabot Lodge and the Search for an American Foreign Policy* (Berkeley: University of California Press, 1980), p. 34.

11. Quoted in Merrill D. Peterson, *The Jefferson Image in the American Mind* (New York: Oxford University Press, 1960), p. 223.

12. Quoted in H. W. Brands, *T.R.: The Last Romantic* (New York: Basic Books, 1997), p. 573.

13. Brands, *T.R.: The Last Romantic*, p. 9.

14. Ibid., p. 19.

15. Ibid., p. 17.

16. Kathleen Dalton, *Theodore Roosevelt: A Strenuous Life* (New York: Knopf, 2002), pp. 33, 34.

17. Brands, *T.R.: The Last Romantic*, p. 26.

18. Ibid., p. 32.

19. Quoted ibid., p. 35.

20. Brands, *T.R.: The Last Romantic*, p. 28.

21. Ibid., p. 57.

22. Ibid., p. 119.

23. Ibid., pp. 9, 80.

24. Ibid., p. 87.

25. Ibid., p. 94.

26. Ibid., p. 114.

27. Quoted ibid., p. 118.

28. Brands, *T.R.: The Last Romantic*, pp. 123, 124.

29. Ibid., p. 134.

30. Ibid., pp. 134, 135.

31. Ibid., pp. 136, 137.

32. David McCullough, *Mornings on Horseback* (New York: Simon & Schuster, 1981), p. 265.

33. Brands, *T.R.: The Last Romantic*, p. 140.

34. Paul Grondahl, *I Rose like a Rocket* (New York: Free Press, 2004), p. 107.

35. Ibid., p. 109.

36. Dalton, *Theodore Roosevelt: A Strenuous Life*, p. 91.

37. Richard W. Turk, *The Ambiguous Relationship: Theodore Roosevelt and Alfred Thayer Mahan* (Westport, CT: Greenwood Press, 1987), p. 14.
38. Grondahl, *I Rose like a Rocket*, p. 183.
39. Ibid., p. 185.
40. Ibid., p. 187.
41. Edmund Morris, *The Rise of Theodore Roosevelt* (New York: Coward, McCann & Geoghegan, 1979), p. 398.
42. Ibid., p. 401.
43. Ibid., p. 401.
44. Grondahl, *I Rose like a Rocket*, p. 190.
45. Morris, *The Rise of Theodore Roosevelt*, p. 402.
46. Ibid., p. 403.
47. Grondahl, *I Rose like a Rocket*, p. 191.
48. Ibid., p. 194.
49. Ibid., pp. 191, 192.
50. Ibid., p. 202.
51. Ibid., p. 214.
52. Brands, *T.R.: The Last Romantic*, p. 276.
53. Grondahl, *I Rose like a Rocket*, pp. 230, 231.
54. Quoted ibid., p. 224.
55. Theodore Roosevelt, *An Autobiography* (New York: Macmillan, 1913), p. 211.
56. Brands, *T.R.: The Last Romantic*, p. 292.
57. Morris, *The Rise of Theodore Roosevelt*, p. 200.
58. Brands, *T.R.: The Last Romantic*, p. 154.
59. Ibid., p. 158.
60. Dalton, *Theodore Roosevelt: A Strenuous Life*, p. 98.
61. Brands, *T.R.: The Last Romantic*, p. 156.
62. Ibid., p. 157.
63. Dalton, *Theodore Roosevelt: A Strenuous Life*, p. 102.
64. Brands, *T.R.: The Last Romantic*, p. 210.
65. Morris, *The Rise of Theodore Roosevelt*, p. 372.
66. Ibid., p. 374.
67. Roosevelt, *An Autobiography*, p. 185.
68. Ibid., p. 70.
69. Thomas Hobbes, *Leviathan*, chapter XIII, "Of the Natural Condition of Mankind as Concerning their Felicity and Misery" (1651).
70. See, for example, T. S. Ashton, *The Industrial Revolution, 1760–1830* (London: Oxford University Press, 1948); John U. Nef, *War and Human Progress: An Essay on the Rise of Industrial Civilization* (Chicago: University of Chicago Press, 1950); F. A. Hayek, ed., *Capitalism and the Historians* (Chicago: University of Chicago Press, 1954); William H. McNeill, *The Rise of the West* (Chicago: University of Chicago Press, 1963); David S. Landes, *The Unbound Prometheus: Technological Change and Industrial Development in Western Europe from 1750 to the Present* (New York: Cambridge University Press, 1969); Douglass C. North and Robert Paul Thomas, *The Rise of the Western World: A New Economic History* (Cambridge: Cambridge University Press, 1973); Fernand Braudel, *Civilization and Capitalism*, vol. 2 (New York, Harper & Row, 1982); Julian L. Simon, *The Ultimate Resource* (Princeton: Princeton University Press, 1981); J. M. Roberts, *The*

Triumph of the West (New York: Little, Brown, 1985); Nathan Rosenberg and L. E. Birdzell Jr., *How the West Grew Rich* (New York: Basic Books, 1986); Rondo Cameron, *A Concise Economic History of the World* (New York: Oxford University Press, 1989); and Joel Mokyr, *The Lever of Riches: Technological Creativity and Economic Progress* (New York: Oxford University Press, 1990).

71. *Historical Statistics of the United States, Colonial Times to 1970* (Washington, DC: Bureau of the Census, 1975), part 1, p. 105.

72. Jacob Riis, *How the Other Half Lives: Studies Among the Tenements of New York* (New York), ch. 1, "Genesis of the Tenement."

73. Jacob Riis, *Theodore Roosevelt: The Citizen* (New York: Outlook Company, 1904), p. 116.

74. Roosevelt, *An Autobiography*, p. 187.

75. Riis, *Theodore Roosevelt: The Citizen*, p. 57.

76. Herbert Spencer, *The Man Versus the State* (1892; repr., Caldwell, ID: Caxton Press, 1940), p. 91. Decades later in the United States, federal urban renewal programs destroyed low-income housing without replacing much of it, thereby displacing large numbers of poor people. See, for example, Martin Anderson, *The Federal Bulldozer: A Critical Analysis of Urban Renewal, 1949–1962* (Cambridge: MIT Press, 1964).

77. Brands, *T.R.: The Last Romantic*, p. 275.

78. Riis, *Theodore Roosevelt: The Citizen*, p. 48.

79. Henry Adams, *The Education of Henry Adams* (1907; repr., Boston: Houghton Mifflin, 2000), pp. 418, 417.

CHAPTER TWO

1. Theodore Roosevelt, address at the Naval War College, June 2, 1897.

2. Ralph Barton Perry, *The Thought and Character of William James* (Boston: Little, Brown, 1936), p. 246.

3. Theodore Roosevelt, *The Strenuous Life* (New York: Century, 1901), p. 16.

4. Carl Schurz, letter to James Pryor, September 1904, in Carl Schurz, *Speeches, Correspondence and Political Papers* (New York: Putnam, 1913), pp. 397–399.

5. Theodore Roosevelt, letter to Henry Cabot Lodge, October 20, 1899, in *Selections from the Correspondence of Theodore Roosevelt and Henry Cabot Lodge, 1884–1918*, vol. 1 (New York: Scribner, 1925), p. 422.

6. Warren Zimmerman, *First Great Triumph: How Five Americans Made Their Country a World Power* (New York: Farrar, Straus and Giroux, 2002), pp. 28, 29.

7. Cited ibid., p. 32.

8. Quoted ibid., p. 24.

9. *Historical Statistics of the United States, Colonial Times to 1970* (Washington, DC: Bureau of the Census, 1975), part 1, p. 224 (estimated U.S. gross national product); part 2, p. 903 (value of exports).

10. *Historical Statistics of the United States, Colonial Times to 1970*, part 2, pp. 903, 904.

11. Walter A. McDougall, *Promised Land, Crusader State: The American Encounter with the World Since 1776* (Boston: Houghton Mifflin, 1997), p. 106.

12. Alden Hatch, *The Lodges of Massachusetts* (New York: Hawthorn Books, 1973), p. 32.

13. Ibid., p. 33.

14. William C. Widenor, *Henry Cabot Lodge and the Search for an American Foreign Policy* (Berkeley: University of California Press, 1980), p. 19.
15. Robert Endicott Osgood, *Ideals and Self-Interest in America's Foreign Relations* (Chicago: University of Chicago Press, 1953), p. 31.
16. David McCullough, *The Path Between the Seas: The Creation of the Panama Canal, 1870–1914* (New York: Simon & Schuster, 1977), p. 250.
17. Robert Seager II, *Alfred Thayer Mahan: The Man and His Letters* (Annapolis: Naval Institute Press, 1977), p. 131.
18. Ibid., p. 134.
19. Ibid., p. 141.
20. Warren Zimmerman, *First Great Triumph*, p. 89.
21. Richard W. Turk, *The Ambiguous Relationship: Theodore Roosevelt and Alfred Thayer Mahan* (Westport, CT: Greenwood Press, 1987), p. 15.
22. Ibid., p. 11.
23. Roosevelt to Mahan, May 12, 1890, quoted ibid., p. 22.
24. Zimmerman, *First Great Triumph*, pp. 100, 101.
25. Seager, *Alfred Thayer Mahan*, p. 214.
26. Ibid., p. 215.
27. Ibid., p. 216.
28. Turk, *The Ambiguous Relationship*, p. 16.
29. Seager, *Alfred Thayer Mahan*, p. 248.
30. Quoted ibid., p. 249.
31. Seager, *Alfred Thayer Mahan*, p. 250.
32. Ibid., p. 256.
33. Ibid., pp. 279, 281.
34. Ibid., p. 280.
35. Robert McElroy, *Grover Cleveland: The Man and Statesman*, vol. 2 (New York: Harper & Brothers, 1923), p. 46.
36. Ibid.
37. Ibid., p. 47.
38. Quoted ibid.
39. Ibid., pp. 47, 48.
40. Gavan Davis, *Shoal of Time: A History of the Hawaiian Islands* (Honolulu: University Press of Hawaii, 1968), p. 271.
41. Alyn Brodsky, *Grover Cleveland: A Study in Character* (New York: Truman Talley Books, 2000), p. 299.
42. Ibid., p. 300.
43. Ibid., p. 299.
44. Ibid., p. 300.
45. Ibid., p. 299.
46. Ibid., pp. 300, 301.
47. Quoted ibid., p. 303.
48. Walter LaFeber, *The New Empire: An Interpretation of American Expansion, 1860–1898* (Ithaca: Cornell University Press, 1998), p. 205.
49. Zimmerman, *First Great Triumph*, p. 150.
50. Walter Karp, *The Politics of War: The Story of Two Wars Which Altered Forever the Political Life of the American Republic, 1890–1920* (New York: Harper & Row, 1979), p. 67.

51. Quoted in H. Wayne Morgan, *William McKinley and His America* (Syracuse: Syracuse University Press, 1963), p. 34.
52. Quoted in Karp, *The Politics of War*, p. 66.
53. Kevin Phillips, *William McKinley* (New York: Times Books, 2003), p. 93.
54. Ibid.
55. William Henry Harbaugh, *Power and Responsibility: The Life and Times of Theodore Roosevelt* (New York: Farrar, Straus & Cudahy, 1961), p. 94.
56. Quoted in Karp, *The Politics of War*, p. 77.
57. Edmund Morris, *The Rise of Theodore Roosevelt* (New York: Coward, McCann & Geoghegan, 1979), p. 568.
58. Quoted ibid., p. 569.
59. Karp, *The Politics of War*, p. 78.
60. Ibid., p. 79.
61. Ibid., p. 83.
62. Ibid., p. 83.
63. Quoted ibid., p. 84.
64. Quoted in Walter Millis, *The Martial Spirit: A Study of Our War with Spain* (New York: Viking, 1965), p. 105.
65. Millis, *The Martial Spirit*, p. 109.
66. Ibid., p. 110.
67. Quoted in W. A. Swanberg, *Citizen Hearst: A Biography of William Randolph Hearst* (New York: Scribner, 1961), pp. 107, 108.
68. Quoted ibid., p. 137.
69. Quoted ibid., p. 138.
70. Quoted ibid.
71. Quoted ibid., p. 135.
72. Quoted in H. W. Brands, *T.R.: The Last Romantic* (New York: Basic Books, 1997), p. 324.
73. Quoted in Harbaugh, *Power and Responsibility*, p. 96.
74. Quoted in Brands, *T.R.: The Last Romantic*, p. 327.
75. Quoted in Brands, *T.R.: The Last Romantic*, p. 328.
76. W. A. Swanberg, *Citizen Hearst*, p. 144.
77. Brian McAllister Linn, *The Philippine War, 1899–1902* (Lawrence: University Press of Kansas, 2000), p. 8.
78. Ibid., p. 6.
79. Karp, *The Politics of War*, p. 98.
80. Linn, *The Philippine War, 1899–1902*, p. 5.
81. Quoted ibid.
82. Quoted in Karp, *The Politics of War*, p. 101.
83. Zimmerman, *First Great Triumph*, p. 309.
84. Ibid., p. 307.
85. Ibid.
86. Linn, *The Philippine War, 1899–1902*, p. 14.
87. Ibid., p. 325.
88. David Haward Bain, *Sitting in Darkness: Americans in the Philippines* (Boston: Houghton Mifflin, 1984), p. 93.
89. Linn, *The Philippine War, 1899–1902*, pp. 186, 187.
90. Quoted in Brands, *T.R.: The Last Romantic*, p. 333.
91. Brands, *T.R.: The Last Romantic*, p. 337.

92. Quoted ibid., p. 340.
93. Zimmerman, *First Great Triumph*, pp. 296, 298.
94. Millis, *The Martial Spirit*, p. 293.
95. Quoted in Brands, *T.R.: The Last Romantic*, p. 360.
96. Zimmerman, *First Great Triumph*, p. 297.
97. Ibid., p. 298.
98. Ibid., p. 314.
99. Quoted in Brodsky, *Grover Cleveland: A Study in Character*, p. 303.
100. Quoted ibid.
101. Stanley Karnow, *In Our Image: America's Empire in the Philippines* (New York: Random House, 1989), p. 136.
102. Quoted ibid.
103. October 16, 1900, interview, in Frederick Anderson, ed., *A Pen Warmed-Up in Hell: Mark Twain in Protest* (New York: Perennial Library, 1972), p. 10.
104. "The War-Prayer," ibid., p. 111.
105. "The Conquest of the United States by Spain," in *War and Other Essays by William Graham Sumner*, ed. Albert Galloway Keller (New Haven: Yale University Press, 1914), pp. 323–325.
106. Karnow, *In Our Image*, p. 138.
107. Brands, *T.R.: The Last Romantic*, p. 376.
108. McCullough, *The Path Between the Seas*, pp. 246, 247.
109. Quoted in Brands, *T.R.: The Last Romantic*, p. 386.
110. Quoted ibid.
111. Quoted in Bain, *Sitting in Darkness*, p. 88.
112. Linn, *The Philippine War, 1899–1902*, p. 7.
113. Ibid., p. 325.
114. Ibid., p. 323.
115. Ibid., p. 206.
116. Quoted ibid., p. 212.
117. Linn, *The Philippine War, 1899–1902*, p. 213.
118. Quoted ibid., p. 223.
119. Quoted in Bain, *Sitting in Darkness*, pp. 88, 89.
120. Quoted ibid., p. 88.
121. Karp, *The Politics of War*, p. 111.
122. Samuel Flagg Bemis, *The Latin American Policy of the United States: An Historical Perspective* (New York: Harcourt, Brace, 1943), p. 146.
123. Harbaugh, *Power and Responsibility*, p. 191.
124. Ibid., p. 192.
125. Quoted in Bemis, *The Latin American Policy of the United States*, p. 147.
126. Bemis, *The Latin American Policy of the United States*, p. 148.
127. Quoted in Harbaugh, *Power and Responsibility*, p. 194.
128. Bemis, *The Latin American Policy of the United States*, p. 155.
129. Harbaugh, *Power and Responsibility*, p. 196.
130. Quoted in John Morton Blum, *The Republican Roosevelt* (Cambridge: Harvard University Press, 1977), p. 136.
131. Bemis, *The Latin American Policy of the United States*, p. 149.
132. Harbaugh, *Power and Responsibility*, p. 199.
133. Quoted ibid.
134. McCullough, *The Path Between the Seas*, p. 255.

135. Ibid., p. 266.
136. Ibid., p. 326.
137. Ibid., p. 269.
138. Quoted ibid., p. 334.
139. Quoted ibid.
140. Quoted ibid., p. 338.
141. McCullough, *The Path Between the Seas*, p. 336.
142. Quoted ibid., p. 354.
143. McCullough, *The Path Between the Seas*, p. 356.
144. Quoted ibid., p. 381.
145. Quoted ibid., p. 383.
146. Quoted ibid.
147. Theodore Roosevelt, *An Autobiography* (New York: Macmillan, 1913), p. 564.
148. Bemis, *The Latin American Policy of the United States*, p. 151.

CHAPTER THREE

1. Theodore Roosevelt, *An Autobiography* (New York: Macmillan, 1913), p. 462.
2. Ibid.
3. Ibid.
4. Ibid., p. 463.
5. Ibid.
6. Ibid.
7. Ibid.
8. John Morton Blum, *The Republican Roosevelt* (Cambridge: Harvard University Press, 1977), p. 76.
9. *Historical Statistics of the United States, Colonial Times to 1970* (Washington, DC: Bureau of the Census, 1975), part 1, p. 14.
10. Ibid.
11. Ibid., p. 224.
12. *Historical Statistics of the United States, Colonial Times to 1970* (Washington, DC: Bureau of the Census, 1975), part 2, pp. 693, 694.
13. *Historical Statistics of the United States, Colonial Times to 1970*, part 1, p. 588.
14. *Historical Statistics of the United States, Colonial Times to 1970*, part 2, p. 690.
15. Ibid., p. 699.
16. Ibid.
17. Ibid., p. 958.
18. Rothschild Peterson Patent Model Museum, www.patentmodel.org/history.html.
19. Ernest L. Bogart and Donald L. Kemmerer, *Economic History of the American People* (New York: Longmans, Green, 1942), p. 542.
20. Harper Leech and John Charles Carroll, *Armour and His Times* (New York: D. Appleton-Century, 1938), p. 121.
21. Gabriel Kolko, *Main Currents in Modern American History* (New York: Harper & Row, 1976), p. 4.
22. Stuart Bruchey, *Enterprise: The Dynamic Economy of a Free People* (Cambridge: Harvard University Press, 1990), pp. 339–343, 345–348.
23. Joy Hakim, *Freedom: A History of US* (New York: Oxford University Press, 2003), pp. 212–216.

24. Stanley Lebergott, *The Americans: An Economic Record* (New York: Norton, 1984), p. 324.
25. Ibid., p. 328.
26. Ibid., p. 305.
27. Douglass C. North, *Growth and Welfare in the American Past* (Englewood Cliffs, NJ: Prentice-Hall, 1966), p. 111.
28. George J. Stigler, "The Origin of the Sherman Act," *Journal of Legal Studies*, January 1985, p. 2.
29. North, *Growth and Welfare in the American Past*, p. 109.
30. Bogart and Kemmerer, *Economic History of the American People*, pp. 549, 550.
31. *Historical Statistics of the United States, Colonial Times to 1970*, part 2, p. 912.
32. Phillip Areeda, *Antitrust Cases: Problems, Text, Cases* (Boston: Little, Brown, 1981), p. 48.
33. A. D. Neale, *The Antitrust Laws of the U.S.A.* (Cambridge, Eng.: Cambridge University Press, 1970), p. 12.
34. Sanford D. Gordon, "Attitudes Toward Trusts Prior to the Sherman Act," *Southern Economic Journal*, October 1963, p. 158.
35. Thomas J. DiLorenzo, "The Origins of Antitrust: An Interest-Group Perspective," *International Review of Law and Economics*, June 1985, p. 76.
36. Bruchey, *Enterprise*, p. 336.
37. Henry Demarest Lloyd, *Wealth Against Commonwealth* (New York: Harper, 1898), p. 1.
38. "Mr. Sherman's Hopes and Fears," *New York Times*, October 1, 1890, p. 2
39. Frank W. Taussig, *The Tariff History of the United States* (New York: Putnam, 1931), p. 259.
40. Ibid., p. 268.
41. Randolph Paul, *Taxation in the United States* (Boston: Little, Brown, 1954), p. 31.
42. John Sherman, *Recollections of Forty Years*, vol. 2 (Chicago: Werner Company, 1895), p. 1083.
43. Blum, *The Republican Roosevelt*, p. 77.
44. Quoted in Earl Kintner, *The Legislative History of the Federal Antitrust Laws and Related Statutes* (New York: Chelsea House, 1978), p. 245.
45. Quoted ibid., p. 271.
46. Quoted in DiLorenzo, "The Origins of Antitrust," p. 82.
47. Christopher Grandy, "Original Intent and the Sherman Antitrust Act: A Re-Examination of the Consumer-Welfare Hypothesis," *Journal of Economic History*, June 1993, pp. 369, 370.
48. DiLorenzo, "The Origins of Antitrust," pp. 79, 80.
49. Ibid., p. 80.
50. Thomas W. Hazlett, "The Legislative History of the Sherman Act Re-examined," *Economic Inquiry*, April 1992, p. 11.
51. "Mr. Sherman's Hopes and Fears."
52. Franklin Pierce, *The Tariff and the Trusts* (New York: Macmillan, 1913), pp. 51, 52.
53. George Bittlingmayer, "Antitrust and Business Activity," *Business History Review*, Autumn 1996, p. 29.
54. Willard L. King, *Melville Weston Fuller, Chief Justice of the United States, 1888–1910* (New York: Macmillan, 1950), p. 111.
55. *United States v. E. C. Knight Co.*, 156 U.S. 1 (1895).

56. Ibid.

57. Dominick T. Armentano, *Antitrust and Monopoly: Anatomy of a Policy Failure* (New York: Holmes & Meier, 1990), p. 51.

58. Ralph L. Nelson, *Merger Movements in American History, 1895–1956* (Princeton: Princeton University Press, 1959), pp. 154–162.

59. Arthur D. Dewing, *Corporate Promotions and Reorganizations* (Cambridge: Harvard University Press, 1914), pp. 225, 268, 304, 411, 463, 549.

60. Gabriel Kolko, *The Triumph of Conservatism: A Reinterpretation of American History, 1900–1916* (Chicago: Quadrangle, 1963), pp. 24, 25.

61. Bittlingmayer, "Antitrust and Business Activity," p. 29.

62. Albro Martin, *James J. Hill and the Opening of the Northwest* (New York: Oxford University Press, 1976), p. 37.

63. Ibid., p. 54.

64. Ibid., p. 71.

65. Ibid., pp. 91, 92.

66. Ibid., p. 92.

67. Ibid., p. 116.

68. Ibid., p. 119.

69. Ibid., p. 228.

70. Ibid., p. 97.

71. Ibid., p. 190.

72. Ibid., p. 192.

73. Ibid., p. 207.

74. Ibid., p. 197.

75. Ibid., p. 226.

76. Ibid., p. 285.

77. Ibid., p. 324.

78. Ibid., p. 270.

79. Ibid., p. 239.

80. Ibid., p. 265.

81. Ibid., p. 247.

82. Ibid., p. 287.

83. Ibid., pp. 229, 278.

84. Ibid., p. 431.

85. Ibid., p. 227.

86. Quoted ibid., p. 300.

87. Martin, *James J. Hill and the Opening of the Northwest*, p. 390.

88. Quoted ibid.

89. Martin, *James J. Hill and the Opening of the Northwest*, p. 396.

90. Ibid., p. 414.

91. Ibid., p. 415.

92. Ibid., p. 411.

93. Ibid., p. 440.

94. Quoted ibid., p. 411.

95. Martin, *James J. Hill and the Opening of the Northwest*, p. 425.

96. Ibid., p. 441.

97. Ibid., p. 444.

98. Ibid., p. 445.

99. Maury Klein, *The Life and Legend of E. H. Harriman* (Chapel Hill: University of North Carolina Press, 2000), p. xiii.
100. Maury Klein, *Union Pacific: The Rebirth, 1894–1969* (New York: Doubleday, 1989), p. 13.
101. Ibid., p. 15.
102. Ibid., p. 13.
103. Ibid., p. 22.
104. Ibid., p. 24.
105. Klein, *The Life and Legend of E. H. Harriman*, p. 225.
106. Ibid., p. 238.
107. Ibid., p. 241.
108. Edmund Morris, *Theodore Rex* (New York: Random House, 2001), p. 59.
109. H. W. Brands, *T.R.: The Last Romantic* (New York: Basic Books, 1996), p. 439.
110. Ibid., p. 436.
111. Quoted in Morris, *Theodore Rex*, p. 139.
112. Bittlingmayer, "Antitrust and Business Activity," p. 10.
113. *Northern Securities Co. v. United States*, 193 U.S. 197 (1904).
114. Ibid.
115. Ibid.
116. Ibid.
117. Ibid.
118. Holmes to Frederick Pollock, February 9, 1921, in Mark DeWolfe Howe, ed., *Holmes-Pollock Letters: The Correspondence of Mr. Justice Holmes and Sir Frederick Pollock, 1874–1932*, vol. 2 (Cambridge: Harvard University Press, 1946), pp. 63, 64.
119. Taussig, *The Tariff History of the United States*, pp. 174–75.
120. Henry George, *Protection or Free Trade* (1886; repr., New York: Robert Schalkenbach Foundation, 1980), p. 169.
121. Henry F. Pringle, *Theodore Roosevelt: A Biography* (New York: Harcourt, Brace, 1931), p. 433.
122. Ibid., p. 434.
123. Milton Friedman and Anna Jacobson Schwartz, *A Monetary History of the United States, 1867–1960* (Princeton: Princeton University Press, 1963), p. 158.
124. Pringle, *Theodore Roosevelt: A Biography*, p. 439.
125. Friedman and Schwartz, *A Monetary History of the United States*, p. 160.
126. Pringle, *Theodore Roosevelt: A Biography*, p. 435.
127. Ibid., p. 442.
128. Ibid., p. 445.
129. Ibid., p. 445.
130. *Standard Oil Co. of New Jersey v. United States*, 223 U.S. 1 (1910).
131. Quoted in Daniel Yergin, *The Prize: The Epic Quest for Oil, Money and Power* (New York: Simon & Schuster, 1991), p. 108.
132. Dominick T. Armentano, *The Myths of Antitrust: Economic Theory and Legal Cases* (New Rochelle, NY: Arlington House, 1972), pp. 77, 78.
133. Ibid., p. 83.
134. Ida M. Tarbell, *The History of Standard Oil*, vol. 1 (1904; repr., New York: Macmillan, 1925), pp. 43, 44.
135. Armentano, *The Myths of Antitrust*, p. 66.

136. Ibid., p. 67.
137. Tarbell, *The History of Standard Oil*, vol. 1, p. 46.
138. Ibid., p. 48.
139. Ibid., p. 49.
140. Ibid., p. 49.
141. Ron Chernow, *Titan: The Life of John D. Rockefeller, Sr.* (New York: Random House, 1998), p. 113.
142. Ibid., p. 116.
143. Tarbell, *The History of Standard Oil*, vol. 1, p. 61; Chernow, *Titan*, pp. 135, 136.
144. Tarbell, *The History of Standard Oil*, vol. 1, p. 102.
145. Ibid., p. 97.
146. Ibid.
147. Ibid., p. 102.
148. Tarbell, *The History of Standard Oil*, vol. 2 (repr., New York: Macmillan, 1925), p. 231.
149. Tarbell, *The History of Standard Oil*, vol. 1, p. 212.
150. Ibid.
151. Ibid., p. 210.
152. Tarbell, *The History of Standard Oil*, vol. 2, pp. 256, 257.
153. Armentano, *The Myths of Antitrust*, p. 68.
154. Ibid., p. 70.
155. Tarbell, *The History of Standard Oil*, vol. 1, p. 51.
156. Armentano, *The Myths of Antitrust*, p. 75.
157. John S. McGee, "Predatory Price Cutting: The Standard Oil Case," *Journal of Law and Economics*, October 1958, p. 146.
158. Ibid.
159. Ibid., p. 147.
160. Ibid.
161. Ida M. Tarbell, *All in A Day's Work: The Autobiography of the Foremost Muckraker of Her Time* (1939; repr. Boston: G. K. Hall, 1985), p. 233.
162. Quoted in Chernow, *Titan*, p. 264.
163. Randall Mariger, "Predatory Price Cutting: The Standard Oil of New Jersey Case, Revisited," *Explorations in Economic History*, March 1978, pp. 341–367.
164. Armentano, *The Myths of Antitrust*, p. 75.
165. Ibid., p. 76.
166. Ibid.
167. Ibid., p. 77.
168. Ibid.
169. Ibid., p. 77.
170. Tarbell, *The History of Standard Oil*, vol. 1, p. 209.
171. Armentano, *The Myths of Antitrust*, p. 78.
172. Sunoco website: www.sunocoinc.com/aboutsunoco/sunhistoryf.htm.
173. Unocal website: www.unocal.com/aboutucl/history/.
174. Armentano, *The Myths of Antitrust*, p. 78.
175. Ralph W. Hidy and Muriel E. Hidy, *Pioneering in Big Business: History of the Standard Oil Company (New Jersey), 1882–1911* (New York: Harper & Brothers, 1955), p. 296.
176. Ibid., p. 355.
177. Ibid., p. 267.

178. Kathleen Brady, *Ida Tarbell: Portrait of a Muckraker* (Pittsburgh: University of Pittsburgh Press, 1984), p. 153.

179. Chernow, *Titan*, p. 462.

180. Ibid., pp. 6, 7, 9, 10, 16, 37, 42, 43.

181. Henry Pringle, *William Howard Taft: The Life and Times*, vol. 2 (Newtown, CT: American Political Biography Press, 1998), p. 660.

182. *Standard Oil Co. of New Jersey v. United States*, 223 U.S. 1 (1910).

183. *United States v. Standard Oil Co.*, 173 F.179 (1909).

184. *Standard Oil Co. of New Jersey v. United States*, 223 U.S. 1 (1910).

185. Ibid.

186. Yergin, *The Prize*, p. 110.

187. Louis Galambos and Joseph C. Pratt, *The Rise of the Corporate Commonwealth: U.S. Business and Public Policy in the Twentieth Century* (New York: Basic Books, 1988), p. 2.

CHAPTER FOUR

1. *Historical Statistics of the United States, Colonial Times to 1970* (Washington, DC: Bureau of the Census, 1975), part 2, p. 740.

2. Ibid., p. 728.

3. Ibid., p. 735.

4. Robert W. Fogel, *Railroads and American Economic Growth: Essays in Econometric History* (Baltimore: Johns Hopkins University Press, 1964), p. 211.

5. Ibid., pp. 219–220.

6. Ibid., p. 4.

7. Ibid., p. 80.

8. Albro Martin, *Enterprise Denied: Origins of the Decline of American Railroads, 1897–1917* (New York: Columbia University Press, 1971), p. 151.

9. Nathan Miller, *Theodore Roosevelt: A Life* (New York: William Morrow, 1992), p. 456.

10. Edmund Morris, *Theodore Rex* (New York: Random House, 2001), p. 433.

11. Ibid., p. 447.

12. Clifford F. Theis, "The American Railroad Network During the Early Nineteenth Century: Private Versus Public Enterprise," *Cato Journal*, Fall 2002, p. 233.

13. Ernest L. Bogart and Donald L. Kemmerer, *Economic History of the American People* (New York: Longmans, Green, 1942), p. 321.

14. Ibid., p. 321.

15. Thies, "The American Railroad Network," p. 234.

16. Bogart and Kemmerer, *Economic History of the American People*, p. 326.

17. Ibid., p. 324; Theis, "The American Railroad Network," p. 234.

18. Theis, ibid., pp. 234, 235.

19. Ibid., pp. 233, 234.

20. Ibid., p. 233.

21. Ibid., p. 234.

22. Bogart and Kemmerer, *Economic History of the American People*, p. 325.

23. Ibid., p. 326.

24. Ibid., p. 326.

25. George H. Miller, *Railroads and the Granger Laws* (Madison: University of Wisconsin Press, 1971), p. 50.

26. Albro Martin, *Railroads Triumphant: The Growth, Rejection, and Rebirth of a Vital American Force* (New York: Oxford University Press, 1992), p. 16.

27. Ibid.

28. Bogart and Kemmerer, *Economic History of the American People*, p. 327.

29. Thies, "The American Railroad Network," p. 237.

30. Ibid.

31. Ibid., p. 230.

32. Miller, *Railroads and the Granger Laws*, p. 51.

33. Arthur Grinath III, John Joseph Wallis, and Richard E. Sylla, "Debt, Default and Revenue Structure: The American State Debt Crisis in the Early 1840s," National Bureau of Economic Research, *NBER Historical Working Paper No. 97*, March 1997, p. 3.

34. Quoted in Miller, *Railroads and the Granger Laws*, p. 54.

35. David Haward Bain, *Empire Express: Building the First Transcontinental Railroad* (New York: Viking, 1999), p. 704.

36. Justin Kaplan, *Mr. Clemens and Mark Twain* (New York: Simon & Schuster, 1966), p. 162.

37. Bain, *Empire Express*, p. 695.

38. Stanley Lebergott, *The Americans: An Economic Record* (New York: Norton, 1984), p. 277.

39. Hugo Richard Meyer, *Government Regulation of Railway Rates: A Study of the Experience of the United States, Germany, France, Austria-Hungary, Russia, and Australia* (New York: Macmillan, 1905), pp. 216, 217.

40. *Historical Statistics of the United States, Colonial Times to 1970*, part 2, pp. 728, 731.

41. Jean Strouse, *Morgan: American Financier* (New York: Random House, 1999), p. 256.

42. Miller, *Railroads and the Granger Laws*, p. 15.

43. Ibid., p. 11.

44. Ibid., p. 13.

45. Fogel, *Railroads and American Economic Growth*, p. 51.

46. Ibid., p. 24.

47. Ibid., pp. 80, 81.

48. Ibid., p. 49.

49. Harold F. Williamson and Arnold R. Daum, *The American Petroleum Industry: The Age of Illumination, 1859–1899* (Evanston: Northwestern University Press, 1959), p. 345.

50. Stanley Lebergott, *The Americans: An Economic Record* (New York: Norton, 1984), p. 284.

51. Ibid., pp. 286, 287.

52. Paul W. MacAvoy, *The Economic Effects of Regulation: The Trunk-Line Railroad Cartels and the Interstate Commerce Commission Before 1900* (Cambridge: MIT Press, 1965), p. 41.

53. Quoted ibid., p. 51.

54. John M. Peterson and Ralph Gray, *Economic Development of the United States* (Homewood, IL: Irwin, 1969), p. 266.

55. Miller, *Railroads and the Granger Laws*, p. 34.

56. Ibid., p. 38.

57. Ibid., p. 35.

58. Ibid., p. 36.
59. Ibid., p. 39.
60. Ibid., p. 100.
61. Werner Troesken, "The Letters of John Sherman and the Origins of Antitrust," *Review of Austrian Economics*, vol. 15, no. 4 (2002), p. 279.
62. Ibid., 280.
63. Lebergott, *The Americans*, p. 290.
64. Hepburn Committee testimony in Alfred D. Chandler and Stuart Bruchy, eds., *Railroads: America's First Big Business: Sources and Readings* (Manchester, NH: Harcourt, Brace & World, 1981), p. 171.
65. John F. Stover, *The Life and Decline of the American Railroad* (New York: Oxford University Press, 1970), p. 91.
66. Miller, *Railroads and the Granger Laws*, p. 162.
67. *Munn v. Illinois*, 94 U.S. 113 (1877).
68. *Wabash, St. Louis & Pacific Railway Co. v. Illinois*, 118 U.S. 557 (1886).
69. *Historical Statistics of the United States, Colonial Times to 1970* (Washington, DC: Bureau of the Census, 1975), part 1, p. 458.
70. Meyer, *Government Regulation of Railway Rates*, p. 218.
71. Miller, *Railroads and the Granger Laws*, p. 17.
72. Ibid.
73. Gabriel Kolko, *Railroads and Regulation, 1877–1916* (New York: Norton, 1965), pp. 30–45.
74. MacAvoy, *The Economic Effects of Regulation*, p. 118.
75. Lebergott, *The Americans*, p. 294.
76. MacAvoy, *The Economic Effects of Regulation*, pp. v, 201.
77. *Chicago, Milwaukee & St. Paul Railway Co. v. Minnesota*, 134 U.S. 418 (1890).
78. Meyer, *Government Regulation of Railway Rates*, pp. 415, 416.
79. Ibid., pp. 450, 451.
80. John Morton Blum, *The Republican Roosevelt*, 2nd ed. (Cambridge: Harvard University Press, 1977), pp. 74–75.
81. Morris, *Theodore Rex*, p. 360.
82. Martin, *Enterprise Denied*, p. 85.
83. Milton Friedman and Anna Jacobson Schwartz, *A Monetary History of the United States, 1867–1960* (Princeton: Princeton University Press, 1963), p. 135.
84. Albro Martin, *Enterprise Denied*, p. 39.
85. Quoted in Blum, *The Republican Roosevelt*, p. 80.
86. Martin, *Enterprise Denied*, p. 146.
87. I. Leo Sharfman, *The American Railroad Problem: A Study in War and Reconstruction* (New York: Century, 1921), p. 50.
88. Miller, *Theodore Roosevelt: A Life*, p. 457.
89. Quoted ibid., p. 459.
90. Martin, *Enterprise Denied*, p. 57.
91. Ibid.
92. Ibid.
93. Ibid., p. 58.
94. Ibid., p. 124.
95. Friedman and Schwartz, *A Monetary History of the United States*, p. 135.
96. Sharfman, *The American Railroad Problem*, p. 41.
97. Martin, *Enterprise Denied*, p. 130.

98. Ibid., p. 135.
99. Ibid., p. 133.
100. Ibid.
101. Ibid., p. 134.
102. Ibid., p. 146.
103. Ibid., p. 184.
104. Meyer, *Government Regulation of Railway Rates.*
105. Hugo Richard Meyer, *Municipal Ownership in Great Britain* (New York: Macmillan, 1906).
106. Hugo Richard Meyer, *The British State Telegraphs: A Study of the Problem of a Large Body of Civil Servants in a Democracy* (New York: Macmillan, 1907).
107. Martin, *Enterprise Denied*, p. 141.
108. Ibid., pp. 140, 141.
109. Ibid., p. 141.
110. Ibid.
111. Ibid., p. 187.
112. Ibid., p. 190.
113. Ibid., p. 144.
114. Ibid., p. 145.
115. Ibid., p. 354.
116. Ibid., p. 354.
117. John F. Stover, *The Life and Decline of the American Railroad* (New York: Oxford University Press, 1970), p. 173.
118. Martin, *Enterprise Denied*, p. 283.
119. Ibid., p. 33.
120. Ibid., p. 361.
121. Ibid., p. 363.

CHAPTER FIVE

1. Theodore Roosevelt, State of the Union message, December 3, 1906.
2. Michael R. Haines, "Estimated Life Tables for the United States, 1850–1900," National Bureau of Economic Research, *NBER Historical Working Paper No. 59*, September 1994, p. 2.
3. Ibid., Table 1.
4. Clayton A. Coppin and Jack High, *The Politics of Purity: Harvey Washington Wiley and the Origins of Federal Food Policy* (Ann Arbor: University of Michigan Press, 1999), p. 31.
5. *Historical Statistics of the United States, Colonial Times to 1970* (Washington, DC: Bureau of the Census, 1975), part 1, p. 58.
6. Judith Walzer Leavitt, *Typhoid Mary: Captive to the Public's Health* (Boston: Beacon Press, 1996).
7. Quoted in Gustavus A. Weber, *The Food, Drug, and Insecticide Administration: Its History, Activities and Organization* (Baltimore: Johns Hopkins University Press, 1928), p. 10.
8. Maguelonne Toussaint-Samat, *A History of Food* (Cambridge: Blackwell, 1992), p. 738.
9. Ibid., p. 737.

10. Ibid., p. 739.
11. Reay Tannehill, *Food in History* (New York: Stein & Day, 1973), pp. 356, 357.
12. James Trager, *The Enriched, Fortified, Concentrated, Country-Fresh, Lip-Smacking, Finger-Licking, International, Unexpurgated Food Book* (New York: Grossman, 1970), pp. 406, 407.
13. Coppin and High, *The Politics of Purity*, p. 20.
14. Harper Leech and John Charles Carroll, *Armour and His Times* (New York: D. Appleton-Century, 1938), p. 51.
15. Douglas Collins, *America's Favorite Food: The Story of the Campbell Soup Company* (New York: Abrams, 1994), p. 30.
16. Ibid., p. 66.
17. Robert C. Alberts, *The Good Provider: H. J. Heinz and His 57 Varieties* (Boston: Houghton Mifflin, 1973), p. 7.
18. Toussaint-Samat, *A History of Food*, p. 750.
19. Ibid., p. 751.
20. S. F. Riepma, *The Story of Margarine* (Washington, DC: Public Affairs Press, 1970), pp. 108, 109.
21. Ibid., p. 110.
22. Coppin and High, *The Politics of Purity*, p. 26.
23. Ibid., p. 21.
24. Leech and Carroll, *Armour and His Times*, pp. 3, 7.
25. Ibid., p. 7.
26. Ibid., p. 10.
27. See Gavin Weightman, *The Frozen Water Trade* (New York: Hyperion, 2003).
28. Leech and Carroll, *Armour and His Times*, p. 126.
29. Mary Yeager, *Competition and Regulation: The Development of Oligopoly in the Meat Industry* (Greenwich, CT: Jai Press, 1981), p. 54.
30. Leech and Carroll, *Armour and His Times*, p. 129.
31. Jimmy M. Skaggs, *Prime Cut: Livestock Raising and Meatpacking in the United States, 1607–1983* (College Station: Texas A & M University Press, 1986), p. 93.
32. Ibid., p. 94.
33. Leech and Carroll, *Armour and His Times*, p. 57.
34. Ibid., p. 129.
35. Quoted ibid., p. 46.
36. Carolyn Dimitri, "Agricultural Marketing Institutions: A Response to Quality Disputes," *Journal of Agricultural and Food Industrial Organization*, vol. 1 (2003), p. 7.
37. Gary Libecap, "The Rise of the Chicago Packers and the Origins of Meat Inspection and Antitrust," *Economic Inquiry*, April 1992, p. 250.
38. Leech and Carroll, *Armour and His Times*, p. 169.
39. Libecap, "The Rise of the Chicago Packers," p. 250.
40. Gabriel Kolko, *The Triumph of Conservatism: A Reinterpretation of American History, 1900–1916* (Glencoe, IL: Free Press, 1963), p. 98.
41. Libecap, "The Rise of the Chicago Packers," p. 244.
42. Dimitri, "Agricultural Marketing Institutions," p. 7.
43. Libecap, "The Rise of the Chicago Packers," p. 253.
44. *Minnesota v. Barber*, 136 U.S. 313 (1890).
45. Kolko, *The Triumph of Conservatism*, p. 99.

46. Ibid., p. 102.
47. Libecap, "The Rise of the Chicago Packers," p. 245; Dimitri, "Agricultural Marketing Institutions," p. 17.
48. Ivan Musicant, *The Spanish-American War and the Dawn of the American Century* (New York: Henry Holt, 1998), p. 637.
49. Kathleen Dalton, *Theodore Roosevelt: A Strenuous Life* (New York: Knopf, 2002), p. 175.
50. Leon Harris, *Upton Sinclair, American Rebel* (New York: Crowell, 1975).
51. Musicant, *The Spanish-American War and the Dawn of the American Century,* p. 639.
52. Leech and Carroll, *Armour and His Times,* p. 325.
53. Musicant, *The Spanish-American War and the Dawn of the American Century,* p. 640.
54. Leech and Carroll, *Armour and His Times,* p. 324.
55. Libecap, "The Rise of the Chicago Packers," p. 246.
56. Dimitri, "Agricultural Marketing Institutions," p. 9.
57. Kolko, *The Triumph of Conservatism,* p. 101.
58. Charles Edward Russell, *The Greatest Trust in the World* (New York: Ridgway-Thayer, 1905; repr., New York: Arno Press, 1975).
59. Kolko, *The Triumph of Conservatism,* p. 103.
60. James Harvey Young, *Pure Food: Securing the Federal Food and Drugs Act of 1906* (Princeton: Princeton University Press, 1989), p. 222.
61. Ibid., p. 224.
62. Upton Sinclair, *Autobiography of Upton Sinclair* (New York: Harcourt, Brace & World, 1962), p. 122.
63. Ibid., p. 120.
64. Theodore Roosevelt to William Allen White, July 31, 1906, in Elting E. Morrison, John M. Blum, and John J. Buckley, eds, *The Letters of Theodore Roosevelt,* vol. 5 (Cambridge: Harvard University Press, 1951–1954), p. 340.
65. H. W. Brands, *T.R.: The Last Romantic* (New York: Basic Books, 1997), p. 549.
66. Kolko, *The Triumph of Conservatism,* p. 105.
67. Ibid., p. 106.
68. Ibid., p. 107.
69. Quoted ibid., p. 103.
70. Weber, *The Food, Drug, and Insecticide Administration,* p. 13.
71. Ibid., p. 7.
72. Ibid., p. 13.
73. Ibid., pp. 3, 4.
74. Ibid., p. 9.
75. Ibid., p. 10.
76. Ibid., p. 49.
77. Ibid., p. 20.
78. Coppin and High, *The Politics of Purity,* p. 28.
79. Ibid., p. 28.
80. Ibid., p. 29.
81. James Harvey Young, *The Medical Messiahs: A Social History of Health and Quackery in Twentieth-Century America* (Princeton: Princeton University Press, 1992), p. 33.
82. Quoted in Coppin and High, *The Politics of Purity,* p. 36.

83. Coppin and High, *The Politics of Purity*, p. 37.
84. Donna J. Wood, *Strategic Uses of Public Policy: Business and Government in the Progressive Era* (Marshfield, MA: Pittman, 1986), p. 79.
85. Coppin and High, *The Politics of Purity*, p. 55.
86. Ibid., p. 54.
87. Ibid., p. 52.
88. Quoted ibid., p. 68.
89. Quoted ibid., p. 74.
90. Coppin and High, *The Politics of Purity*, p. 74.
91. Quoted ibid., p. 57.
92. Coppin and High, *The Politics of Purity*, p. 68.
93. Ibid., p. 67.
94. Ibid., p. 103.
95. Ibid., p. 62.
96. Ibid., p. 78.
97. Ibid., p. 59.
98. Ibid., p. 60.
99. Ibid., p. 63.
100. Ibid., p. 67.
101. Ibid., p. 66.
102. Ibid., p. 65.
103. Ibid., p. 66.
104. Ibid., p. 79.
105. Ibid., p. 69.
106. Ibid., p. 84.
107. Ibid., p. 75.
108. Young, *Pure Food*, p. 195.
109. Coppin and High, *The Politics of Purity*, p. 73.
110. Ibid., p. 70.
111. Weber, *The Food, Drug, and Insecticide Administration*, p. 17.
112. *United States v. Johnson*, 221 U.S. 488 (1911).
113. Coppin and High, *The Politics of Purity*, p. 136.
114. Ibid.
115. Ibid., p. 137.
116. Ibid.
117. Ibid., p. 136.
118. Quoted ibid., p. 141.
119. Coppin and High, *The Politics of Purity*, p. 142.
120. Ibid., p. 143.
121. Ibid., p. 145.
122. Ibid., p. 149.
123. Ibid.
124. Ibid., p. 142.
125. Ibid., p. 143.
126. Mark Prendergast, *For God, Country, and Coca-Cola: The Definitive History of the Great American Soft Drink and the Company That Makes It* (New York: Basic Books, 2000), p. 111.
127. Ibid., p. 117.
128. Ibid.

129. Ibid., p. 119.

130. Ibid., p. 118.

131. Coppin and High, *The Politics of Purity*, p. 146.

132. Ibid., p. 158.

133. Quoted ibid., p. 147.

134. Coppin and High, *The Politics of Purity*, p. 147.

135. Quoted ibid., p. 151.

136. *United States v. Forty Barrels and Twenty Kegs of Coca-Cola*, 241 U.S. 265 (1916).

137. Prendergast, *For God, Country, and Coca-Cola*, p. 121.

138. Ibid., p. 122.

139. Coppin and High, *The Politics of Purity*, p. 16.

140. Weber, *The Food, Drug, and Insecticide Administration*, pp. 23, 24.

141. Coppin and High, *The Politics of Purity*, p. 163.

142. Ibid., p. 165.

143. Prendergast, *For God, Country, and Coca-Cola*, p. 120.

144. Ibid.

145. Ibid.

146. Coppin and High, *The Politics of Purity*, p. 167.

147. Harvey Washington Wiley, *An Autobiography* (Indianapolis: Bobbs-Merrill, 1930), p. 241.

148. Theodore Roosevelt to Henry Hurd Rusby, January 7, 1909, in Elting Morison, ed., *The Letters of Theodore Roosevelt* (Cambridge: Harvard University Press, 1951–54), vol. VI, pp. 1467–1468.

CHAPTER SIX

1. Samuel P. Hays, *Conservation and the Gospel of Efficiency: The Progressive Conservation Movement, 1890–1920* (Pittsburgh: University of Pittsburgh Press, 1999).

2. Ibid.

3. Ibid., pp. 137, 138.

4. E. Louise Peffer, *The Closing of the Public Domain: Disposal and Reservation Policies, 1900–1950* (Stanford, CA: Stanford University Press, 1951), p. 8.

5. Andro Linklater, *Measuring America: How an Untamed Wilderness Shaped the United States and Fulfilled the Promise of Democracy* (New York: Walker, 2002), p. 36.

6. William Bradford, *Of Plymouth Plantation, 1620–1647* (New York: Knopf, 1997), p. 120.

7. Linklater, *Measuring America*, p. 43.

8. Ibid., p. 169.

9. Ibid., p. 149.

10. Paul Wallace Gates, *Landlords and Tenants on the Prairie Frontier: Studies in American Land Policy* (Ithaca: Cornell University Press, 1973), p. 51.

11. Ibid., p. 27.

12. *Green v. Biddle*, 21 U.S. 1 (1821).

13. Hernando de Soto, *The Mystery of Capital* (New York: Basic Books, 2000), p. 135.

14. Ibid., p. 134.

15. Ibid., p. 128.
16. Paul W. Gates, "The Homestead Act: Free Land Policy in Operation, 1862–1935," in *Public Land Policies: Management and Disposal*, ed. Paul Wallace Gates (New York: Arno Press, 1979), p. 37.
17. Ibid., p. 39.
18. Ibid., p. 35.
19. *Historical Statistics of the United States, Colonial Times to 1970* (Washington, DC: Bureau of the Census, 1975), part 1, p. 460.
20. Linklater, *Measuring America*, p. 175.
21. Theodore Roosevelt, *An Autobiography* (New York: Macmillan, 1913), p. 395.
22. Marc Reisner, *Cadillac Desert: The American West and Its Disappearing Water* (New York: Penguin Books, 1993), p. 106.
23. Ibid., p. 107.
24. Ibid., p. 109.
25. Hays, *Conservation and the Gospel of Efficiency*, p. 10.
26. Ibid., p. 13.
27. Peffer, *The Closing of the Public Domain*, p. 33.
28. Hays, *Conservation and the Gospel of Efficiency*, p. 12.
29. Peffer, *The Closing of the Public Domain*, p. 21.
30. Reisner, *Cadillac Desert*, p. 113.
31. Peffer, *The Closing of the Public Domain*, p. 33.
32. Reisner, *Cadillac Desert*, p. 60.
33. Roosevelt, *An Autobiography*, p. 434.
34. Peffer, *The Closing of the Public Domain*, pp. 148, 149.
35. Reisner, *Cadillac Desert*, p. 116.
36. Ibid., p. 183.
37. Roosevelt, *An Autobiography*, p. 434.
38. Western Water Alliance, "Case Studies in Bureau of Reclamation Mismanagement," www.westernwateralliance.org/dwnld/case_studies.pdf.
39. Roosevelt, *An Autobiography*, p. 434.
40. Ibid.
41. Hays, *Conservation and the Gospel of Efficiency*, p. 249.
42. Reisner, *Cadillac Desert*, p. 115.
43. Ibid., p. 68.
44. Ibid., p. 82.
45. Ibid., p. 83.
46. Ibid., p. 84.
47. Ibid., p. 93.
48. Ibid., p. 117.
49. Robert William Fogel, *Railroads and American Economic Growth: Essays in Econometric History* (Baltimore: Johns Hopkins University Press, 1964), p. 5.
50. Hays, *Conservation and the Gospel of Efficiency*, p. 139.
51. Ibid., p. 110.
52. Quoted ibid., pp. 105–106.
53. Quoted ibid., p. 108.
54. Quoted ibid., p. 110.
55. Hays, *Conservation and the Gospel of Efficiency*, p. 203.
56. Roosevelt, *An Autobiography*, p. 429.

57. Theodore Roosevelt, "The Forest in the Life of a Nation," *Proceedings* of the American Forest Congress held at Washington, DC, January 2–6, 1905, under the auspices of the American Forestry Association (Washington, DC: Suter, 1905), p. 8.

58. Ralph W. Hidy, Frank Ernest Hill, and Allan Nevins, *Timber and Men: The Weyerhaeuser Story* (New York: Macmillan, 1963), p. 137.

59. Peffer, *The Closing of the Public Domain*, p. 107.

60. Ibid., p. 45.

61. Ibid., p. 44.

62. Gerald W. Williams, "American Forest Congress, January 2–6, 1905, Washington, DC," February 4, 2004.

63. Quoted in Benjamin Horace Hibbard, *A History of the Public Land Policies* (New York: Peter Smith, 1939), p. 479.

64. Peffer, *The Closing of the Public Domain*, pp. 90, 91.

65. Paul W. Gates, *The Wisconsin Pine Lands of Cornell University: A Study in Land Policy and Absentee Ownership* (Madison: State Historical Society of Wisconsin, 1965), pp. 237–239, 242, 243.

66. Hidy, Hill, and Nevins, *Timber and Men*, pp. 210, 211.

67. Ibid., p. 167.

68. Ibid., p. 215.

69. Sherry H. Olson, *The Depletion Myth: A History of Railroad Use of Timber* (Cambridge: Harvard University Press, 1971), p. 72.

70. Terry L. Anderson and Donald R. Leal, *Free Market Environmentalism* (San Francisco: Pacific Research Institute, 1991), p. 41.

71. Hays, *Conservation and the Gospel of Efficiency*, p. 138.

72. Ibid., p. 33.

73. Ibid.

74. Olson, *The Depletion Myth*, p. 11.

75. Ibid., p. 164.

76. Ibid., p. 11.

77. W. Brad Smith, Patrick D. Miles, John S. Vissage, and Scott A. Pugh, *Forest Resources of the United States, 2002* (Washington, DC: U.S. Department of Agriculture, Forest Service, 2004), p. 3; Olson, *The Depletion Myth*, p. 3.

78. Ernest A. Sterling, "Comment," *American Forestry*, June 1915, p. 731.

CHAPTER SEVEN

1. Theodore Roosevelt, State of the Union address, December 3, 1906.

2. Matthew Josephson: *The Robber Barons, Great American Capitalists, 1861–1901* (New York: Harcourt, Brace, 1934).

3. *Historical Statistics of the United States, Colonial Times to 1970* (Washington, DC: Bureau of the Census, 1975), part 1, pp. 457, 459, 460.

4. Paul W. Gates, "The Homestead Act: Free Land Policy in Operation, 1862–1935," in *Public Land Policies: Management and Disposal*, ed. Paul Wallace Gates (New York: Arno Press, 1979), p. 37.

5. *Historical Statistics of the United States, Colonial Times to 1970*, part 1, p. 462.

6. Roy G. Blakey and Gladys C. Blakey, *The Federal Income Tax* (New York: Longmans, Green, 1940), p. 8.

7. W. A. Swanberg, *Pulitzer* (New York: Scribner, 1967), p. 88.

8. Edwin Robert Anderson Seligman, *The Income Tax: A Study of the History, Theory, and Practice of Income Taxation at Home and Abroad* (New York: Macmillan, 1911), part 1, p. 11.

9. Ibid., p. 35.

10. Ibid., p. 36.

11. Quoted in Richard J. Joseph, *The Origins of the American Income Tax: The Revenue Act and Its Aftermath* (Syracuse: Syracuse University Press, 2004), p. 90.

12. Paolo E. Coletta, *William Jennings Bryan: Political Evangelist, 1860–1908* (Lincoln: University of Nebraska Press, 1964), pp. 17, 18.

13. Quoted in Joseph, *The Origins of the American Income Tax*, p. 90.

14. Adam Smith, *An Inquiry into the Nature and Causes of the Wealth of Nations*, Vol. II (1776; repr., Indianapolis: Liberty Press, 1981), chapter II, part II, article IV, p. 867.

15. Ibid., article II, p. 848.

16. Quoted in Blakey and Blakey, *The Federal Income Tax*, p. 39.

17. William Graham Sumner, "The Absurd Effort to Make the World Over," in *Essays of William Graham Sumner*, vol. 1, ed. Albert Galloway Keller and Maurice R. Davie (1894; repr., New Haven: Yale University Press, 1934), pp. 98, 99.

18. William Graham Sumner, *What Social Classes Owe to Each Other* (1883; repr., Caldwell, ID: Caxton Printers, 1963), pp. 11, 27, 28.

19. John F. Witte, *The Politics and Development of the Federal Income Tax* (Madison: University of Wisconsin Press, 1985), pp. 71, 72.

20. Joseph, *The Origins of the American Income Tax*, p. 61.

21. Coletta, *William Jennings Bryan*, p. 57.

22. Quoted in Randolph E. Paul, *Taxation in the United States* (Boston: Little, Brown, 1954), p. 37.

23. Paul, *Taxation in the United States*, p. 37.

24. Willard L. King, *Melville Weston Fuller, Chief Justice of the United States, 1888–1910* (New York: Macmillan, 1950), p. 194.

25. Quoted in Paul, *Taxation in the United States*, p. 42.

26. Seligman, *The Income Tax*, part 2, pp. 548–555.

27. Quoted in Paul, *Taxation in the United States*, pp. 53, 54.

28. Quoted in Steven R. Weisman, *The Great Tax Wars, Lincoln to Wilson: The Fierce Battles over Money and Power That Transformed the Nation* (New York: Simon & Schuster, 2002), p. 152. Choate based his argument on a brief prepared by his friend Charles F. Southmayd, a retired attorney who, Choate later wrote, had a "very keen and very powerful" sense of the importance of property and "an abiding allegiance to the Constitution, under which the country had so long prospered, and an abhorrence of any violation of it." See Theron G. Strong, *Joseph H. Choate: New Englander, New Yorker, Lawyer, Ambassador* (New York: Dodd, Mead, 1917), p. 165.

29. Seligman, *The Income Tax*, part 2, p. 520.

30. Quoted in Paul, *Taxation in the United States*, p. 43.

31. *Springer v. United States*, 102 U.S. 586 (1880).

32. Paul, *Taxation in the United States*, p. 58.

33. Fuller explained, "Ordinarily, all taxes paid primarily by persons who can shift the burden upon some one else, or who are under no legal compulsion to pay them, are considered indirect taxes; but a tax upon property holders in respect of their

estates, whether real or personal, or of the income yielded by such estates, and the payment of which cannot be avoided, are direct taxes. . . . The law in question, in imposing a tax on the income or rents of real estate, imposes a tax upon the real estate itself; and in imposing a tax on the interest or other income of bonds or other personal property, held for the purposes of income or ordinarily yielding income, imposes a tax upon the personal estate itself; that such tax is a direct tax, and void because imposed without regard to the rule of apportionment; and that by reason thereof the whole law is invalidated." *Pollock v. Farmers' Loan and Trust Company*, 157 U.S. 429 (1895).

34. Paul, *Taxation in the United States*, p. 58.
35. *Pollock v. Farmers Loan & Trust Co.*, 158 U.S. 601 (1895).
36. Ibid.
37. Ibid.
38. *Pollock v. Farmers Loan & Trust Co.*, 157 U.S. 429 (1895).
39. Paul, *Taxation in the United States*, p. 65.
40. Ibid.
41. Ibid., p. 88.
42. Quoted ibid.
43. Theodore Roosevelt, State of the Union address, December 3, 1906.
44. Quoted in Paul, *Taxation in the United States*, p. 89.
45. Weisman, *The Great Tax Wars, Lincoln to Wilson*, p. 223.
46. Cordell Hull, *The Memoirs of Cordell Hull*, vol. 1 (New York: Macmillan, 1948), p. 49.
47. Ibid., p. 48.
48. Quoted in Blakey and Blakey, *The Federal Income Tax*, p. 23.
49. Quoted ibid.
50. *Historical Statistics of the United States, Colonial Times to 1970* (Washington, DC: Bureau of the Census, 1975), part 2, p. 1104.
51. Blakey and Blakey, *The Federal Income Tax*, p. 26.
52. Hull, *The Memoirs of Cordell Hull*, p. 58.
53. Quoted in Paul, *Taxation in the United States*, p. 92.
54. Witte, *The Politics and Development of the Federal Income Tax*, p. 74.
55. Quoted in Blakey and Blakey, *The Federal Income Tax*, p. 39.
56. Weisman, *The Great Tax Wars, Lincoln to Wilson*, p. 228.
57. Blakey and Blakey, *The Federal Income Tax*, pp. 40, 41.
58. Weisman, *The Great Tax Wars, Lincoln to Wilson*, p. 232.
59. Paul, *Taxation in the United States*, p. 95.
60. Blakey and Blakey, *The Federal Income Tax*, p. 46.
61. Ibid., p. 47.
62. Ibid., p. 52.
63. *Flint v. Stone Tracy Co.*, 220 U.S. 107 (1911).
64. Blakey and Blakey, *The Federal Income Tax*, p. 57.
65. Paul, *Taxation in the United States*, p. 94.
66. Quoted ibid., p. 97.
67. Hull, *The Memoirs of Cordell Hull*, p. 61.
68. Blakey and Blakey, *The Federal Income Tax*, p. 68.
69. Ibid., p. 97.
70. Quoted ibid., p. 93.

71. Blakey and Blakey, *The Federal Income Tax*, p. 96.

72. Ibid., p. 91.

73. *Brushaber v. Union Pacific Railroad Co.*, 240 U.S. 1 (1916).

74. W. Elliott Brownlee, *Federal Taxation in America: A Short History* (Cambridge, Eng.: Cambridge University Press, 1996), p. 49.

75. Ibid., p. 51.

CONCLUSION

1. August Heckscher, *Woodrow Wilson* (New York: Scribner, 1991), p. 162.

2. Frank Freidel, *Franklin D. Roosevelt: A Rendezvous with Destiny* (Boston: Little, Brown, 1990), pp. 10, 11, 17, 142, 164.

3. Eric F. Goldman, *The Tragedy of Lyndon Johnson* (New York: Knopf, 1969), p. 57.

4. Quoted in Doris Kearns, *Lyndon Johnson and the American Dream* (New York: Harper & Row, 1976), p. 35.

5. Quoted in Stephen E. Ambrose, *Nixon: The Triumph of a Politician, 1962–1972* (New York: Simon & Schuster, 1989), p. 26.

6. Hyman G. Rickover, *How the Battleship* Maine *Was Destroyed* (Washington, DC: Department of the Navy, Naval History Division, 1976), pp. 94–97, 104–106.

7. Samuel Flagg Bemis, *The Latin American Policy of the United States: An Historical Perspective* (New York: Harcourt, Brace, 1943), p. 157.

8. U.S. Department of State, "Good Neighbor Policy," www.state.gov/r/pa/ho/time/id/17341.htm.

9. Theodore Roosevelt, *An Autobiography* (New York: Macmillan, 1913), p. 551.

10. Arthur M. Schlesinger Jr., *The Imperial Presidency* (Boston: Houghton Mifflin, 1973), p. 88.

11. Tyler Dennett, *Roosevelt and the Russo-Japanese War* (1925, repr., Gloucester, MA: Peter Smith, 1959), p. 2.

12. D. Clayton James, *The Years of MacArthur, 1880–1941* (Boston: Houghton Mifflin, 1970), p. 109.

13. Fred Anderson and Andrew Cayton, *The Dominion of Forcer: Empire and Liberty in North America, 1500–2000* (New York: Viking, 2005), p. 344.

14. Robert A. Caro, *The Years of Lyndon Johnson: Master of the Senate* (New York: Knopf, 2002), p. 38.

15. For more detail on the consequences of Wilson's intervention in World War I, see Jim Powell, *Wilson's War: How Woodrow Wilson's Great Blunder Led to Hitler, Lenin, Stalin, and World War II* (New York: Crown Forum, 2005).

16. Samuel Eliot Morison, Henry Steele Commager, and William E. Leuchtenburg, *The Growth of the American Republic*, vol. 2 (New York: Oxford University Press, 1980), p. 378.

17. Ibid., p. 379.

18. Ibid., p. 380.

19. For details about how the New Deal backfired, see Jim Powell, *FDR's Folly: How Roosevelt and His New Deal Prolonged the Great Depression* (New York: Crown Forum, 2003).

20. Walter Olson, "Meddlers Won't Quit," *USA Today*, November 17, 1997.

21. For the estimate by Crain and Hopkins, the breakdown included environmental regulations ($197 billion), economic regulations ($435 billion), workplace regula-

tions ($82 billion), and tax regulations ($129 billion). On-budget costs of operating federal regulatory agencies added another $18.9 billion. See W. Marl Crain and Thomas D. Hopkins, *The Impact of Regulatory Costs on Small Firms* (Washington, DC: U.S. Small Business Administration, Office of Advocacy, 2000), and Clyde Wayne Crews Jr., *Ten Thousand Commandments: An Annual Snapshot of the Federal Regulatory State* (Washington, DC: Cato Institute, 2003), p. 5.

22. Stephen J. Entin, *The Cost of Government Regulation: Beyond the Initial Impact,* (Washington, DC: Institute for Research on the Economics of Taxation, March 9, 2005), p. 17.

23. "News Release: Gross Domestic Product" (Washington, DC: U.S. Department of Commerce, Bureau of Economic Analysis, February 25, 2005).

24. Paul M. Warburg, *The Federal Reserve: Origin and Growth,* vol. 1 (New York: Macmillan, 1930), p. 78.

25. Allan H. Meltzer, *A History of the Federal Reserve, 1913–1951* (Chicago: University of Chicago Press, 2003), p. 196.

26. Milton Friedman and Anna Jacobson Schwartz, *A Monetary History of the United States, 1867–1960* (Princeton: Princeton University Press, 1963), p. 231.

27. G. Warren Nutter and Henry Adler Einhorn, *Enterprise Monopoly in the United States, 1899–1958* (New York: Columbia University Press, 1969), summarize several of these studies.

28. Dominick T. Armentano, *Antitrust and Monopoly: Anatomy of a Policy Failure* (New York: Wiley, 1982), pp. 59, 60.

29. Dominick T. Armentano, "Antitrust Policy: Reform or Repeal?" Cato Institute, *Policy Analysis No. 21,* January 18, 1983, p. 3.

30. *United States v. Aluminum Co. of America*, 148 F.2d 416 (1945), in Phillip Areeda, *Antitrust Analysis: Problems, Text, Cases* (Boston: Little, Brown, 1981), p. 165.

31. Robert Levy, "Microsoft Is No Monopoly," *USA Today,* January 14, 1999.

32. William F. Long, Richard Schramm, and Robert D. Tollison, "The Economic Determinants of Antitrust Activity," in *The Causes and Consequences of Antitrust: The Public-Choice Perspective,* ed. Fred S. McChesney and William F. Shughart II (Chicago: University of Chicago Press, 1995), p. 104.

33. William F. Shughart II, Jon D. Silverman, and Robert D. Tollison, "Antitrust Enforcement and Foreign Competition," ibid., pp. 181, 182.

34. Paul H. Rubin, "What Do Economists Think About Antitrust? A Random Walk down Pennsylvania Avenue," ibid., p. 57.

35. Richard A. Posner, "A Statistical Study of Antitrust Enforcement," ibid., p. 80.

36. William F. Shughart II, "Private Antitrust Enforcement—Compensation, Deterrence, or Extortion?" *Regulation,* Fall 1990, p. 53.

37. Sam Peltzman, *Regulation of Pharmaceutical Innovation: The 1962 Amendments* (Washington, DC: American Enterprise Institute, 1978), p. 6.

38. Ibid., p. 9.

39. Robert M. Goldberg, "Breaking Up the FDA's Medical Information Monopoly," *Regulation,* Spring 1995, No. 2.

40. Robert M. Goldberg, "Speak No Good: The Tragedy of FDA Gag Rules," National Center for Policy Analysis, *NCPA Brief Analysis No. 214,* September 27, 1996.

41. Peltzman, *Regulation of Pharmaceutical Innovation,* pp. 9, 13, 17, 19, 81.

42. Alexander T. Tabarrok, "Assessing the FDA via the Anomaly of Off-Label Drug Prescribing," *Independent Review,* Summer 2000, p. 30. Tabarrok refers to W. M. Wardell, "A Close Inspection of the 'Calm Look,' Rhetorical Amblyopia and Se-

lective Amnesia at the Food and Drug Administration," *Journal of the American Medical Association,* May 12, 1978, pp. 2004–2011.

43. *Cato Handbook for Congress,* 108th Congress (Washington, DC: Cato Institute, 2003), p. 406.

44. Robert M. Goldberg, "Why Kessler Must Go," *Wall Street Journal,* April 4, 1996.

45. Ibid.

46. Robert M. Goldberg, "FDA Needs a Dose of Reform," *Wall Street Journal,* September 30, 2002.

47. Tabarrok, "Assessing the FDA via the Anomaly of Off-Label Drug Prescribing," p. 32.

48. Ibid., p. 31.

49. Robert M. Goldberg, "The Right Road to Safe Drugs," *New York Post,* December 28, 2004. Dale H. Gieringer, "The Safety and Efficacy of New Drug Approval," *Cato Journal,* Spring/Summer 1985, p. 181.

50. Cited in James Harvey Young, *The Medical Messiahs: A Social History of Health and Quackery in Twentieth-Century America* (Princeton: Princeton University Press, 1992), pp. 35, 36.

51. Alex Berenson and Barnaby Feder, "A Reminder That No Drug Is Risk-Free," *New York Times,* February 19, 2005, p. C1.

52. Roger A. Sedjo and Marion Clawson, "Global Forests," in *The Resourceful Earth,* ed. Julian Simon (Oxford: Basil Blackwell, 1984), p. 142.

53. National Resources Defense Council, "100 Years Later: U.S. Reclamation Bureau Stuck in 19th Century," *San Diego Earth Times,* www.sdearthtimes.com/et0802/et0802s9.html.

54. Testimony of Mr. Adam Werbach, President, Sierra Club, before the Subcommittee on National Parks and Public Lands, and Water and Power Resources, of the House of Representatives, Washington, DC, September 23, 1997.

55. Western Water Alliance, "Case Studies in Bureau of Reclamation Mismanagement," www.westernwateralliance.org/dwnld/case_studies.pdf.

56. Marc Reisner, *Cadillac Desert: The American West and Its Disappearing Water* (New York: Penguin Books, 1993), p. 333.

57. *Omaechevarria v. Idaho,* 246 U.S. 343 (1918).

58. Wesley Calef, *Private Grazing and Public Lands: Studies of the Local Management of the Taylor Grazing Act* (Chicago: University of Chicago Press, 1960), pp. 250, 285.

59. Robert H. Nelson, *A Burning Issue: A Case for Abolishing the U.S. Forest Service* (Lanham, MD: Rowman & Littlefield, 2000), pp. 18, 21.

60. Ibid., p. 46.

61. Ibid., p. 19.

62. Ibid., pp. 19, 94.

63. Ibid., p. 96.

64. W. Brad Smith, Patrick D. Miles, John S. Vissage, and Scott A. Pugh, *Forest Resources of the United States, 2002* (Washington, DC: U.S. Department of Agriculture, Forest Service, 2004), p. 6.

65. "Earth Day at 30: A Progress Report," House Policy Committee, U.S. House of Representatives, December 14, 2001.

66. See Donald R. Leal and Holl L. Fretwell, "Back to the Future to Save Our Parks," Property and Environment Research Center, *PERC Policy Series Issue No. PS-10,* June 1997.

67. "Costly Outhouses Monuments to Red Tape," *USA Today,* December 15, 1997.
68. See, for instance, Alston Chase, *Playing God in Yellowstone: The Destruction of America's First National Park* (Boston: Atlantic Monthly Press, 1986).
69. Roy G. Blakey and Gladys C. Blakey, *The Federal Income Tax* (London: Longmans, Green, 1940), p. 105.
70. Ibid., p. 120.
71. Ibid., p. 121.
72. *Historical Statistics of the United States, Colonial Times to 1970* (Washington, DC: Bureau of the Census, 1975), part 2, p. 1107.
73. Blakey and Blakey, *The Federal Income Tax,* pp. 147, 151, 152, 155.
74. John F. Witte, *The Politics and Development of the Federal Income Tax* (Madison: University of Wisconsin Press, 1985), p. 79.
75. *Historical Statistics of the United States, Colonial Times to 1970,* part 2, p. 1107.
76. It is still true that a minority of taxpayers bears a disproportionate share of the burdens. Based on 2001 data, the top 5 percent of wage earners paid 53 percent of federal income taxes. The top 10 percent paid 64 percent of federal income taxes. The top 50 percent paid 96 percent of federal income taxes. See Internal Revenue Service, "Tax Stats at a Glance," www.irs.gov/taxstats/article/0,,id=102886,00.html.
77. James L. Payne, *Costly Returns: The Burdens of the U.S. Tax System* (San Francisco: Institute for Contemporary Studies, 1993), p. 8.

BIBLIOGRAPHY

ARTICLES

Alchian, Armen and Ruben Kessel, "Competition, Monopoly and the Pursuit of Pecuniary Gain," in *Aspects of Labor Economics* (Princeton, NJ: National Bureau of Economic Research, 1962), pp. 156–183.

Allen, Douglas W. "Homesteading and Property Rights, or 'How the West Was Really Won,'" *Journal of Law and Economics*, April 1991, pp. 1–23.

Averch, H., and L. Johnson. "The Firm Under Regulatory Constraint," *American Economic Review*, December 1962, pp. 1052–1059.

Baack, Bennett D., and Edward John Ray. "The Political Economy of the Origin and Development of the Federal Income Tax," in *Emergence of the Modern Political Economy*, ed. Robert Higgs (Greenwich, CT: JAI Press, 1985).

Baumol, William J., and Janusz A. Ordover. "Use of Antitrust to Subvert Competition," *Journal of Law and Economics*, May 1985, pp. 247–265.

Benson, Bruce L., M. L. Greenhut, and Randall G. Holcombe. "Interest Groups and the Antitrust Paradox," *Cato Journal*, Winter 1987, pp. 801–817.

Bernstein, David E. "Racism, Railroad Unions, and Labor Regulations," *Independent Review*, Fall 2000, pp. 237–247.

Binder, John J. "The Sherman Act and the Railroad Cartels," *Journal of Law and Economics*, October 1988, pp. 443–468.

Bittlingmayer, George. "Antitrust and Business Activity: The First Quarter Century," *Business History Review*, Autumn 1996, pp. 363–401.

———. "Did Antitrust Policy Cause the Great Merger Wave?" *Journal of Law and Economics*, April 1985, pp. 77–118.

———. "Economics and 100 Years of Antitrust," *Economic Inquiry*, April 1992, pp. 203–206.

———. "Regulatory Uncertainty and Investment: Evidence from Antitrust Enforcement," *Cato Journal*, Winter 2001, pp. 295–336.

———. "The Stock Market and Early Antitrust Enforcement," *Journal of Law and Economics*, April 1993, pp. 1–32.

———. "Trust-Busting: Past and Prologue," *Jobs and Capital*, Winter 1997, pp. 3–8.

Blackford, Mansel Griffiths. "Businessmen and the Regulation of Railroads and Public Utilities in California During the Progressive Era," *Business History Review*, August 1970, pp. 307–319.

Bork, Robert H. "Legislative Intent and the Policy of the Sherman Act," *Journal of Law and Economics*, October 1966, pp. 7–48.

———. "Vertical Integration and the Sherman Act: The Legal History of an Economic Misconception," *University of Chicago Law Review*, Autumn 1954, pp. 157–201.

Bradley, Robert L., Jr. "On the Origins of the Sherman Antitrust Act," *Cato Journal*, Winter 1990, pp. 737–742.

Breit, William, and Kenneth G. Elzinga. "Private Antitrust Enforcement: The New Learning," *Journal of Law and Economics*, May 1985, pp. 405–443.

Brozen, Yale. "The Attack on Concentration," *The Freeman*, January 1979.

Burns, Malcolm. "The Competitive Effects of Trust-Busting: A Portfolio Analysis," *Journal of Political Economy*, 1977, pp. 717–739.

———. "Predatory Pricing and the Acquisition Cost of Competitors," *Journal of Political Economy*, April 1986, pp. 226–296.

Caine, Stanley. "Why Railroads Supported Regulation: The Case of Wisconsin, 1905–1910," *Business History Review*, 1970, pp. 175–189.

Capozzola, Christopher. "The Only Badge Needed Is Your Patriotic Fervor: Vigilance, Coercion and the Law in World War I America," *Journal of American History*, March 2002, pp. 1354–1382.

Coase, Ronald H. "Law and Economics at Chicago," *Journal of Law and Economics*, April 1993, pp. 239–254.

Coate, Malcolm B., Richard S. Higgins, and Fred S. McChesney. "Bureaucracy and Politics in FTC Merger Challenges," *Journal of Law and Economics*, October 1990, pp. 463–482.

Courville, Leon. "Regulation and Efficiency in the Electrical Utility Industry," *Bell Journal of Economics*, Spring 1974, pp. 53–74.

Crew, Michael, and Charles Rowley. "Toward a Public Choice Theory of Monopoly Regulation," *Public Choice*, April 1988, pp. 49–67.

Cummings, F. J., and W. E. Ruther. "The Northern Pacific Case," *Journal of Law and Economics*, October 1979, pp. 329–340.

Dam, Kenneth. "Economics as a Guide to Antitrust Regulation," *Journal of Law and Economics*, August 1976, pp. 385–388.

DeBow, Michael E. "The Social Costs of Populist Antitrust: A Public Choice Perspective," *Harvard Journal of Law and Public Policy*, 1991, pp. 205–225.

Demsetz, Harold. "Economics as a Guide to Antitrust Regulation," *Journal of Law and Economics*, August 1976, pp. 371–384.

———. "How Many Cheers for Antitrust's 100 Years?" *Economic Inquiry*, April 1992, pp. 207–217.

———. "Industry Structure, Market Rivalry, and Public Policy," *Journal of Law and Economics*, April 1973, pp. 1–9.

———. "The Trust Behind Antitrust," *International Institute for Economic Research*, Original Paper no. 10, Los Angeles, March 1978.

———. "Why Regulate Utilities?" *Journal of Law and Economics*, April 1968, pp. 55–65.

Dewey, Donald. "The Economic Theory of Antitrust: Science or Religion?" *Virginia Law Review*, April 1964, pp. 413–434.

DiLorenzo, Thomas J. "The Ghost of John D. Rockefeller," *The Freeman*, June 1998, pp. 334–337.

———. "The Origins of Antitrust: An Interest-Group Perspective," *International Review of Law and Economics*, June 1985, pp. 73–90.

DiLorenzo, Thomas J., and Donald J. Boudreaux. "The Protectionist Roots of Antitrust," *Review of Austrian Economics*, 1993, pp. 81–96.

DiLorenzo, Thomas J., and Jack C. High. "Antitrust and Competition, Historically Considered," *Economic Inquiry*, July 1988, pp. 423–435.

Easterbrook, Frank H. "Antitrust and the Economics of Federalism," *Journal of Law and Economics*, April 1983, pp. 23–50.

———. "Detrebling Antitrust Damages," *Journal of Law and Economics*, May 1985, pp. 445–467.

Eis, Carl. "The 1919–1930 Merger Movement in American Industry," *Journal of Law and Economics*, October 1969, pp. 267–296.

Ellison, Sarah Fisher, and Wallace P. Mullin. "Economics and Politics: The Case of Sugar Tariff Reform," *Journal of Law and Economics*, October 1995, pp. 335–366.

Elzinga, Kenneth G. "The Antimerger Law: Pyrrhic Victories?" *Journal of Law and Economics*, April 1969, pp. 43–78.

———. "Predatory Pricing: The Case of the Gunpowder Trust," *Journal of Law and Economics*, April 1970, pp. 223–240.

Elzinga, Kenneth G., and William Breit. "Antitrust Enforcement and Economic Efficiency: The Uneasy Case for Treble Damages," *Journal of Law and Economics*, October 1974, pp. 329–356.

Elzinga, Kenneth G., and David E. Mills. "Testing for Predation: Is Recoupment Feasible?" *Antitrust Law Journal*, Winter 1989, pp. 969–993.

English, William B. "Understanding the Costs of Sovereign Default: American State Debts in the 1840's," *American Economic Review*, March 1996, pp. 259–275.

Ernst, Daniel R. "The New Antitrust History," *New York Law School Law Review*, Vol. 35, No. 4, 1990, pp. 879–891.

Faith, Roger L., and Donald R. Leavens. "Antitrust Pork Barrel," *Journal of Law and Economics*, October 1982, pp. 32–42.

Fogel, Robert William. "The Conquest of High Mortality and Hunger in Europe and America: Timing and Mechanisms," National Bureau of Economic Research, *NBER Historical Working Paper No. 16*, September 1990.

Friedman, David D. "In Defense of the Long Haul/Short Haul Discrimination," *Bell Journal of Economics*, Autumn 1979, pp. 706–708.

Gieringer, Dale H. "The Safety and Efficacy of New Drug Approval," *Cato Journal*, Spring/Summer 1985, pp. 177–201.

Gilligan, Thomas W., William J. Marshall, and Barry R. Weingast. "Regulation and the Theory of Legislative Choice: The Interstate Commerce Act of 1887," *Journal of Law and Economics*, April 1989, pp. 35–61.

Gordon, Sanford D. "Attitudes Toward Trusts Prior to the Sherman Act," *Southern Economic Journal*, October 1963, pp. 156–167.

Grandy, Christopher. "Original Intent and the Sherman Antitrust Act: A Re-Examination of the Consumer-Welfare Hypothesis," *Journal of Economic History*, June 1993, pp. 359–376.

Greenspan, Alan. "Antitrust," in *Capitalism: The Unknown Ideal*, ed. Ayn Rand (New York: Signet, 1966).

Grinath, Arthur, III, John Joseph Wallis, and Richard E. Sylla. "Debt, Default and Revenue Structure: The American State Debt Crisis in the Early 1840s," National Bureau of Economic Research, *NBER Historical Working Paper No. 97*, March 1997.

Haines, Michael R. "Estimated Life Tables for the United States, 1850–1900," National Bureau of Economic Research, *NBER Working Paper No. 59*, September 1994.

Hawley, Ellis W. "The Discovery and Study of a Corporate Liberalism," *Business Historical Review*, Autumn 1978, pp. 309–320.

Hay, George A., and Daniel Kelley. "An Empirical Survey of Price-Fixing Conspiracies," *Journal of Law and Economics*, April 1974, pp. 13–38.

Hays, Samuel P. "The Mythology of Conservation," in *Perspectives on Conservation*, ed. H. Jarrett (Baltimore, Johns Hopkins University Press, 1958).

Hazlett, Thomas W. "Is Antitrust Anticompetitive?" *Harvard Journal of Law and Public Policy*, Spring 1986, pp. 277–336.

———. "The Legislative History of the Sherman Act Reexamined," *Economic Inquiry*, April 1992, pp. 263–276.

High, Jack, and Clayton A. Coppin. "Wiley and the Whiskey Industry: Strategic Behavior in the Passage of the Pure Food Act," *Business History Review*, Summer 1988, pp. 286–309.

Hilton, George W. "The Consistency of the Interstate Commerce Act," *Journal of Law and Economics*, October 1966, pp. 87–113.

Hovenkamp, Herbert. "Antitrust Policy After Chicago," *University of Michigan Law Review*, November 1985, pp. 213–284.

———. "Antitrust's Protected Classes," *University of Michigan Law Review*, October 1989, pp. 1–48.

Ippolito, Richard A., and Robert T. Masson. "The Social Cost of Government Regulation of Milk," *Journal of Law and Economics*, April 1978, pp. 33–65.

Jarrell, Greg. "The Demand for State Regulation of the Electric Utility Industry," *Journal of Law and Economics*, October 1978, pp. 269–295.

Koller, Roland H. "The Myth of Predatory Pricing: An Empirical Study," reprinted in *The Competitive Economy*, ed. Yale Brozen (Morristown, NJ: General Learning Press, 1975), pp. 418–428.

Kovacic, William E. "Failed Expectations: The Troubled Past and Uncertain Future of the Sherman Act as a Tool for Deconcentration," *Iowa Law Review*, July 1989, pp. 1105–1150.

———. "The Federal Trade Commission and Congressional Oversight of Antitrust Enforcement," *Tulsa Law Journal*, 1982, pp. 587–671.

Law, Marc T. "The Origins of State Pure Food Regulation," *Journal of Economic History*, December 2003, pp. 1103–1130.

Leone, Robert A. "The Real Costs of Regulation," *Harvard Business Review*, November/December 1977, pp. 57–66.

Letwin, William. "Congress and the Sherman Antitrust Law," *University of Chicago Law Review*, Winter 1956, pp. 221–258.

Leuchtenburg, William E. "Progressivism and Imperialism: The Progressive Movement and Foreign Policy, 1898–1916," *Mississippi Valley Historical Review*, December 1952, pp. 483–504.

Libecap, Gary D. "The Rise of the Chicago Packers and the Origins of Meat Inspection and Antitrust," *Economic Inquiry*, April 1992, pp. 242–262.

Libecap, Gary D., and Marc T. Law. "Corruption and Reform? The Emergence of the 1906 Pure Food and Drug Act and the 1906 Meat Inspection Act," International Centre for Economic Research, *Working Paper No. 20*, 2003.

Liebeler, Wesley J. "Antitrust and Economic Efficiency: Comment," *Journal of Law and Economics*, May 1985, pp. 335–343.

———. "Market Power and Competitive Superiority in Concentrated Markets," *UCLA Law Review*, 1978, pp. 1243–1250.

Long, William F., Richard Schramm, and Robert D. Tollison. "The Economic Determinants of Antitrust Activity," *Journal of Law and Economics*, October 1973, pp. 351–364.

Manne, Henry G. "Mergers and the Market for Corporate Control," *Journal of Political Economy*, April 1965, pp. 110–120.

McChesney, Fred S. "Antitrust," in *The Fortune Encyclopedia of Economics*, ed. David R. Henderson (New York: Warner Books, 1993).

———. "Antitrust and Regulation: Chicago's Contradictory Views," *Cato Journal*, Winter 1991, pp. 775–798.

———. "Law's Honour Lost: The Plight of Antitrust," *Antitrust Bulletin*, Summer 1986, pp. 359–382.

Mariger, Randall. "Predatory Price Cutting, The Standard Oil of New Jersey Case, Revisited," *Explorations in Economic History*, October 1978, pp. 341–367.

May, James. "Antitrust in the Formative Era: Political and Economic Theory in Constitutional and Antitrust Analysis, 1880–1918," *Ohio State Law Journal*, 1989, pp. 257–395.

McCraw, Thomas J. "Regulation in America: A Review Article," *Business History Review*, Summer 1975, pp. 159–183.

McCurdy, Charles W. "The *Knight* Sugar Decision of 1895 and the Modernization of American Corporation Law, 1869–1903," *Business History Review*, Autumn 1979, pp. 304–342.

McGee, John S. "Predatory Price Cutting: The Standard Oil (N.J.) Case," *Journal of Law and Economics*, October 1958, pp. 137–169.

———. "Predatory Pricing Revisited," *Journal of Law and Economics*, October 1980, pp. 289–330.

———. "Professor Weiss on Concentration [The Extent and Effects of Aggregate Concentration]," *Journal of Law and Economics*, June 1983, pp. 457–465.

Miller, Geoffrey P. "The Origins of Utility Regulation and the 'Theories of Regulation' Debate: Comment," *Journal of Law and Economics*, April 1993, pp. 325–329.

Miller, James C., III. "Use of Antitrust to Subvert Competition: Comment," *Journal of Law and Economics*, May 1985, pp. 267–270.

Miller, James C., III, and Paul Pautler. "Predation: The Changing View in Economics and the Law," *Journal of Law and Economics*, May 1985, pp. 495–502.

Millon, David. "The Sherman Act and the Balance of Power," *Southern California Law Review*, 1988, pp. 1219–1292.

Mitchell, William C. "Chicago Political Economy: A Public Choice Perspective," *Public Choice*, 1989, pp. 283–292.

Mitnick, Barry M. "Myths of Creation and Fables of Administration: Explanation and the Strategic Use of Regulation," *Public Administration Review*, May/June 1980, pp. 275–286.

Moore, Thomas Gale. "Antitrust and Economic Efficiency," *Journal of Law and Economics*, May 1985, pp. 245–246.

———. "The Effectiveness of Regulation of Electric Utility Prices," *Southern Economic Journal*, April 1969, pp. 365–375.

Moshe, Kim. "The Beneficiaries of Trucking Regulation, Revisited," *Journal of Law and Economics*, April 1984, pp. 227–241.

Mott, Frank Luther. "The Magazine Revolution and Popular Ideas in the Nineties," *Proceedings of the American Antiquarian Society*, April 21, 1954, pp. 195–203.

Newmark, Craig M. "Is Antitrust Enforcement Effective?" *Journal of Political Economy*, December 1988, pp. 1315–1328.

Niskanen, William A. "Bureaucrats and Politicians," *Journal of Law and Economics*, December 1975, pp. 617–643.

Olson, William J., and Alan Woll. "Executive Orders and National Emergencies: How Presidents Have Come to 'Run the Country' by Usurping Legislative Power," Cato Institute, *Policy Analysis*, October 28, 1999.

Page, William H. "Capture, Clear Articulation, and Legitimacy: A Reply to Professor Wiley," *University of Southern California Law Review*, 1988, pp. 1343–1355.

———. "The Chicago School and the Evolution of Antitrust: Characterization, Antitrust Injury, and Evidentiary Sufficiency," *University of Virginia Law Review*, 1989, pp. 1221–1308.

———. "Interest Groups, Antitrust, and State Regulation: *Parker v. Brown* in the Economic Theory of Legislation," *Duke Law Journal*, 1987, pp. 618–668.

Parsons, Donald O., and Edward John Ray. "The United States Steel Consolidation: The Creation of Market Control," *Journal of Law and Economics*, April 1975, pp. 181–219.

Pasour, Ernest C., Jr. "We Can Do Better Than Government Inspection of Meat," *The Freeman*, May 1998, pp. 290–295.

Peltzman, Sam. "The Causes and Consequences of Rising Industrial Concentration," *Journal of Law and Economics*, April 1979, pp. 209–211.

———. "The Gains and Losses from Industrial Concentration," *Journal of Law and Economics*, October 1977, pp. 229–263.

———. "The Growth of Government," *Journal of Law and Economics*, October 1980, pp. 209–287.

———. "Toward a More General Theory of Regulation," *Journal of Law and Economics*, August 1976, pp. 211–240.

Peterman, John L. "The Brown Shoe Case," *Journal of Law and Economics*, April 1975, pp. 81–146.

———. "The Federal Trade Commission v. Brown Shoe Company," *Journal of Law and Economics*, October 1975, pp. 361–419.

Peterson, Laura Bennett. "Comment on Antitrust Remedies [Detrebling Antitrust Damages] [Private Antitrust Enforcement: The New Learning]," *Journal of Law and Economics*, May 1985, pp. 483–488.

Poole, Keith T., and Howard Rosenthal. "The Enduring Nineteenth-Century Battle for Economic Regulation: The Interstate Commerce Act Revisited," *Journal of Law and Economics*, October 1993, pp. 837–860.

Posner, Richard A. "The Chicago School of Antitrust Analysis," *University of Pennsylvania Law Review*, 1979, pp. 925–948.

———. "The Federal Trade Commission," *University of Chicago Law Review*, 1969, pp. 48–89.

———. "Oligopoly and the Antitrust Laws: A Suggested Approach," *Stanford Law Review*, June 1969, pp. 1562–1606.

———. "The Rule of Reason and the Economic Approach: Reflections on the Sylvania Decision," *University of Chicago Law Review*, 1977, pp. 1–20.

———. "The Social Costs of Monopoly and Regulation," *Journal of Political Economy*, August 1975, pp. 807–827.

———. "A Statistical Study of Antitrust Enforcement," *Journal of Law and Economics*, October 1970, pp. 365–419.

————. "Theories of Economic Regulation," *Bell Journal of Economics and Management Science*, Autumn 1974, pp. 335–358.

Prager, Robin A. "Using Stock Price Data to Measure the Effects of Regulation: The Interstate Commerce Act and the Railroad Industry," *Rand Journal of Economics*, 20, Summer 1989, pp. 280–290.

Pratt, Joseph A. "The Petroleum Industry in Transition: Antitrust and the Decline of Monopoly Control in Oil," *Journal of Economic History*, December 1980, pp. 815–837.

Priest, George L. "The Origins of Utility Regulation and the 'Theories of Regulation' Debate," *Journal of Law and Economics*, April 1993, pp. 289–323.

Reder, Melvin W. "Chicago Economics: Permanence and Change," *Journal of Economic Literature*, March 1982, pp. 1–38.

Roback, Jennifer. "The Political Economy of Segregation: The Case of Segregated Streetcars," *Journal of Economic History*, December 1986, pp. 893–917.

Rosenbluth, Gideon. "Economics as a Guide to Antitrust Regulation: Comment," *Journal of Law and Economics*, August 1976, pp. 389–392.

Ross, Thomas W. "Store Wars: The Chain Tax Movement," *Journal of Law and Economics*, April 1986, pp. 125–137.

————. "Winners and Losers Under the Robinson-Patman Act," *Journal of Law and Economics*, October 1984, pp. 243–271.

Rothbard, Murray N. "Origins of the Welfare State in America," *Journal of Libertarian Studies*, Fall 1996, pp. 193–232.

————. "Richard T. Ely: Paladin of the Welfare-Warfare State," *Independent Review*, Spring 2002, pp. 585–589.

————. "World War I as Fulfillment: Power and the Intellectuals," *Journal of Libertarian Studies*, Winter 1989, pp. 81–125.

Scherer, F. M. "Causes and Consequences of Rising Industrial Concentration," *Journal of Law and Economics*, April 1979, pp. 191–208.

Schwartzman, D. "The Burden of Monopoly," *Journal of Political Economy*, December 1960, pp. 727–730.

Seltzer, Alan L. "Woodrow Wilson as Corporate-Liberal: Toward a Reconsideration of Left Revisionist Historiography," *Western Political Quarterly*, June 1977, pp. 183–212.

Shepherd, John, Jr. "A Capture Theory of Antitrust Federalism" *Harvard Law Review*, 1986, pp. 713–789.

————. "After Chicago: An Exaggerated Demise," *Duke Law Journal*, 1986, pp. 1003–1013.

Shughart, William F., II. "Private Antitrust Enforcement—Compensation, Deterrence, or Extortion," *Regulation*, Fall 1990, pp. 53–61.

Shughart, William F., II, and Robert D. Tollison. "The Employment Consequences of the Sherman and Clayton Acts," *Journal of Institutional and Theoretical Economics*, 1991, pp. 38–52.

————. "The Positive Economics of Antitrust Policy: A Survey Article," *International Review of Law and Economics*, June 1985, pp. 39–57.

Siegfried, John. "The Determinants of Antitrust Activity," *Journal of Law and Economics*, October 1975, pp. 559–574.

Sims, Joe, and Robert H. Lande. "The End of Antitrust—Or a New Beginning," *Antitrust Bulletin*, 1986, pp. 301–322.

Sinclair, Upton. "The Condemned-Meat Industry: A Reply to Mr. Ogden Armour," in

Shaking the Foundations: 200 Years of Investigative Journalism, ed. Bruce Shapiro (New York: Avalon, 2002), pp. 112–135.

Sobel, Russell S. "Public Health and the Placebo: The Legacy of the 1906 Pure Food and Drugs Act," *Cato Journal*, Winter 2002, pp. 463–479.

Spiller, Pablo T. "Comments on Easterbrook and Synder [Detrebling Antitrust Damages][Efficient Assignment of Rights to Sue for Antitrust Damages]," *Journal of Law and Economics*, May 1985, pp. 489–494.

Spitzer, Matthew L. "Antitrust Federalism and Rational Choice Political Economy: A Critique of Capture Theory," *University of Southern California Law Review*, 1988, pp. 1293–1326.

Sproul, Michael F. "Antitrust and Prices," *Journal of Political Economy*, 1993, pp. 741–754.

Stigler, George J. "The Economists and the Problem of Monopoly," in *The Economist as Preacher and Other Essays* (Chicago: University of Chicago Press, 1982), pp. 38–54.

———. "The Origin of the Sherman Act," *Journal of Legal Studies*, January 1985, pp. 1–11.

———. "The Theory of Economic Regulation," *Bell Journal of Economics and Management Science*, Spring 1971, pp. 3–21.

Stigler, George J., and Claire Friedland. "What Can Regulators Regulate? The Case of Electricity," *Journal of Law and Economics*, October 1962, p. 1–16.

Stillman, Robert. "Examining Anti-Trust Policy Towards Horizontal Mergers," *Journal of Financial Economics*, April 1983, pp. 225–240.

Stone, Christopher D. "ICC: Some Reminiscences on the Future of American Transportation," *New Individualist Review*, Spring 1963, pp. 3–15.

Tabarrok, Alexander T. "Assessing the FDA via the Anomaly of Off-Label Drug Prescribing," *Independent Review*, Summer 2000, pp. 25–53.

Taubes, Gary. "What If It's All Been a Big Fat Lie?" *New York Times Magazine*, July 7, 2002, p. 22.

Theis, Clifford F. "The American Railroad Network During the Early 19th Century: Private Versus Public Enterprise," *Cato Journal*, Fall 2002, pp. 229–260.

Tollison, Robert D. "Chicago Political Economy," *Public Choice*, 1989, pp. 293–297.

Troesken, Werner. "Antitrust Enforcement Before the Sherman Act: The Break-up of the Chicago Gas Trust Company," *Explorations in Economic History*, January 1995, pp. 109–136.

Troesken, Werner, ed. "The Letters of John Sherman and the Origin of Antitrust," *Review of Austrian Economics*, October 2002, pp. 275–295.

Tullock, Gordon. "The Welfare Costs of Monopolies, Tariffs, and Theft," *Western Economic Journal*, June 1967, pp. 224–232.

Warren, Christian. "Toxic Purity: The Progressive Era Origins of America's Lead Paint Poisoning Epidemic," *Business History Review*, Winter 1999, pp. 705–736.

Weiss, Leonard. "The Extent and Effects of Aggregate Concentration," *Journal of Law and Economics*, June 1983, pp. 429–455.

Wood, Donna. "The Strategic Use of Public Policy: Business Support for the 1906 Food and Drug Act," *Business History Review*, Autumn 1985, pp. 403–432.

Young, Allyn A. "The Sherman Act and the New Anti-Trust Legislation," *Journal of Political Economy*, April 1915, pp. 305–326.

Zerbe, Richard. "The American Sugar Refining Company, 1887–1914: The Story of a Monopoly," *Journal of Law and Economics*, October 1969, pp. 339–375.

———. "Monopoly, the Emergence of Oligopoly and the Case of Sugar Refining," *Journal of Law and Economics*, October 1970, pp. 501–515.

BOOKS

Anderson, Avis H. *The Story of the Great Atlantic and Pacific Tea Company* (Dover, NH: Arcadia, 2002).

Anderson, Terry L. *Free Market Environmentalism* (New York: Palgrave, 2001).

Anderson, Terry L., and Peter J. Hill, ed. *The Political Economy of the American West* (Lanham, MD: Rowman & Littlefield, 1994).

Anderson, Terry L., and Alexander James. *The Politics and Economics of Park Management* (Lanham, MD: Rowman & Littlefield, 2001).

Areeda, Phillip. *Antitrust Analysis: Problems, Text, Cases* (Boston: Little, Brown, 1981).

Armentano, Dominick T. *Antitrust and Monopoly: Anatomy of a Policy Failure* (New York: Wiley, 1982).

———. *The Myths of Antitrust: Economic Theory and Legal Cases* (New Rochelle: Arlington House, 1972).

Auerbach, Alan J., ed., *Corporate Takeovers: Causes and Consequences* (Chicago: University of Chicago Press, 1988).

Bain, David Haward. *Sitting in Darkness: Americans in the Philippines* (Boston: Houghton Mifflin, 1984).

Baker, Ray Stannard. *American Chronicle: Autobiography* (New York: Scribner, 1945).

Barger, Harold. *The Transportation Industries, 1889–1946: A Study of Output, Employment and Productivity* (New York: National Bureau of Economic Research, 1951).

Barrow, Clyde W. *More than a Historian: The Political and Economic Thought of Charles A. Beard* (New Brunswick, NJ: Transaction, 2000).

Baskerville, Stephen W. *Of Laws and Limitations: An Intellectual Portrait of Louis Dembitz Brandeis* (Rutherford, NJ: Fairleigh Dickinson University Press, 1994).

Beale, Howard K. *Theodore Roosevelt and the Rise of America to World Power* (Baltimore: Johns Hopkins University Press, 1961).

Beale, Howard K., ed. *Charles A. Beard, an Appraisal* (New York: Octagon, 1976).

Beard, Charles A. *An Economic Interpretation of the Constitution of the United States* (1913; repr., New York: Free Press, 1986).

———. *Economic Origins of Jeffersonian Democracy* (New York: Macmillan, 1915).

———. *The Supreme Court and the Constitution* (New York: Macmillan, 1912).

Beard, Mary Ritter. *The Making of Charles A. Beard, an Interpretation* (New York: Exposition Press, 1955).

Behr, Edward. *Prohibition: The 13 Years That Changed America* (New York: Arcade, 1996).

Benson, Lee. *Merchants, Farmers, and Railroads: Railroad Regulation and New York Politics, 1850–1887* (Cambridge: Harvard University Press, 1955).

———. *Turner and Beard* (Westport, CT: Greenwood Press, 1980).

Bishop, Joseph Bucklin. *Theodore Roosevelt and His Time Shown in His Own Letters*, 2 vols. (New York: Scribner, 1920).

Blum, John Morton. *The Progressive Presidents: Roosevelt, Wilson, Roosevelt and Johnson* (New York: Norton, 1980).

———. *The Republican Roosevelt*, 2nd ed. (Cambridge: Harvard University Press, 1977).

Bork, Robert. *The Antitrust Paradox* (New York: Basic Books, 1978).

Borning, Bernard C. *The Political and Social Thought of Charles A. Beard* (Westport, CT: Greenwood Press, 1984).

Brady, Kathleen. *Ida Tarbell: Portrait of a Muckraker* (Pittsburgh: University of Pittsburgh Press, 1989).

Brandeis, Louis D. *The Curse of Bigness: Miscellaneous Papers*, ed. Osmond K. Fraenkel (Port Washington, NY: Kennikat Press, 1965).

Brands, H. W. *Bound to Empire: The United States and the Philippines* (New York: Oxford University Press, 1992).

———. *T.R.: The Last Romantic* (New York: Basic Books, 1998).

Bringhurst, Bruce. *Antitrust and the Oil Monopoly: The Standard Oil Cases, 1890–1911* (Westport, CT: Greenwood Press, 1979).

Brown, Robert Eldon. *Charles Beard and the Constitution: A Critical Analysis of an Economic Interpretation of the Constitution* (Princeton: Princeton University Press, 1956).

Brownlee, W. Elliott. *Federal Taxation in America: A Short History* (Cambridge, Eng.: Cambridge University Press, 1996).

Brozen, Yale. *Concentration, Mergers, and Public Policy* (New York: Macmillan, 1982).

Bruchey, Stuart. *Enterprise: The Dynamic Economy of a Free People* (Cambridge: Harvard University Press, 1990).

Buchanan, James, Robert Tollison, and Gordon Tullock. *Toward a Theory of the Rent-Seeking Society* (College Station: Texas A&M University Press, 1980).

Buenker, John D. *The Income Tax and the Progressive Era* (New York: Garland, 1985).

Burton, David H. *Theodore Roosevelt, American Politician: An Assessment* (Madison, NJ: Fairleigh Dickinson Press, 1997).

Burton, Theodore E. *John Sherman* (New York: Houghton Mifflin, 1906).

Busch, Noel F. *T.R.: The Story of Theodore Roosevelt and His Influence on Our Times* (New York: Reynal, 1963).

Butt, Archibald Willingham. *Taft and Roosevelt: The Intimate Letters of Archie Butt* (Garden City, NY: Doubleday, Doran, 1930).

Caine, Stanley P. *The Myth of a Progressive Reform: Railroad Regulation in Wisconsin, 1903–1910* (Madison: State Historical Society of Wisconsin, 1970).

Calef, Wesley Carr. *Private Grazing and Public Lands: Studies of the Local Management of the Taylor Grazing Act* (Chicago: University of Chicago Press, 1960).

Caro, Robert A. *The Years of Lyndon Johnson: Master of the Senate* (New York: Knopf, 2002).

Carson, Clarence B. *The Growth of America, 1878–1928* (Greenville, AL: American Textbook Committee, 1985).

———. *Throttling the Railroads* (Indianapolis: LibertyFund, 1971).

Carstensen, Vernon Roscoe. *Farms or Forests* (New York: Arno Press, 1979).

Carstensen, Vernon Roscoe, ed. *The Public Lands—Studies in the History of the Public Domain* (Madison: University of Wisconsin Press, 1962).

Carter, Susan B., and Richard Sutch. "Historical Perspectives on the Economic Consequences of Immigration into the United States," National Bureau of Economic Research, *NBER Historical Working Paper No. 106*, December 1997.

Chandler, Alfred D. *The Visible Hand* (Cambridge: Harvard University Press, 1977).

Chandler, Alfred D., and Stuart Bruchey, ed. *Railroads, America's First Big Business: Sources and Readings* (Manchester, NH: Harcourt, Brace & World, 1981).

Chernow, Ron. *The House of Morgan: An American Banking Dynasty and the Rise of Modern Finance* (New York: Simon & Schuster, 1990).

———. *Titan: The Life of John D. Rockefeller* (New York: Random House, 1998).

Chessmen, G. Wallace. *Theodore Roosevelt and the Politics of Power* (Boston: Little, Brown, 1969).

Coffey, Thomas M. *The Long Thirst: Prohibition in America, 1920–1933* (New York: Norton, 1975).

Coletta, Paolo E. *The Presidency of William Howard Taft* (Lawrence: University Press of Kansas, 1973).

———. *William Jennings Bryan: Political Evangelist, 1860–1908* (Lincoln, University of Nebraska Press, 1964).

———. *William Jennings Bryan: Political Puritan, 1915–1925* (Lincoln: University of Nebraska Press, 1971).

———. *William Jennings Bryan: Progressive Politician and Moral Statesman, 1909–1915* (Lincoln: University of Nebraska Press, 1969).

Collins, Michael L. *That Damned Cowboy: Theodore Roosevelt and the American West, 1883–1898* (New York: Peter Lang, 1989).

Coppin, Clayton, and Jack High. *The Politics of Purity: Harvey Washington Wiley and the Origins of Federal Food Policy* (Ann Arbor: University of Michigan Press, 1999).

Crawford, Jay Boyd. *The Crédit Mobilier of America: Its Origin and History, Its Work Constructing the Union Pacific Railroad and the Relation of Members of Congress Therewith* (1880; repr., Westport, CT: Greenwood Press, 1969).

Dalton, Kathleen. *A Strenuous Life* (New York: Random House, 2002).

Dawes, Charles G., and Bascom N. Timmons. *A Journal of the McKinley Years* (Chicago: Lakeside Press, 1950).

Dawes, Gavan. *Shoal of Time: A History of the Hawaiian Islands* (Honolulu: University of Hawaii Press, 1974).

Demsetz, Harold. *Efficiency, Competition and Policy: The Organization of Economic Activity* (Oxford: Blackwell, 1989).

Dennett, Tyler. *Roosevelt and the Russo-Japanese War* (1925; repr., Gloucester, MA: Peter Smith, 1959).

Denson, John V., ed. *Reassessing the Presidency: The Rise of the Executive State and the Decline of Freedom* (Auburn, AL: Ludwig von Mises Institute, 2001).

Destler, Chester McArthur. *Henry Demarest Lloyd and the Empire of Reform* (Philadelphia: University of Pennsylvania Press, 1963).

Dewing, Arthur S. *Corporate Promotions and Reorganizations* (New York: Harper & Row, 1969).

Diggins, John P. *The Bard of Savagery: Thorstein Veblen and Modern Social Theory* (New York: Seabury Press, 1978).

———. *Thorstein Veblen: Theorist of the Leisure Class* (New York: New American Library, 1957).

Dixon, Frank Haigh, and Julius H. Parmelee. *War Administration of the Railways of the United States and Great Britain* (New York: Oxford University Press, 1919).

Donovan, Timothy Paul. *Henry Adams and Brooks Adams* (Norman: University of Oklahoma Press, 1961).

Dorfman, Joseph. *Economic Mind in American Civilization*, vols. 3 and 4 (Clifton, NJ: Augustus M. Kelley, 1959).

―――. *Thorstein Veblen and His America* (New York: Viking, 1947).

Dos Passos, John. *The Bitter Drink: A Biography of Thorstein Veblen* (San Francisco: Grabhorn Press, 1939).

―――. *USA Trilogy: The Forty-Second Parallel; Nineteen Nineteen; The Big Money* (Boston: Houghton Mifflin, 1969).

Dowd, Douglas. *Thorstein Veblen* (New York: Washington Square Press, 1966).

Duffus, Robert L. *Innocents at Cedro: A Memoir of Thorstein Veblen and Some Others* (New York: Macmillan, 1944).

Eisenach, Eldon J. *The Lost Promise of Progressivism* (Lawrence: University Press of Kansas, 1994).

Ekirch, Arthur A. Jr. *Man and Nature in America* (New York: Columbia University Press, 1963).

―――. *Progressivism in America: A Study of the Era from Theodore Roosevelt to Woodrow Wilson* (New York: New Viewpoints, 1974).

Ely, James W., Jr. *The Chief Justiceship of Melville W. Fuller, 1888–1910* (Columbia: University of South Carolina Press, 1995).

―――. *The Fuller Court: Justices, Rulings and Legacy* (Santa Barbara, CA: ABC-Clio Supreme Court Handbooks, 2003).

―――. *Railroads and American Law* (Lawrence: University Press of Kansas, 2001).

Ely, Richard T. *Ground Under Our Feet: An Autobiography* (New York: Macmillan, 1938).

Elzinga, Kenneth G., and William Breit. *The Antitrust Penalties: A Study in Law and Economics* (New Haven: Yale University Press, 1976).

Emmet, Boris, and John E. Jeuck. *Catalogs and Counters: A History of Sears, Roebuck & Company* (Chicago: University of Chicago Press, 1950).

Epstein, Richard A. *Forbidden Grounds: The Case Against Employment Discrimination Laws* (Cambridge: Harvard University Press, 1992).

Fabricant, Solomon. *The Output of Manufacturing Industries, 1899–1937* (New York: National Bureau of Economic Research, 1940).

Fleming, Thomas. *Illusion of Victory: America in World War I* (New York: Basic Books, 2003).

Fogel, Robert William. *Railroads and Economic Growth* (Baltimore: Johns Hopkins University Press, 1964).

―――. *The Union Pacific Railroad* (Baltimore: Johns Hopkins University Press, 1960).

Fogel, Robert William, and Stanley L. Engerman, ed. *The Reinterpretation of American Economic History* (New York: Harper & Row, 1971).

Fradkin, Philip L. *A River No More: The Colorado River and the West* (Berkeley: University of California Press, 1996).

Freidel, Frank. *Franklin D. Roosevelt: A Rendezvous with Destiny* (Boston: Little, Brown, 1990).

Friedenberg, Robert V. *Theodore Roosevelt and the Rhetoric of Militant Decency* (Westport, CT: Greenwood Press, 1990).

Friedman, Milton, and Anna Jacobson Schwartz. *A Monetary History of the United States, 1867–1960* (Princeton: Princeton University Press, 1963).

Fuer, A. B. *America at War: The Philippines, 1898–1913* (Westport, CT: Praeger, 2002).

Furer, Howard B. *The Fuller Court, 1888–1910* (Millwood, NY: Associated Faculty Press, 1986).

Furnas, J. C. *The Life and Times of the Late Demon Rum* (New York: Putnam, 1965).

Garraty, John A. *Henry Cabot Lodge: A Biography* (New York: Knopf, 1953).

Gates, Paul Wallace. *The History of Public Land Law Development* (New York: Arno Press, 1979). Originally written for the Public Land Law Commission (1968).

————. *Landlords and Tenants on the Prairie Frontier: Studies in American Land Policy* (Ithaca: Cornell University Press, 1973).

————. *The Wisconsin Pine Lands of Cornell University: A Study in Land Policy and Absentee Ownership* (Madison: State Historical Society of Wisconsin, 1965).

Gates, Paul Wallace, ed. *The Fruits of Land Speculation* (New York: Arno Press, 1979).

————. *Public Land Policies, Management and Disposal* (New York: Arno Press, 1979).

————. *The Rape of Indian Lands* (New York: Arno Press, 1979).

Gilbert, James. *Designing the Industrial State: The Intellectual Pursuit of Collectivism in America, 1880–1940* (Chicago: Quadrangle Books, 1972).

Gillon, Steven. *That's Not What We Meant to Do: Reform and Its Unintended Consequences in the Twentieth Century* (New York: Norton, 2000).

Goldin, Claudia, and Gary D. Libecap, ed. *The Regulated Economy: A Historical Approach to Political Economy* (Chicago: University of Chicago Press, 1994).

Goldman, Eric F. *The Tragedy of Lyndon Johnson* (New York: Knopf, 1969).

Goldschmidt, H., M. Mann, and F. Weston, eds. *Industrial Concentration: The New Learning* (Boston: Little, Brown, 1974).

Goodrich, Carter. *Government Promotion of American Canals and Railroads* (New York: Columbia University Press, 1960).

Gosnell, Harold F. *Boss Platt and His New York Machine: A Study of the Political Leadership of Thomas C. Platt, Theodore Roosevelt and Others* (Chicago: University of Chicago Press, 1924).

Gould, Louis L. *The Presidency of Theodore Roosevelt* (Lawrence: University Press of Kansas, 1991).

————. *The Presidency of William McKinley* (Lawrence: University Press of Kansas, 1980).

————. *The Spanish-American War and President McKinley* (Lawrence: University Press of Kansas, 1982).

Grandy, Christopher. *New Jersey and the Fiscal Origins of Modern American Corporation Law* (New York: Garland, 1993).

Grantham, Dewey W., ed. *Theodore Roosevelt* (Engelwood Cliffs, NJ: Prentice-Hall, 1971).

Haar, Charles M., ed. *Zoning and the American Dream: Promises Still to Keep* (Chicago: American Planning Association, 1989).

Hage, Wayne. *Storm over Rangelands: Private Rights in Federal Lands* (Bellevue, WA: Free Enterprise Press, 1989).

Harbaugh, William Henry. *Power and Responsibility: The Life and Times of Theodore Roosevelt* (New York: Farrar, Straus & Cudahy, 1961).

Harris, Leon. *Merchant Princes: An Intimate History of Jewish Families Who Built Great Department Stores* (New York: Harper, 1979).

————. *Upton Sinclair, American Rebel* (New York: Crowell, 1975).

Hatch, Alden. *The Lodges of Massachusetts* (New York: Hawthorn Books, 1973).

Haynes, Sam W. *James K. Polk and the Expansionist Impulse* (New York: Longman, 1997).

Hays, Samuel P. *Conservation and the Gospel of Efficiency: The Progressive Conservation Movement, 1890–1929* (Cambridge: Harvard University Press, 1959).

————. *The Response to Industrialism, 1885–1914* (Chicago: University of Chicago Press, 1957).

Heckscher, August. *Woodrow Wilson* (New York: Scribner, 1991).

Hendrickson, Robert. *The Grand Emporiums: The Illustrated History of America's Great Department Stores* (New York: Stein & Day, 1979).

Hibbard, Benjamin Horace. *A History of the Public Land Policies* (Madison: University of Wisconsin Press, 1965).

Hidy, Ralph W., and Muriel E. Hidy. *History of Standard Oil Company (N.J.): Pioneering in Big Business, 1882–1911* (New York: Harper, 1955).

Hidy, Ralph W., Frank Ernest Hill, and Alan Nevins. *Timber and Men: The Weyerhaeuser Story* (New York: Macmillan, 1963).

Higgs, Robert M. *Crisis and Leviathan, Critical Episodes in the Growth of American Government* (New York: Oxford University Press, 1987).

————. *The Transformation of the American Economy, 1865–1914: An Essay in Interpretation* (New York: Wiley, 1971).

Higgs, Robert M., ed. *The Emergence of Modern Political Economy: Research in Economic History*, Suppl. 4 (Greenwich, CT: JAI Press, 1985).

Himmelberg, Robert F., ed. *The Growth of the Regulatory State, 1900–1917: State and Federal Regulation of Railroads and Other Enterprises* (New York: Garland, 1994).

Hinich, Melvin J., and Richard Staelin. *Consumer Protection Legislation and the U.S. Food Industry* (New York: Pergamon Press, 1980).

Hoffer, Peter Charles. *Law and People in Colonial America* (Baltimore: Johns Hopkins University Press, 1998).

Howland, Harold. *Theodore Roosevelt and His Times: A Chronicle of the Progressive Movement* (New Haven: Yale University Press, 1921).

Hoyt, Edwin P. *That Wonderful A&P* (New York: Hawthorn Books, 1969).

Hughes, Jonathan R. T. *The Governmental Habit: Economic Controls from Colonial Times to the Present* (New York: Basic Books, 1971).

Johnson, Ronald N., and Gary D. Libecap, eds. *The Federal Civil Service System and the Problem of Bureaucracy: The Economics and Politics of Institutional Change* (Chicago: University of Chicago Press, 1994).

Johnson, Walter. *William Allen White's America* (New York: Henry Holt, 1947).

Joseph, Richard J. *The Origins of the American Income Tax: The Revenue Act of 1894 and Its Aftermath* (Syracuse: Syracuse University Press, 2004).

Josephson, Matthew. *The Robber Barons: The Great American Capitalists, 1861–1901* (New York: Harcourt, Brace, 1935).

Juergens, George. *Joseph Pulitzer and the New York World* (Princeton: Princeton University Press, 1966).

Kallett, Arthur. *100,000,000 Guinea Pigs: Dangers in Everyday Foods, Drugs, and Cosmetics* (New York: Grossett & Dunlap, 1935).

Kaplan, Justin. *Lincoln Steffens: A Biography* (New York: Simon & Schuster, 1974).

Karnow, Stanley. *In Our Image: America's Empire in the Philippines* (New York: Random House, 1989).

Karp, Walter. *Indispensable Enemies: The Politics of Misrule in America* (New York: Franklin Square Press, 1993).

———. *The Politics of War: The Story of Two Wars Which Altered Forever the Political Life of the American Republic, 1890–1920* (New York: Harper & Row, 1979).

Katzmann, Robert A. *Regulatory Bureaucracy: The Federal Trade Commission and Antitrust Policy* (Cambridge: MIT Press, 1980).

Kaysen, Carl, and Donald F. Turner. *Antitrust Policy: An Economic and Legal Analysis* (Cambridge: Harvard University Press, 1959).

Kearns, Doris. *Lyndon Johnson and the American Dream* (New York: Harper & Row, 1976).

Kennan, George. *The Chicago and Alton Case: A Misunderstood Transaction* (New York: Arno Press, 1981).

Kerr, K. Austin. *American Railroad Politics, 1914–1920: Rates, Wages, Efficiency.* (Pittsburgh: University of Pittsburgh Press, 1969).

King, Judson. *The Conservation Fight: From Theodore Roosevelt to the Tennessee Valley Authority* (Washington, DC: Public Affairs Press, 1959).

King, Willard L. *Melville Fuller: Chief Justice of the United States, 1888–1910* (New York: Macmillan, 1950).

Kintner, Earl W. *The Legislative History of the Federal Antitrust Laws and Related Statutes* (New York: Chelsea House, 1978).

Klein, Maury. *The Life and Legend of E. H. Harriman* (Chapel Hill: University of North Carolina Press, 2000).

———. *Unfinished Business: Railroads in American Life* (Hanover, NH: University Press of New England, 1994).

———. *Union Pacific: Birth of a Railroad, 1862–1893* (New York: Doubleday, 1987).

———. *Union Pacific: Rebirth, 1894–1969* (New York: Doubleday, 1990).

Klingman, David C., and Richard K. Vedder, eds. *Essays on the Economy of the Old Northwest* (Athens: Ohio University Press, 1987).

Kobler, John. *Ardent Spirits: The Rise and Fall of Prohibition* (New York: Putnam, 1973).

Kolko, Gabriel. *Century of War: Politics, Conflict and Society* (New York: New Press, 1995).

———. *Main Currents in Modern American History* (New York: Harper & Row, 1976).

———. *Railroads and Regulation: 1877–1916* (New York: Norton, 1965).

———. *The Triumph of Conservatism: A Reinterpretation of American History, 1900–1916* (Chicago: Quadrangle, 1963).

Krass, Peter. *Carnegie* (New York: Wiley, 2002).

Kwoka, John, and Lawrence J. White, eds. *The Antitrust Revolution* (New York: HarperCollins, 1989).

LaFeber, Walter. *The New Empire: An Interpretation of American Expansion, 1860–1898* (Ithaca: Cornell University Press, 1993).

Lamoreaux, Naomi R. *The Great Merger Movement in American Business, 1895–1904* (Cambridge, Eng.: Cambridge University Press, 2002).

Landau, Richard L., ed. *Regulating New Drugs* (Chicago: University of Chicago Press, 1973).

Lane, Franklin Knight. *Letters, Personal and Political* (Boston: Houghton Mifflin, 1922).

Lasswell, Harold D. *Propaganda Technique in the World War* (New York: Peter Smith, 1938).

Leavitt, Judith Walzer. *Typhoid Mary: Captive to the Public's Health* (Boston: Beacon Press, 1996).

Lebergott, Stanley. *The American Economy* (Princeton: Princeton University Press, 1976).

———. *The Americans: An Economic Record* (New York: Norton, 1984).

———. *Manpower in Economic Growth: The American Record Since 1800* (New York: McGraw-Hill, 1964).

Lebhar, Godfrey M. *Chain Stores in America, 1859–1950* (New York: Chain Store Publishing, 1952).

Leech, Harper, and John Charles Carroll. *Armour and His Times* (Freeport, NY: Books for Libraries Press, 1971).

Letwin, William. *Law and Economic Policy in America: The Evolution of the Sherman Antitrust Act* (New York: Random House, 1965).

Libecap, Gary D. *Contracting for Property Rights* (Cambridge, Eng.: Cambridge University Press, 1989).

———. *Locking Up the Range: Federal Land Controls and Grazing* (San Francisco: Pacific Institute for Public Policy Research, 1981).

Link, Arthur S. *Woodrow Wilson and the Progressive Era, 1900–1917* (New York: Harper, 1954).

Linn, Brian McAllister. *Guardians of Empire: The U.S. Army and the Pacific, 1902–1940* (Chapel Hill: University of North Carolina Press, 1999).

———. *The Philippine War, 1899–1902* (Lawrence: University Press of Kansas, 2000).

———. *The U.S. Army and Counterinsurgency in the Philippine War, 1899–1902* (Chapel Hill: University of North Carolina Press, 1989).

Lodge, Henry Cabot. *Early Memories* (New York: Scribner, 1913).

Lustig, Jeffrey. *Corporate Liberalism: The Origins of Modern American Political Theory, 1890–1920* (Berkeley: University of California Press, 1982).

Lyon, Peter. *Success Story: The Life and Times of S. S. McClure* (New York: Scribner, 1963).

MacAvoy, Paul W. *The Crisis of the Regulatory Commissions: An Introduction to a Current Issue of Public Policy* (New York: Norton, 1970).

———. *The Economic Effects of Regulation: The Trunk-Line Railroad Cartels and the Interstate Commerce Commission Before 1900* (Cambridge: MIT Press, 1965).

Mackay, Robert J., James C. Miller III, and Bruce Yandle, eds. *Public Choice and Regulation: A View from inside the Federal Trade Commission* (Stanford, CA: Hoover Institution Press, 1987).

Martin, Albro. *Enterprise Denied: Origins of the Decline of American Railroads, 1897–1917* (New York: Columbia University Press, 1971).

———. *James J. Hill and the Opening of the Northwest* (New York: Oxford University Press, 1976).

———. *Railroads Triumphant: The Growth, Rejection, and Rebirth of a Vital American Force* (New York: Oxford University Press, 1992).

McChesney, Fred S., and William F. Shughart, eds. *The Causes and Consequences of Antitrust: The Public Choice Perspective* (Chicago: University of Chicago Press, 1995).

McCraw, Thomas K., ed. *Regulation in Perspective: Historical Essays* (Cambridge: Harvard University Press, 1981).

McClure, S. S. *Autobiography* (Lincoln: University of Nebraska Press, 1997).

McCullough, David. *Mornings on Horseback* (New York: Simon & Schuster, 1981).

——. *The Path Between the Seas: The Creation of the Panama Canal, 1870–1914* (New York: Simon & Schuster, 1977).

McDonald, Forrest. *A Constitutional History of the United States* (Malabar, FL: Robert E. Krieger, 1986).

——. *We the People: The Economic Origins of the Constitution* (New Brunswick, NJ: Transaction, 1992).

McGeary, Nelson. *Gifford Pinchot, Forester-Politician* (Princeton: Princeton University Press, 1960).

McGrane, Reginald Charles. *Foreign Bondholders and American State Debts* (New York: Macmillan, 1935).

——. *The Panic of 1837: Some Problems of the Jacksonian Era* (Chicago: University of Chicago Press, 1965).

Meltzer, Allan H. *A History of the Federal Reserve, 1913–1951* (Chicago: University of Chicago Press, 2003).

Merk, Frederick. *Manifest Destiny and Mission in American History: A Reinterpretation* (New York: Knopf, 1963).

Meyer, Hugo Richard. *The British State Telegraphs: A Study of the Problem of a Large Body of Civil Servants in a Democracy* (New York: Macmillan, 1907).

——. *Government Regulation of Railway Rates: A Study of the Experience of the United States, Germany, France, Austria-Hungary, Russia and Australia* (New York: Macmillan, 1905).

——. *Municipal Ownership in Great Britain* (New York: Macmillan, 1906).

——. *Public Ownership and the Telephone in Great Britain: Restriction of the Industry by the State and the Municipalities* (New York: Macmillan, 1907).

Miller, George H. *Railroads and the Granger Laws* (Madison: University of Wisconsin Press, 1971).

Miller, Nathan. *Theodore Roosevelt: A Life* (New York: Morrow, 1992).

Millis, Walter. *The Martial Spirit: A Study of Our War with Spain* (Boston: Houghton Mifflin, 1931).

Mock, James R., and Cedric Larson. *Words That Won the War: The Story of the Committee on Public Information, 1917–1919* (Princeton: Princeton University Press, 1939).

Morgan, H. Wayne. *From Hayes to McKinley: National Party Politics, 1872–1896* (Syracuse: Syracuse University Press, 1969).

——. *William McKinley and His America* (Syracuse: Syracuse University Press, 1963).

Morris, Edmund. *The Rise of Theodore Roosevelt* (New York: Modern Library, 2001).

——. *Theodore Rex* (New York: Random House, 2001).

Mowry, George E. *The Era of Theodore Roosevelt and the Birth of Modern America* (New York: Harper, 1958).

——. *Theodore Roosevelt and the Progressive Movement* (Madison: University of Wisconsin Press, 1947).

Musicant, Ivan. *Empire by Default: The Spanish-American War and the Dawn of the American Century* (New York: Henry Holt, 1998).

Nasaw, David. *The Chief: The Life of William Randolph Hearst* (Boston: Houghton Mifflin, 2000).

National Emergency Powers (Washington, DC: Library of Congress, Congressional Research Service, September 18, 2001).

Neale, A. D. *The Antitrust Laws of the U.S.A.* (Cambridge, Eng.: Cambridge University Press, 1970).

Nelson, Ralph L. *Merger Movements in American History, 1895–1956* (Princeton: Princeton University Press, 1959).

Nelson, Robert H. *A Burning Issue: A Case for Abolishing the U.S. Forest Service* (Lanham, MD: Rowman & Littlefield, 2000).

———. *Public Lands and Private Rights: The Failure of Scientific Management* (Lanham, MD: Rowman & Littlefield, 1995).

Niskanen, William A. *Bureaucracy and Representative Government* (Chicago: Aldine-Atherton, 1971).

Nore, Ellen. *Charles A. Beard: An Intellectual Biography* (Carbondale: Southern Illinois University Press, 1983).

North, Douglass C. *Growth and Welfare in the American Past: A New Economic History* (Engelwood Cliffs, NJ: Prentice-Hall, 1966).

Olson, Sherry H. *The Depletion Myth: A History of Railroad Use of Timber* (Cambridge: Harvard University Press, 1971).

Osgood, Robert Endicott. *Ideals and Self-Interest in America's Foreign Relations: The Great Transformation of the Twentieth Century* (Chicago: University of Chicago Press, 1964).

Passer, Harold. *The Electrical Manufacturers, 1875–1900: A Study of Competition, Entrepreneurship, Technical Change and Economic Growth* (New York: Arno Press, 1972).

Paul, Randolph E. *Taxation in the United States* (Boston: Little, Brown, 1954).

Pease, Otis. ed. *The Progressive Years: The Spirit and Achievement of American Reform* (New York: George Braziller, 1962).

Peffer, E. Louise. *The Closing of the Public Domain: Disposal and Reservation Policies, 1900–1950* (Stanford, CA: Stanford University Press, 1951).

Pegram, Thomas R. *Battling Demon Rum: The Struggle for a Dry America, 1800–1933* (Chicago: Ivan R. Dee, 1998).

Peltzman, Sam. *Regulation of Pharmaceutical Innovation* (San Francisco: Troubadour Press, 1974).

Peterson, Horace Cornelius, and Gilbert C. Fite. *Opponents of War, 1917–1918* (Madison: University of Wisconsin Press, 1957).

Pierce, Franklin. *The Tariff and the Trusts* (New York: Macmillan, 1907).

Posner, Richard A. *Antitrust Law: An Economic Perspective* (Chicago: University of Chicago Press, 1976).

Prendergast, Mark. *For God, Country and Coca-Cola: The Definitive History of the Great American Soft Drink and the Company That Makes It* (New York: Macmillan, 1994).

Pringle, Henry F. *The Life and Times of William Howard Taft*, 2 vols. (New York: Archon Books, 1964).

———. *Theodore Roosevelt: A Biography* (New York: Harcourt, Brace, 1931).

Qualey, Carlton C., ed. *Thorstein Veblen* (New York: Columbia University Press, 1968).

Ratchford, B. U. *American State Debts* (Durham, NC: Duke University Press, 1941).

Rees, Albert. *Real Wages in Manufacturing, 1890–1914* (Princeton: Princeton University Press, 1961).

Reisner, Marc. *Cadillac Desert: The American West and Its Disappearing Water* (New York: Penguin Books, 1993).

Riepma, S. F. *The Story of Margarine* (Washington, DC: Public Affairs Press, 1970).

Rippy, J. Fred. *Latin America: A Modern History* (Ann Arbor: University of Michigan Press, 1958).

Robbins, Roy M. *Our Landed Heritage: The Public Domain, 1776–1970* (Lincoln: University of Nebraska Press, 1976).

———. *Preëmption: A Frontier Triumph* (Cedar Rapids, IA: Torch Press, 1931).

Rohrbough, Malcolm J. *The Land Office Business: The Settlement and Administration of American Public Lands, 1789–1837* (New York: Oxford University Press, 1968).

Roosevelt, Theodore. *America and the World War* (New York: Scribner, 1915).

———. *An Autobiography* (New York: Macmillan, 1913).

———. *Gouverneur Morris* (Cambridge: Houghton, Mifflin, 1896).

———. *Letters*, 8 vols., selected and edited by Elting E. Morison (Cambridge: Harvard University Press, 1951–1954).

———. *Oliver Cromwell* (New York: Scribner, 1900).

———. *The Rough Riders* (1899; repr., Lincoln: University of Nebraska Press, 1998).

———. *The Winning of the West*, 6 vols. (New York: Current Literature Publishing Co., 1904–1906).

Schlesinger, Arthur M., Jr. *The Imperial Presidency* (Boston: Houghton Mifflin, 1973).

Schweikart, Larry. *The Entrepreneurial Adventure: A History of Business in the United States* (Fort Worth, TX: Harcourt, Brace, 2000).

Seager, Robert, II. *Alfred Thayer Mahan* (Annapolis: Naval Institute Press, 1977).

Seager, Robert, II, and Doris D. Maguire, eds. *Letters and Papers of Alfred Thayer Mahan* (Annapolis: Naval Institute Press, 1975).

Sedgwick, Ellery. *The Happy Profession* (Boston: Little, Brown, 1946).

Shaffer, Butler D. *In Restraint of Trade: The Business Campaign Against Competition, 1918–1938* (Lewisburg, PA: Bucknell University Press, 1997).

Sharfman, I. Leo. *The American Railroad Problem* (New York: Century, 1921).

Sherman, John. *Recollections of Forty Years*, vol. 2 (Chicago: Werner Company, 1895).

Shughart, William F. II. *Antitrust Policy and Interest Group Politics* (New York: Quorum Books, 1990).

———. *The Organization of Industry* (Homewood, IL: Irwin, 1990).

Sinclair, Upton. *The Autobiography* (New York: Harcourt, Brace & World, 1962).

Skaggs, Jimmy. *Prime Cut: Livestock Raising and Meatpacking in the United States, 1607–1983* (College Station: Texas A&M University Press, 1986).

Skowronek, Stephen. *Building a New American State: The Expansion of National Administrative Capacities, 1877–1920* (NY: Cambridge University Press, 1982).

Smith, Adam. *An Inquiry into the Nature and Causes of the Wealth of Nations*, 2 vols. (1776; repr., Indianapolis: LibertyPress, 1981).

Steel, Ronald. *Walter Lippman and the American Century* (Boston: Little, Brown, 1980).

Steffens, Lincoln. *Autobiography* (New York: Harcourt, Brace, 1931).

Stigler, George J. *The Economist as Preacher and Other Essays* (Chicago: University of Chicago Press, 1982).

Storey, Moorfield, and Marcial P. Lichauco. *The Conquest of the Philippines by the United States, 1898–1925* (New York: Putnam, 1925).

Strong, Theron G. *Joseph H. Choate: New Englander, New Yorker, Lawyer, Ambassador* (New York: Dodd, Mead, 1917).

Strouse, Jean. *Morgan, American Financier* (New York: Random House, 1999).

Stover, John F. *The Life and Decline of the American Railroad* (New York: Oxford University Press, 1970).

Strum, Philippa. *Louis Brandeis: Beyond Progressivism* (Lawrence: University of Kansas Press, 1993).

Sumner, William Graham. *Essays*, 2 vols., ed. Albert Galloway Keller and Maurice R. Davie (New Haven: Yale University Press, 1934).

———. *What Social Classes Owe to Each Other* (1883; repr., Caldwell, ID: Caxton Printers, 1963).

Swanberg, W. A. *Citizen Hearst: A Biography of William Randolph Hearst* (New York: Scribner, 1961).

———. *Pulitzer* (New York: Scribner, 1967).

Swift, Louis Franklin. *The Yankee of the Yards: The Biography of Gustavus Franklin Swift* (New York: AMS Press, 1970).

Tabrah, Ruth M. *Hawaii: A History* (New York: Norton, 1980).

Tannehill, Reray. *Food in History* (New York: Stein & Day, 1973).

Tarbell, Ida M. *All in a Day's Work: An Autobiography* (New York: Macmillan, 1939).

———. *The History of the Standard Oil Company* (1904; repr., New York: Peter Smith, 1950).

———. *Life of Napoleon Bonaparte* (New York: Macmillan, 1926).

———. *The Tariff in Our Times* (New York: Macmillan, 1911).

Taussig, Frank W. *The Tariff History of the United States* (New York: Putnam, 1931).

Taylor, George Rogers. *The Transportation Revolution, 1815–1860* (New York: Rinehart, 1951).

Taylor, Robert Lewis. *Vessel of Wrath: The Life and Times of Carrie Nation* (New York: New American Library, 1966).

Thayer, William Roscoe. *The Life and Letters of John Hay* (Boston: Houghton Mifflin, 1929).

———. *Theodore Roosevelt: An Intimate Biography* (Boston: Houghton Mifflin, 1919).

Thelen, David P. *Robert M. La Follette and the Insurgent Spirit* (Madison: University of Wisconsin Press, 1976).

Thorelli, Hans. *The Federal Antitrust Policy: Origination of an American Tradition* (Baltimore: Johns Hopkins University Press, 1955).

Tilman, Rick. *Thorstein Veblen and His Critics, 1891–1963: Conservative, Liberal and Radical Perspectives* (Princeton: Princeton University Press, 1992).

Timberlake, James H. *Prohibition and the Progressive Movement, 1900–1920* (New York: Atheneum, 1970).

Timberlake, Richard. *Monetary Policy in the United States* (Chicago: University of Chicago Press, 1993).

Tollison, Robert D., ed., *The Political Economy of Antitrust* (Lexington, MA: Lexington Books, 1980).

Tompkins, Mary E. *Ida M. Tarbell* (New York: Twayne, 1974).

Toussaint-Samat, Maguelonne. *A History of Food* (Cambridge: Blackwell, 1987).

Troesken, Werner. *Why Regulate Utilities? The New Institutional Economics and the Chicago Gas Industry, 1849–1924* (Ann Arbor: University of Michigan Press, 1996).

Turk, Richard W. *The Ambiguous Relationship: Theodore Roosevelt and Alfred Thayer Mahan* (Westport, CT: Greenwood Press, 1987).

Turner, Frederick Jackson. *The Frontier in American History* (NY: Henry Holt, 1920).

Twain, Mark. *A Pen Warmed Up in Hell: Mark Twain in Protest*, ed. Frederick Anderson (New York: Perennial Library, 1972).

Urofsky, Melvin I. *Louis D. Brandeis and the Progressive Tradition* (Boston: Little, Brown, 1981).

Walsh, William I. *The Rise and Decline of the Great Atlantic and Pacific Tea Company* (Secaucus, NJ: Lyle Stuart, 1986).

Warburg, Paul M. *The Federal Reserve Systems, Origin and Growth*, 2 vols. (New York: Macmillan, 1930).

Warren, Christian. *Brush with Death: A Social History of Lead Poisoning* (Baltimore: Johns Hopkins University Press, 2000).

Weber, Gustavus Adolphus. *The Food, Drug, and Insecticide Administration: Its History, Activities, and Organization* (Baltimore: Johns Hopkins University Press, 1928).

Weil, Gordon L. *Sears Roebuck USA: The Great American Catalog Store and How It Grew* (New York: Stein & Day, 1977).

Weinstein, James. *The Corporate Ideal in the Liberal State, 1900–1918* (Boston: Beacon Press, 1969).

Wengert, Norman. *Natural Resources and the Political Struggle* (New York: Doubleday, 1955).

Widenor, William C. *Henry Cabot Lodge and the Search for an American Foreign Policy* (Berkeley: University of California Press, 1980).

Wiebe, Robert. *Businessmen and Reform: A Study of the Progressive Movement* (Chicago: Quadrangle Books, 1962).

———. *The Search for Order, 1877–1920* (New York: Hill and Wang, 1967).

Wiley, Harvey Washingon. *An Autobiography* (Indianapolis: Bobbs-Merrill, 1930).

———. *Foods and Their Adulteration* (Philadelphia: Blakiston, 1907).

———. *The History of a Crime Against the Food Law* (1929; repr., Milwaukee: Lee Foundation for Nutritional Research, 1955).

Williams, William Appleman. *The Tragedy of American Diplomacy* (NY: Dell, 1972).

Williamson, H. F., and A. R. Dam. *The American Petroleum Industry: The Age of Illumination, 1859–1899* (Westport, CT: Greenwood Press, 1981).

Wood, Donna J. *Strategic Uses of Public Policy: Business and Government in the Progressive Era* (Boston: Pitman, 1986).

Worster, Donald. *Rivers of Empire: Water, Aridity, and the Growth of the American West* (New York: Oxford University Press, 1992).

Yeager, Mary. *Competition and Regulation: The Development of Oligopoly in the Meat Packing Industry* (Greenwich, CT: Jai Press, 1981).

Young, James Harvey. *The Early Years of Federal Food and Drug Control* (Madison, WI: American Institute of the History of Pharmacy, 1982).

———. *Pure Food: Securing the Federal Food and Drugs Act of 1986* (Princeton: Princeton University Press, 1989).

Zimmerman, Warren. *First Great Triumph: How Five Americans Made Their Country a World Power* (New York: Farrar, Straus & Giroux, 2002).

Zwick, Jim. ed. *Mark Twain's Weapons of Satire: Anti-Imperialist Writings on the Philippine-American War* (Syracuse: Syracuse University Press, 1992).

ACKNOWLEDGMENTS

I SPENT SOME FORMATIVE YEARS of my youth in the shadow of Sagamore Hill, Theodore Roosevelt's fabled home in Oyster Bay, Long Island. I was a classmate with one of his charming great-granddaughters. An enterprising great-grandson was two years ahead of me in high school. So TR's legendary name has always meant something to me.

Later, at the University of Chicago, where I got to know Milton Friedman, George Stigler, Yale Brozen, Sam Peltzman, and other empirical economists, I learned to evaluate the often unintended consequences of presidential policies.

I became fascinated to see how frequently major political historians ignore empirical evidence about their subjects, developed by researchers outside their field. While historians feel free to write about economic issues, for instance, they seldom consult the findings of economists—certainly not economists who challenge their views. Presidential historians continue to focus on personalities, speeches, political campaigns, and other topics that reveal little or nothing about bottom-line consequences.

Having chronicled misadventures of Franklin Delano Roosevelt and Woodrow Wilson in my previous books, I began to explore the empirical literature on Theodore Roosevelt, who promoted many ideas they embraced. The literature is substantial, and I expect that in the future it will play out in more books critical of the "progressive" era.

Of particular importance are studies by Terry L. Anderson, Dominick T. Armentano, Bruce L. Benson, George Bittlingmayer, Robert L. Bradley, James M. Buchanan, Clayton A. Coppin, Thomas J. DiLorenzo, Samuel P. Hays, Thomas W. Hazlett, Jack High, Robert M. Higgs, Walter Karp, Stanley Lebergott, Gary D. Libecap, Albro Martin, Fred S. McChesney, John S. McGee, James C. Miller III, Robert H. Nelson, William A. Niskanen, Ernest C. Pasour Jr., Sam Peltzman, William F. Shughart II, Russell S. Sobel, Robert D. Tollison, George J. Stigler, Alexander T. Tabarrok, Clifford F. Theis, Werner Troesken, and Donna Wood.

Among Theodore Roosevelt's contemporaries, I believe the most perceptive critic, an unsung hero, was Hugo Richard Meyer. He was a University of Chicago economist who, defying "progressive" trends toward more government intervention in the economy, showed how federal regulations disrupted markets and suppressed competition. Meyer reported how European governments—from which many American "progressives" drew inspiration—disrupted the development of vital industries, including iron, steel, and railroads.

I appreciate the assistance of reference librarians at Yale University and Harvard University's Theodore Roosevelt Collection. I made extensive use of interlibrary loan services at the Westport (Connecticut) Public Library. To help accelerate research, I acquired hundreds of books through Internet used-book databases.

I deeply appreciate being named the R. C. Hoiles Senior Fellow at the Cato Institute in Washington, D.C. Funding was kindly arranged by Cato's Tom Palmer together with Richard Wallace at Freedom Communications in Irvine, California. This helped assure timely completion of the book. Raymond Cyrus Hoiles (1878–1970) was the founder of the Freedom Newspaper chain, whose news pages offered factual reporting and whose editorial pages were distinguished by refreshing libertarian views. Hoiles maintained that political power was the principal threat to liberty and prosperity. He had some firsthand experience—during the course of exposing corrupt politicians, his home was dynamited, and there were attempts to dynamite his office and his car. Freedom Communications has continued to uphold the principles that Hoiles so valiantly defended.

I'm grateful, as always, for steadfast support from Cato president Ed Crane and executive vice president David Boaz. I'm proud of my association with Cato, which goes back eighteen years (and counting).

I want to thank my Crown Forum editor, Jed Donahue, for another thoughtful collaboration. Jed is certainly doing his part to help rewrite American history.

I regret that Frank and Madeline couldn't be with me on this adventure.

Thanks to Marisa, Justin, Kristin, and Rosalynd, who made it all worthwhile.

INDEX

ABOUT THE AUTHOR

Historian Jim Powell is the author of *Wilson's War: How Woodrow Wilson's Great Blunder Led to Hitler, Lenin, Stalin, and World War II; FDR's Folly: How Roosevelt and His New Deal Prolonged the Great Depression;* and *The Triumph of Liberty: A 2,000-Year History Told Through the Lives of Freedom's Greatest Champions.* He has given talks at Harvard, Stanford, and other universities across the United States, as well as in England, Germany, Japan, Argentina, and Brazil. He has written for the *New York Times,* the *Wall Street Journal,* the *Chicago Tribune, Money* magazine, *Reason, Barron's, Esquire,* the *Christian Science Monitor,* and numerous other national publications. Currently the R. C. Hoiles Senior Fellow at the Cato Institute, Powell served as editor of Laissez Faire Books for eleven years. He studied history at the University of Chicago under Daniel Boorstin and William McNeill. Jim Powell lives with his family in Westport, Connecticut.